The Gay Nineties

AN ANTHOLOGY OF
CONTEMPORARY
GAY FICTION

Edited by
Phil Willkie & Greg Baysans

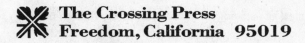 **The Crossing Press**
Freedom, California 95019

Richard Hall's story, *A Rose in Murcia*, is reprinted by permission of The Grey Fox Press, San Francisco, California.
James White's *Journal 1979* is reprinted by permission of the James L. White Estate, Kate Green, Executor.

Cover design: Elise Huffman
Cover photograph: John Wulpe, from Remy Charlip's *Ten Men*
Printed in the U.S.A.

Library of Congress Cataloging-in-Publication Data

The Gay Nineties: an anthology of contemporary gay fiction / edited by Phil Wilkie
& Greg Baysans.
     p. cm.
   ISBN 0-89594-473-1 (cloth)   ISBN 0-89594-472-3 (pbk.)
    1. Gay men—Fiction. 2. Short stories, American I. Wilkie, Phil. II. Baysans, Greg.
PS648.H57G39 1991
813'.0108353—dc20   91–7506
                                                  CIP

Table of Contents

Introduction

GREG BAYSANS / PHILIP WILLKIE

It is easy, given the differences between the previous decades, to be curious about what gay literature will express in the 1990s. The American gay movement had its embryonic beginnings in the '50s with the fledgling Mattachine Society and *One* magazine, which was sold under the counter at newsstands in big cities. That secretive and repressive era lasted until the late '60s when dissent emerged at Stonewall. The closet door was opened with popular books like *The Front Runner*. The mid to late '70s often saw coming out stories and Fire Island-Key West pickup stories.

The '80s, because we are not yet far enough from that decade, are more difficult to characterize. Clearly, the decade was marked by the appearance of AIDS, which would affect us all, gay and straight, in the ensuing years. But it was also a decade for the diversification of gay culture. The stories in this book are a documentation of that diversification. They first appeared in the pages of the gay men's literary quarterly, *The James White Review*.

One facet of the gay experience is, of course, love. Richard Hall's "A Rose in Murcia" is a double love story, encompassing the main character's present lover and his first lover many years earlier. In style, it is as smooth as a turbulence-free airplane flight, building methodically and powerfully, hallmarks of Hall's much-collected fiction.

Lucas Dedrick's "The Beach" is not a romantic love story but a moving love story, nonetheless. With a poet's economy, Dedrick includes colorful incidental characters in this story of devotion for a dying friend. The story's treatment of AIDS is deft—not sentimentalized or morbid.

Daniel Mangin's "Dressing a Wound" is a light comedy about loving oneself. It's told as a monologue, funny and touching at once. "After girls in phone booths and the assorted perversions of hustling, I got into leather for a change of pace. It was supposed to be a joke, but the nice thing about people is they'll take you at your own word and since I *looked* butch, they figured I was," Mangin writes, one of many clever observations of human nature.

"Sex and Love," by Peter McGehee, falls back to primarily being a pickup story. The main character has a lover but picks up a teenager and they have safe sex. Literature, more than politics, is willing to expose truths. McGehee exposes lust for youth as a common phenomenon in our culture.

Jim White's journals, "October 1979," gets at a different truth. "On the surface I appeared a gentle and kind man. That is one of the useful lies of my life. I think that's one of the useful lies of being homosexual: We appear to be what we are not and our terrible anger is masked." White cuts through hyperbole, leaving himself totally naked.

Another sort of self-discovery is related in Doug Federhart's "Learning Secrets." A teenager discovers sex at the public library and later explores relationships through the small town's florist. Federhart's ever-present style makes the reader feel as though he is the one coming to terms with this new and forbidden desire in the confines of a toilet stall.

Louis Crew's "Ben's Eyes" is a story of rediscovery. The narrator is at his grandmother's funeral and recalls a crush on an older cousin. "I liked being with Ben even better outdoors on the tractor leaning against his lap, or taking a break in the shade at the far end of the field or having him snuggle up after he thought I'd gone to sleep." Though Ben has no memory of the intensity of their relationship, the narrator is comforted by the memory.

In Isaac Jackson's "Ruby's Red Slippers," the death of a grandmother motivates the author to reach for the past through his good friend, an older drag queen. Their warm relationship is captured in their tender repartee.

"Alida," by Wes Muchmore, is a story of more than returning to the past but of avenging it. What starts as a bit of nostalgia becomes menacing and cathartic. It is a story not without its share of suspense. And pain.

Pain is, unfortunately, a common element in much writing of our gay experience. It is perhaps a saving aspect of that pain that it can result in some astonishingly powerful writing. This writing can aid us in remembering the mistakes and injustices of the past. Such is the importance of James Tushinski's "Remembering," a story set in 1965 when it was not uncommon for gay men and women to undergo electroshock "therapy."

Another vividly painful but powerful story is Walter Rico Burrell's "Rites of Passage." The story of a pre-teen's social and sexual awakening, it is brutally memorable and unflinchingly honest in its depiction of youth and power. A common theme is given an uncommon strength in Burrell's writing.

A different piece of history, the Holocaust, is retold in David Steinberg's "I See Your Cup Is Empty." The argument raised but not wholly resolved is a comparison of the Holocaust and the AIDS epidemic. Steinberg skillfully makes the comparison yet neither the Holocaust nor AIDS lose their individual differences.

Sam Rudy's "Sheet Music" is a unique story in its inclusion of AIDS. Here the main character is a married man who lives in a rural area and takes over the care of a younger man who has returned from the big cities in the final stages of AIDS.

AIDS in a humorous story? Only the talent of David Feinberg could make it work. "I decided to take the Test after I discovered that two former sexual partners of mine had AIDS by reading articles in the *New York Times*. The first article dealt with AIDS in the workplace. 'Why look! There's Ralph,' I said to myself, coughing up breakfast and several meals from the past two weeks. The second was a human interest story about AZT in action. 'Gee, didn't know Mark was on AZT these days,' I commented from a supine position on the floor, having just fainted." Feinberg's ability to follow a giggle with a loud guffaw is the mark of a gifted comic. His inclusiveness and control in bringing comedy to the plane of pathos are marks of a gifted writer.

Another comic venture is Thomas McKague's "Flying Low." The humor here is, however, less broad, wonderfully witty. Characterizations are made in fine and loving detail despite the narrator's seeming cynicism. In an early episode the narrator relates the story of his nosy neighbors and how "they *did* send their minister over to our house once, an imposing woman with a Bible and huge breasts (actually, her shape resembled the continent of Africa). She told us that two men living together in sin . . . didn't necessarily preclude damnation. I told her that we were already members of the Church for Fallen-Away Catholics, and asked if she would like to join us in a drink."

Donald Vining's "D.O.M." is a funny tale of a "dirty old man" just moved into a retirement home, the perfect character to embody Vining's appreciation for male beauty. He complains, "On the soap operas . . .

doctors were unfailingly handsome. That wasn't the reality of the nursing home . . . One hoped for visitors who might be easy on the eyes, an occasional son or grandson."

"A Somewhat Imperfect Landing" by the prolific Felice Picano, is an adventure told in panic as the narrator is in flight from Turkey to New York City with some recently purchased hashish. In flashback, the narrator tells the strange encounters he had while procuring the hashish. The story then comes back to the flight where the narrator tries to rid himself of the substance in the only way he knows. It is a story full of unexpected and delightful ironies.

Leonard Tirado's "Hector and the Madrina" shows another kind of flight, a Latino tradition in a gay perspective. The main character's grandmother leads him to a spiritual belief that affirms homosexuality.

In putting together this collection, we wish to acknowledge and thank the hundreds of people who sent manuscripts to us. Variety has been a determining factor in selecting these stories. Here we present authors of different generations, races, ethnic and economic backgrounds. Perhaps only in a gay anthology can such real and artificial barriers be crossed.

We are particularly grateful for editorial assistance from Laurence Roberts, Clif Mayhood and Brent Derowitsch.

Greg Baysans and Phil Willkie
Minneapolis, Minnesota, October 1990

I See Your Cup Is Empty

DAVID STEINBERG

At ten o'clock the cafe was uncrowded. Lively new wave music poured out through the open doors and windows, and despite the music and the traffic on Market Street, there was a calmness in the air. My lover, Ronnie, went inside for drinks while I found a table under the big gnarl of wisteria that hung from one of the glass walls of the cafe.

Ronnie's father, Edward Eisenberg, lowered himself onto a chair with the help of his cane, and lighting a cigarette, stared out at the busy street, smoking quietly. Though Ronnie was gone only minutes, I squirmed in my seat and cracked my knuckles, unable to think of anything to say. Finally Ronnie appeared with two glasses of red wine, a Dubonnet for his father.

Edward's visit was his first trip to the United States, and the first time he'd seen his son since Ronnie moved to San Francisco three years ago. Edward walked with an ever-present cane, and the frequent pains in his legs seemed to have frozen his face in a grimace that made him appear unfriendly, hostile. At the age of eighty-four, only a fringe of grey hair circled his head, and the thick lens of his heavy, tortoise shell glasses magnified clear, gray eyes that looked out of a face webbed with wrinkles.

The first morning of his stay, his hand, unsteady from Parkinson's, shook the coffee out of his cup. Whenever he spoke, his gruff voice, a thick blend of British, Hebrew, and German accents, was hard to understand and put me off at first. Often, after saying something I half understood, he

1

would pause and smile, a clue he'd made some joke. In our early conversations I found him eager to discuss anything, from panhandlers on the street to the evening news. At first I had enjoyed bantering with him about politics, but after three days with Edward, his brusque demeanor still intimidated me, and I was unsure if I liked him, or if he liked me. After all, I was his son's lover, the "homo" Ronnie was "sexual" with. And what was my relationship with him? Friend? Son-in-law? Guest to tolerate for two weeks?

Earlier in the evening we had stood outside synagogue after Kol Nidre services, three good, non-fasting Jews, deciding where to go for a drink. It was one of those rare, warm evenings in San Francisco, the first after weeks of fog, and I wanted to walk, but it was too far from the synagogue on Eureka Street to Cafe Flor for Edward.

"Some days I walk five minutes and my legs say 'That's it!'" said Edward, "but mind you, I'm not too tired for a drink." I wasn't used to an elderly person or the constant accommodations I made for this Old World gentleman who put on a suit jacket and tie to go to the corner store for milk or cigarettes. We squeezed into our small economy car, and as I drove up Castro Street, I caught Ronnie's eye in the rearview mirror.

My high-strung, handsome Ronnie—even in the nighttime light, his wide, doe eyes glistened, wet moons hovering above the dark curve of his thick, black mustache. We hadn't had more than five minutes alone since Edward arrived.

Ronnie rolled his eyes at me in exaggerated exasperation in the rearview mirror, then leaned forward and began talking to Edward in a loud, eager-to-please voice that irritated me. Edward was deaf in his right ear and used a hearing aid in his left ear, and could only hear if you shouted.

"Ronnie, you want to give me a break? I'm trying to drive and you're screaming in my ear." I instantly regretted snapping at him, but it was out of my mouth like a shot.

"I didn't mean to scream in your ear, I just wanted to speak up so Edward could hear me in the front seat, ok?" I snapped my head back to scowl at him. Ronnie shot back in his seat, shrugging his shoulders and mouthing "Sorry!", a wounded look on his face.

We were visibly tense, edgy tonight, even though the evening had gone as Ronnie had planned. Although he'd come out to Edward years ago, he was anxious to show Edward as positive a picture of his new gay life in San Francisco as he could. Part of that plan included Kol Nidre services at a lesbian-gay synagogue with me, his Jewish-American lover of two years. This idea didn't faze Edward in any way I could discern when Ronnie proposed it during dinner the night Edward arrived.

"Sure that's fine with me. I'm always interested in something new and different," was all he said.

"You're certainly open-minded for an eighty-four-year-old," I remarked a little too brightly that first night, then cringed at what I'd said.

"Eighty-four, forty-eight, I was always the same young man," he replied without looking up from his plate.

During the Kol Nidre service Edward sat listening and observing, smiling whenever the women who lead portions of the service used "she" instead of "he" when referring to God. During the Yizkor service, the ritual of remembrance for the dead, many people, mostly men, stood in turn:

"For my lover, Michael, who died in July."

"Arnie, my roommate, who died last week."

And several women as well:

"In remembrance of Jack, my best friend of twelve years."

I stood, reluctantly, and felt Ronnie and Edward's eyes on me:

"For my best friend, Kevin, who died three weeks ago today." I sat down, staring straight ahead, but saw Edward out of the corner of my eye raising his eyebrows at Ronnie, who slid his arm around my shoulders and leaned against me. It was the first time we touched in front of Edward. I'd known Kevin nearly ten years, the first close friend I'd made after moving to San Francisco. We talked often on the phone, two or three times a week, for hours. Long, intense conversations, like I hadn't had since college days, about art, painters, poetry, AIDS, anything. I had gotten so used to those hours-long conversations, where the mask of the telephone allowed our real selves to pour out.

Each time the phone had rung in the last three weeks, I had wanted it to be him, and felt crushed to hear the voice of someone else on the line. To never hear his bright, sardonic voice on the phone again—how was I going to get used to that? I took Ronnie's hand as my chest heaved, and struggled not to cry.

"Will everyone please rise? Even if you haven't lost anyone personally in the past year," said the Rabbi, "we can recite Kaddish together for all those in the community who have died, and for all who perished in the Holocaust and have no one to say Kaddish for them."

Kaddish, the prayer that simply affirms belief in God and never once mentions the dead. I stood with a surge of bitterness and confusion. What *was* I doing in a synagogue after so many years? But with the arrival of the viral holocaust, too many questions stirred in me. Why were all my friends dying? Why them, not me? A yearning for something found me dressed in the traditional white shirt for the High Holy Days, black tie, black jeans and jacket for Kevin, and a tallis draped around my shoulders.

Kaddish came effortlessly to my lips, memorized years ago in Saturday morning services on another coast in another town. The words returned without pause and, surprisingly, the same wave of gooseflesh when the rabbi intoned:

"May the Almighty, who establishes peace in the heaven, grant us peace on earth. Amen."

I sat down overwhelmed by the tumult of emotion inside me, and let the rest of the service wash over me. For Ronnie, Kol Nidre brought back memories of his Jerusalem childhood, of the singing that flowed out of the synagogues into the quiet streets empty of cars. Ronnie had told me once that what he liked most about services was all the songs and no one complaining about his terrible singing. During the service he sat between Edward and me and sang loudly, like a little boy in his off-key voice. I sat holding his warm hand, watching him sing the closing prayer, longing to be home, to be in bed.

"Well, here we are, my holy, non-fasting Jews," said Ronnie raising his glass of wine, "L'chaim, g'mar hatima tova, may you be inscribed in the book of life," he said for my benefit. I'd never mastered Hebrew all those years ago.

"L'chaim," grumbled Edward looking into his drink.

I sipped my wine and, glancing around, noticed a young guy a ways off to my right, his spiky hair bleached to let black roots show. He sat smoking a joint and drinking coffee as he scribbled in his journal, and I wished I were doing the same.

"Cafe Hair-Do's and Diaries," I sniffed.

"Hmm? What's that you're saying?" said Edward in his gravelly accent, leaning forward and turning his "good" ear toward me. I hated shouting so Edward could hear me. It made every conversation sound like an argument.

"Oh, that guy over there writing in his journal. It's so pretentious when people come here and play 'writer.' I don't know any real writers who write here. I've tried, but I always see someone I know. You do see the best collection of hair-do's here though."

"So you're a writer?" asked Edward. "Have you a book then?"

"No, but I've published a number of poems in magazines here and there."

"And how much do you get paid for this writing, if you don't mind my asking?"

4

I heard the challenge in his voice and was suddenly defensive. This was happening in nearly every conversation we had, and I didn't like defending myself, watching every move, like a chess game.

"I don't get *paid*, Edward, I'm lucky to get published. Everyone writes poetry these days." Unnerved by his questions, I wanted to get off the subject fast. It brought up too much — the books I hadn't published, the rejection slips, the little victories that never matched the hours spent writing, the struggle to scrape out a few hours to write after work.

"You mean to tell me that if some magazine wants your writing they don't pay you something? Don't you insist they pay if they want your poem, or do you write for free then? Bloody hell, I don't understand this!" Edward's glowering face demanded an answer, but I felt knocked off balance by this spiteful antagonism that kept bursting out at me.

"Oh, come on," I spat back, "is that all that counts? You only do something if there's money in it? I already do that five days a week, word processing for the corporations downtown. Besides, I'm not writing poetry to make money."

"Well, tell me then, what the bloody hell do you write it for if you please?"

I wanted to avoid the argument Edward was pushing me toward. Last night's fierce altercations, about IRA bombings in London where Edward lived, ended in a tense silence I regretted.

"Because I like to write, if you please. Is that okay with you, Edward?"

"Come on, you two," said Ronnie, shifting nervously in his seat, "not another go round, tonight, hey? Let's talk about something else. Are you feeling okay, Edward?" Ronnie always addressed his father by his first name, Ronnie's habit from hippie days, but it did nothing to make them like friends. Even I felt like I was with my father.

"No, no, I'm fine," Edward replied, his voice softening, his hand shaking a bit as he lifted his glass.

"How about another drink?" I asked, jumping up from the table. I went for another round, and when I returned, slouched low in my chair, drinking my glass of wine too quickly. I so much wanted to hit it off with Ronnie's father this first visit, but every time we talked . . . and eleven more days in our small apartment. I drained my glass and drifted off on the wine when I heard Edward say to Ronnie:

" . . . during the Yizkor, when so many stood to say who their Kaddish was for, I must say I was a bit shocked, so many young people, it reminded me of shul after the war, just after I was at Belsen . . ."

"You were at Belsen, Bergen-Belsen?" I said, snapping out of my reverie. "Are you a survivor of the camps?"

"Well, put it this way, I'm a survivor, yes and no. I wasn't a prisoner in the camps, no small thanks for that. No, I marched into Belsen with the British army right before the end of the war."

"I've never heard about this," said Ronnie. "How come you never said anything before?"

"Ach, I'm not like those old cockehs sitting around with nothing better to talk about than what heroes they were in the war. Besides, I don't like to remember. But sometimes, like tonight, the memories come back of their own."

"Edward, I'm really shocked," Ronnie said, hovering on the edge of his seat like a boy, leaning closer to his father. "All these years, how come you've never told me before?"

Edward shifted in his seat, shrugging his shoulders. "What, when you were a little boy, you wanted I should tell you then? Yad Vashem wasn't enough for you to see, you wanted to hear it from me, too?"

"Of course, you're my father. I mean, you suddenly let this drop like it's nothing."

"Look," said Edward, "why burden you with what I saw? When you were born I was so happy to have a child and to watch you grow up in Israel. I simply wanted to forget, that's all."

"But Edward," continued Ronnie, "not everyone's father has seen what you've seen. I want to hear about what you saw at Belsen, especially since what we're living through is a holocaust for us," said Ronnie, glancing at me.

"I beg your pardon? You have the nerve to say that what's happening in San Francisco is a holocaust, Ronnie? You, who I raised in Israel and should know better? Let me tell you something, it's tragic what's happening, and God forbid it happens to either of you," he said, his voice trembling momentarily. "But a holocaust? No!" he said, slamming his hand on the table.

"For us AIDS is a kind of holocaust, Edward. In its own way," I said quietly.

"Ah, that's nonsense. No one rounded you up and did this to you, you gave it to each other."

"Edward," Ronnie snapped. "No one knew the virus was around, you think we'd deliberately spread this to each other?"

"No, of course not. You misunderstand me. I know it's terrible," he said looking at me, "to lose friends in the prime of life. But please," he said, waving a dismissive hand at me, "no one's rounding you up."

"No, Nazis aren't rounding us up," I said. "But let me tell you, some things seem frightening similar. My friend Kevin I said Kaddish for tonight?"

"Yes, I saw."

"A few weeks ago I watched him choke to death on fluids from edema that filled him from his feet to his lungs. I sat with him after he died, looking at his body for a long time. He looked bizarre—five-foot-five-inch Kevin weighed 180 lbs. from all the fluids, but his arms were so thin, skeletal nearly, like someone out of the death camps. And it made me wonder. . . . All that's left of him now is a plastic bag of ashes. No, Edward, it's not happening for the same reasons, or the same way, but Kevin's not the first friend who's nothing but ashes and he won't be the last, this year, or next."

"I'm very sorry about your friend, my condolences to you," said Edward curtly, "but please understand that while I sympathize, you cannot say it's the same. What happened to the Jews in Europe was a deliberate political plan. This is a catastrophe, more like one of your earthquakes, or some natural disaster."

"Probably," Ronnie said.

"What do you mean, probably?"

"Maybe it's not an accident," said Ronnie. "After all, a virus planted in a bathhouse would be less trouble than camps and trains and gas chambers, wouldn't it?"

"Ah, you've got to be joking," said Edward.

"He's not the only one who thinks so," I said.

"Ah, that's crazy nonsense," snorted Edward.

"No crazier than what they're telling us—that some African monkeys bit and infected Africans who spread the virus to an airline steward who caused simultaneous outbreaks of AIDS in New York, L.A. and San Francisco," said Ronnie, off and running with his pet conspiracy theory, "I don't think anyone's going to tell us if it was planted, do you?"

"No, but this 'conspiracy' idea of yours is the most unbelievable nonsense," said Edward.

"No more nonsensical than the European settlers of America who deliberately sold blankets infected with smallpox to wipe out the Native Americans," I said.

"This I know nothing about so I can't say."

"It couldn't happen here in the 'New World' as you call it, could it, Edward?" My heart pounding in my chest told me I was too worked up again. Kevin's death. I knew that at some wrong moment I'd go off in a rage at the wrong person, or start sobbing, but I didn't want that to happen now, not with Edward.

"Look," Edward intoned, "I know nothing of your 'conspiracy theory,' but suppose it was even half-true? What then, eh, Ronnie, what would that change? It wouldn't bring your friends back to life, or suddenly cure those afflicted, would it?"

"No," said Ronnie, "but . . . I don't know, I've had it with this epidemic, I can't handle it anymore, I guess I want to have someone to blame."

"Everyone wants a scapegoat for a catastrophe, it's only natural to want to blame someone, but what in bloody fact does that change?"

"Well, even if it was deliberately planted, which they're not about to tell us anyway, the government response is nothing but disgraceful and at least warrants burning down the Federal Building," I said.

"And to what good purpose, that?" asked Edward.

"Get some of this anger off our collective chests. Better anger than this communal mope we're all bogged down in. Besides, this right-wing government deserves a good bash from someone, may as well be from us fags. Coffee, anyone?" I said, standing up, then leaned over to rub the back of Ronnie's neck. His brown eyes glistened in the lights of the cafe, and his smile, half-grimace, told me he too wished we were alone.

"Coffee with cream for me," he said.

"Black for me," said Edward.

Offended and provoked, I realized standing in line for coffee that I'd never talked to a witness of the Holocaust. I was now. He was now eighty-four years old. Would I have the chance to talk with Edward again? I returned with the coffees and took a deep breath.

"So tell us what you saw that morning at the *real* holocaust at Belsen," I said, more edge in my voice than I intended. After a moment Edward asked:

"So you really want to know?"

"I do," I said, "for some strange reason." Ronnie nodded his head.

Edward fiddled with his cup, looking into it, quiet for a long time before he spoke.

"It's strange to remember so long ago, but I can see it as clearly as this coffee cup. I don't know . . ." he said, voice trailing off. "After so many years . . . why remember?" A change came over his face, his expression suddenly sad.

"I'd like to hear what you . . . It's important to remember," I said quietly. "You know, there's a wacko organization in L.A., the Institute for Hysterical Review I call it. They claim the Holocaust never happened, that it was propaganda put together by Jews to get U.S. aid for Israel."

"I beg your pudding?" said Edward, one of his stock phrases he used when he heard something he didn't believe. "You mean to tell me that . . . Well, that's the Americans for you. What a visit I'm having in your meshugge country."

"It was in the papers a few years ago, and they're still saying the Holocaust's a hoax."

"Well, strange as it may be, it's not the first time. There was an exhibition during the war, in London, photos and some drawings smuggled out of the camps. Everyone knew Jews were being deported to the camps, but we thought this exhibition was propaganda cooked up in Mr. Churchill's war offices, something in the midst of the Blitz to make us dig in our heels and want to go kill all the bloody Germans. No one believed the photos, it was unthinkable that people were doing such things only just across the Channel."

After a long pause Edward spoke again. "But when I walked through the gates of Bergen-Belsen I saw with my own eyes it was no propaganda."

I hesitated a moment. "How did you end up going to Belsen?" I asked. I thought of Kevin's thin arms. I had only seen photographs, read accounts. A voyeur rose up in me, and I wanted to see what Edward had seen, wanted it made real.

"I went to Belsen because I'd signed up with Her Majesty's bloody army. I was in the Jewish battalion of the British Army that liberated Belsen, but believe me, there wasn't much left to liberate by the time we got there."

"The Jewish battalion? They had separate sections for Jews?" I asked.

"Sure, like your American army with the blacks during the war. It was the same damn thing. The British have no great love for the Jews, let me tell you, but they needed every man to fight Hitler during the war."

"So what exactly happened, Edward," I asked hesitatingly, "what do you remember about that day at Belsen?"

"How clear the sky was that morning, how mild the air was, how sweet it smelled. I'll never forget that day, April 15 it was. We were camped in the woods, we could have been on holiday, but we'd been inside Germany a few days and knew the war wouldn't last much longer. By then we had the bloody devils running backwards to Berlin. When winter finally came to an end that year, we knew the end of the thousand-year Reich was coming too.

"At breakfast we received our orders to march toward this concentration camp between these two small towns, Bergen and Belsen, yeah?

"It was believed the Germans had fled, but no one was certain. No one knew what we were marching toward, mind you, it was the first camp freed by the Allies. So, off we go, brave heroes, down this country road through beautiful pine woods, they were so fragrant in the sun. We arrived by mid-afternoon, around 5:00 I remember. It wasn't much at first glance, the usual fence topped with barbed wire and rows of barracks.

"At first it seemed empty. 'Bloody hell,' I thought, 'just like the British to march us on their rotten breakfast to an empty camp. Nobody home!'

"But then we saw this thing like I don't know what. Not like a man, more like a ghost in that striped uniform they all wore, yeah? Then another and another walked up to the gates, all of them quiet as can be. We walked up to the gates and saw the place was full of people. Some walked up to the gates and simply stood there without so much as a 'Hello.' You'd think they'd be cheering for joy when they saw us, but no. Quiet as can be, and all around, these bloody birds chirping. We walked in and found more of these skeletons with a bit of skin holding their insides in, most too weak to move, sitting or lying on the ground, many in puddles of their own excrement and . . ."

He broke off, staring at the table in front of him.

"What did you see then, Edward?" I asked. Voyeur. Ronnie's eyes said, "Don't push."

Staring at the table Edward continued:

"We went on to 'inspect' the camp further. As we passed one of the women's barracks near the rear of the camp, one woman came rushing out at us yelling, 'Back there, further back past those trees, go look, go look.' We thought there were Nazis back there, so off we go with guns at the ready till we came upon, quite suddenly, heaps of bodies, some in pits, most in stacks. They didn't even look like people anymore, those piles of starved corpses. It took me a moment to understand that these had been human beings like myself. Then the smell hit me. I hadn't noticed it at first, I guess I was in shock. I didn't smell the pine trees anymore."

He turned his head to the side and stared at the ground. For a moment I was afraid he would be sick. Had I asked too much?

"Edward, if it's too painful for you to talk about this, we can . . ." Can what? Forget it? Do this another time? My question felt shallow, learned in some '80s support group. "Do you want to stay with this now and process it?"

"No," he said. "Not painful. It's just . . . gruesome to remember. Gruesome."

He looked at me, then Ronnie. "You've seen the photographs. They took footage of everything so the whole world could see. But a photograph is only a photograph. Every man that marched in with Her Majesty's Army broke down. When I stopped weeping, I pulled my razor from my kit and cut off my payess." Payess, the strange side-curls of hair that embarrassed me when I was a child.

"You wore payess in the army?" asked Ronnie, incredulous. "I didn't know you were ever so religious."

"Sure, it's how I was raised. My father was rabbi for the British

Consulate in Berlin where I was born, which is how I happened to be born a British citizen in Germany, yeah?

"After I cut off both my payess I yanked my shirt over my head and tore off the tallis I wore underneath my shirt like a good Jew. I shredded it with my own hands and threw it with the payess into those stinking pits the Nazis left uncovered, and that was the end of God for me, because I knew after what I saw there was no God.

"And after I threw God away I wept again and when I was done I joined my mates to set up a make-shift hospital and kitchen. Most of the poor buggers threw up whatever food we gave them, so we made a clear broth to help their skin and bones remember what food was, but it was too late for too many. I threw myself into whatever work needed doing, from sun-up till late, and any little thing I had to do I was glad for it, because in between you'd sit with your head in your hands and try to understand what didn't make bloody sense, but there it was in front of us. That was the dangerous thing, if you sat too long thinking. Then you were in trouble. You'd start to go bloody bugger all."

I became aware of people passing by, cars on the street. I was at a cafe outdoors. I felt blurred around the edges. Ronnie, silent most of this time, fiddled with his coffee cup. No, I thought, it's similar, what we're going through with AIDS, but not the same.

It was a new year by the Jewish calendar, and the new year that would come in January would bring more diagnoses, more deaths, and endless caring for the sick, for the friends and lovers left behind. There was something more I needed to know.

"How did you . . . go on after that?" I asked. I couldn't answer anymore about how I went on, year after year of the epidemic, never knowing who was next, or if it would be Ronnie or me. My heart kept beating, I breathed automatically, but I wasn't sure that meant I was alive anymore. Months ago I realized I didn't cry anymore. I steeled myself when someone called with the latest bad news, and kept telling myself I could handle it. But I couldn't. I was going numb inside, and didn't know how to stop it from happening.

Edward looked at me. "How did I go on? I said good-bye to God and looked for the next thing to do to help those poor sods. I talked with the survivors and listened to their stories, what happened, what they had to do to survive. I wept as often as I could. I did not pray, although I wanted to. I assisted at the hospital with my amateur nurse routine and, as I'm a good cook, I cooked frequently. I polished my boots every morning. I stuck to my routines and did the next thing that needed doing. Then one day the war was over. Another day came and with it my orders to leave. Another day I was at Calais waiting for the ferry and spat on the last piece of the Continent my feet ever touched. And then one day I was back in London and looking for a place to live, a job.

"I went on because what else was there to do? Join them in the pits? There were days when I thought why wasn't it me instead of them? It could have been me if my father, may he rest in peace, hadn't worked for the British and had been living in the Embassy. I would have been a German citizen otherwise."

"Did you feel guilty because you . . . because you survived?"

"Guilty? Sometimes, sure, because in all of God's bloody creation was there any reason in it? Why them and not me? It's over forty years since that day at Belsen and I'll tell you. I'm an old man now and still, the only question I have is 'Why?'

"Guilty? I suppose everyone felt guilty once the rest of the world saw. In London before the war, the bloody churches and synagogues were always full, but after? If I went for a walk in my neighborhood on Sunday morning, you could watch the priest shake hands with himself."

"So why do you go to services on the High Holidays, Edward?" I asked. "I don't know why I go at all. I hadn't gone for years till I met Ronnie and then, after everyone started dying . . ."

"Tonight I went because you and Ronnie wanted me to. I could have sat home and been content."

"Really?" said Ronnie. "To be honest, we went tonight because you're visiting and I thought you'd like to go."

"Ronnie, please don't get religious on my account. If I go to High Holidays, it's not to ask a God I don't believe in to forgive my sins and inscribe me in the book of life for the new year. It's to say Kaddish for your mother, may she rest in peace. And since I'm alive, one day of the year I go to remember what I saw that morning in April, may they not be forgotten."

We sat silent in the warm night. I glanced up at the wisteria drooping off the wall of the cafe, the yellow leaves scattered on the table tops and benches. I reached for Ronnie's hand and suddenly thought of Kevin. Nothing I could do would ever bring him back. My eyes were suddenly wet, and I felt Edward's hand grasp the back of my other hand.

"I see your cup is empty," said Edward. "Let me treat this time, I insist."

Rites of Passage

WALTER RICO BURRELL

"Get that goddamned bird out of here!"

Bunky knew he was wrong to bring the baby bird to the dinner table. He knew his father would scream at him just for having it in the house. Dogs, cats, even fish. It didn't matter.

His father had said it countless times: "Houses are for people. Animals belong outside. If God had wanted animals to be in houses, he'd have made them smart enough to make their own. That's why they have fur and feathers. So they can stay outside."

So Bunky knew he risked getting screamed at if his father saw the bird, but it was so little, so helpless. It would surely die without him, he thought. Actually, his father hadn't really *seen* it. He'd *heard* it. The bird was only two days old and it kept squawking constantly for food. The boy didn't know what baby birds ate. To his nine-year-old way of thinking, birds were supposed to eat seeds, but when he'd borrowed some parakeet feed from his next door neighbor, the baby bird didn't even look at it. Then he tried worms. Everybody knows birds like worms. At least they did on the Saturday morning cartoon shows.

Bunky spent two hours after school digging up the back yard searching for worms under rocks and in his mother's flower beds. When he finally found some fat, wriggly specimens, he thought his problem was solved at least, until the bird sat on them unceremoniously in the corner of the shoe box and showed absolutely no interest in eating even one of the slimy, naked, pink things.

Maybe they were too dirty, Bunky thought. After all, wasn't his mother always telling him to wash his apples and grapes before he ate them? So he washed the worms in the kitchen sink, careful not to let either of his parents see what he was doing.

"What are you doing in that kitchen so long, Bunky," his mom asked without turning her face from the five o'clock news.

"Just washing my hands, mother," Bunky replied, half telling the truth.

He always called her *mother*. Never *mommy*. One of his schoolmates once heard him call her mommy and teased him about it for days. The youngster even told all the kids at school, prolonging Bunky's humiliation.

The little bird, one of the many sparrows that made nests in just about every space or hole or opening they could find, spurned the worms just as it had the seeds. In fact, it hadn't eaten anything at all since Bunky became its excited guardian the previous day. It simply slouched in the corner of the shoe box and shivered, its beady eyes half closed.

It was an ugly little thing with no feathers and bulging eyes atop a cavernous, yellow-rimmed mouth. At first, Bunky held it in his warm hands and breathed on it, hoping to stop the violent shaking. This worked in the beginning, but he soon realized he couldn't keep that up for long. He eventually took one of his socks (not a good one, but one with a hole in the toe) and wrapped it around the pathetic, naked lump of featherless flesh. That helped for a while. But the little boy didn't understand that all his love and concern for the helpless creature simply couldn't give it what it so desperately needed: its parents' special care, including their regurgitation of partially digested food into the baby chick's ever receptive, ever gaping mouth.

Still, Bunky tried. He tried with all the best of intentions. He had even risked getting smacked by his father, who had hit him many times for far less than bringing a bird into the house.

A day ago, the baby bird was with its parents in a nest high in the top fronds of the tall palm tree in Bunky's front yard. The tree was higher than Bunky's house, which was itself two stories tall. Bunky could hear the squeaky, high-pitched voices as they communicated high above him in their leafy penthouse suite. He'd seen the parents scurrying back and forth with bits of string and dried grass and even some strands from his mother's discarded wig as they constructed their tightly-woven nest among the uppermost branches of the tree.

Once the eggs hatched, the chicks' squawking inevitably attracted the attention of some of Bunky's classmates who lived on the street. One afternoon, as some of the boys were wandering idly home after school, they heard the noise in the tree top and stopped to investigate. They could see the edge of the nest perched somewhat precariously on one of the palm branches. One of the boys got the bright idea to shake the tree hard enough to make the nest topple down on to the sidewalk. It took all of the boys' skinny, gangling bodies straining against the tree to shake it even a little bit, but they were determined and finally managed to jar the trunk enough to unsettle the nest.

Bunky protested, of course, but the other boys only laughed at him and called him a sissy for not joining in. When the little nest finally fell onto the sidewalk, scattering its delicate contents over the cold cement, the frenetic fourth graders screeched with delight at the pink, writhing little bodies of the newly hatched chicks, their wide, eager mouths agape, hungry for life and expecting to be fed right there on the sidewalk. But no food was forthcoming, though mama and papa sparrow darted about the boys' heads chattering their frustration and indignation over their family having been so rudely torn apart. But little boys are impervious to such logic and their investigative, pre-adolescent minds often take somewhat sadistic turns.

"Wow!" exclaimed one excited, small voice. "They fell all that way and they're still alive!"

It was Sweetums, so named because every morning as he left for school, his mother called after him, "Have a nice day, sweetums." As soon as the kids were out of her earshot, his friends howled in unison through their laughter, "Have a nice day, *sweetums*!" And the nickname stuck.

"Let's take 'em to school 'n share 'em in homeroom," Sweetums suggested with gleeful abandon.

"I got a better idea," interjected Stink Pot, who earned his nickname the all-too-obvious way. According to a story spread around school, his mother fed him beans every day and he developed a habit of ripping off some terrible farts. Sometimes they were so loud the other kids could hear them all across the school yard. The worst were the silent farts he'd cut loose when things were particularly quiet, like during a test when everyone was concentrating. One of Stink Pot's silent farts could turn a classroom into unbridled Pandemonium.

"Let's go feed 'em to Mama Cat!" Stink Pot managed to scream between bites of his Hershey with almonds.

"Yeah!" agreed Sweetums, his big eyes stretching even wider at the thought.

Mama Cat, whose thick, nappy fur had long ago been white, but which was now a greasy, dingy, matted gray, lived behind the store at the bottom of the hill. Nobody owned Mama Cat. Actually, nobody even wanted her.

Occasionally, some of the neighbors left poison food in the alley behind the store in hopes that she'd eat it and die, but she proved to be crafty enough to avoid it every time. She'd even been attacked by some of the neighborhood dogs, but she survived them, too.

It seemed Mama Cat was always either pregnant or nursing kittens. Understandably, she was always on the prowl for food. Sweetums, Stink Pot and the other boys squealed with delight as they scooped up the baby birds, still squawking to be fed, and scrambled down the street. They paid no attention to Bunky as he pleaded with them to try and put the birds and what remained of the nest back in the tree. They were afire with the idea of feeding this meal to Mama Cat and watching with fascination as she chewed their little heads off. So off they ran, giggling and babbling all the while, skipping toward the bottom of the hill. Bunky ran after them part of the way, though he knew it wouldn't do any good.

Half way down the block the boys were stopped in their tracks unexpectedly by Reverend Cleaver. He lived a few doors down from Bunky with his wife and teenaged son and daughter. Most of the kids in the neighborhood were scared stiff of Reverend Cleaver, and with good reason. First of all, there was the sheer presence of the man. He was so big. Well over six feet tall. And he must have weighed more than 200 pounds. He was what some black folks refer to as a *high yella* black man; very light, reddish-colored skin with lots of freckles and kinky, red hair.

But the scariest thing of all about Reverend Cleaver was his eyes. One was light brown, the other green—exactly, Bunky had observed long ago, like Mama Cat's. But while Mama Cat's eyes were mildly disconcerting to the boy, Reverend Cleaver's virtually terrified him. He often had nightmares about them. In his dreams, the reverend was always chasing him; reaching for the boy as he ran from what he believed, at least in his dreams, to be a life or death situation. But Bunky always managed to wake up before 'ol Cat Eyes caught him.

It was Stink Pot and Sweetums who first ran into Reverend Cleaver, who had been working in his yard and had stepped onto the sidewalk as the boys approached, blocking their path. They had the baby birds in their hands and when they reached the minister, they not-so-discreetly hid their tiny contraband behind their backs.

"What you boys up to?" he growled, addressing Stink Pot, those evil cat eyes burning into the boy's brain.

Stink Pot opened his mouth and tried to speak, but no words would come out. He turned to see if maybe Sweetums was going to respond, but Sweetums was just as terrified as were the rest of the boys. Finally, the reverend moved toward the boys, his face a granite portrait of sternness.

But as he reached out for Stink Pot, all the boys bolted and took off down the hill as fast as their shaky little legs would carry them.

"I'm gon' tell your parents!" 'ol Cat Eyes yelled, cheated of his prey.

"You ought to be home doin' somethin' constructive. God's lookin' at you. He sees everything. You boys better get right while there's still time!"

With that, he went back into his yard and as he turned to shut the wrought iron gate, he noticed Bunky still standing on the sidewalk a couple of houses away. He stopped for a brief, cold moment and smiled in the boy's direction. At least his lips moved slowly to a smile position. The rest of his face wasn't smiling at all.

Even though Bunky was terrified of those mismatched eyes, he didn't panic like the rest of the boys. Instead, he simply looked down at his feet, turned slowly, then walked back to his own house, feeling all the while that the eyes were burning a hole in the back of his shirt. He imagined he could feel heat coming from the minister's stare, but he was proud of himself for not running. It was a small, personal victory that no one else would ever know about. But he knew. And he kept walking.

When he returned to his own house, Bunky noticed something. There, on the sidewalk under the palm tree, was one of the baby birds, obviously overlooked by the boys in their haste. Bunky forgot about the minister the second he laid eyes on the tiny bundle of life. As he kneeled down to pick it up, the parent sparrows watched for a moment from a low-hanging branch, then flew off, obeying some instinctive command urging them not to waste useless energy here, but to start a new family elsewhere. For them, there would be other nests to build, other baby chicks to nurture. Such was the unrelenting, forward surge of nature.

But Bunky's young thoughts were otherwise. To him, saving the little chick was thoroughly possible. He would take the little bird into the house, feed it, care for it until it was strong enough to fly, then set it free. Perhaps it would return periodically and perch on his finger, but for the time being, he'd be careful not to let his father see it. Perhaps he could keep it in the garage behind the clothes dryer. It was always warm there, especially when his mother was drying clothes.

Bunky, in his childish innocence, thought perhaps the chick was lonely for its parents, so he sat down beside it and talked to it, trying to keep it company, but of course that didn't change things. In fact, the bird simply slumped over on its side. If Bunky hadn't seen its labored breathing, he'd have thought it was dead. But it managed to squawk occasionally and open its huge, pleading mouth, still begging for food. The boy had no way of knowing at that point that his was a hopeless undertaking. The Holy Grail of eventual freedom for this tiny spark of life was quite simply unattainable. But only personal experience could teach this lesson to an undauntable nine-year-old, so he continued the scenario, failing to anticipate that the ending to this little episode would be a different, sadder one than he had planned.

It was on the second day that Bunky dared to bring the bird into the house. The pathetic thing was very weak and he didn't want to leave it alone, as if keeping it company would prolong its life. He was hiding it beneath the dinner table when the squawking commenced. His father heard it immediately and Bunky knew what was coming. He accepted his father's chastisement without argument, then took the ailing chick back to the garage, returning to the dinner table only to pick unenthusiastically at his food. How could he stuff himself with all that good food while the little bird wasted away in the shoe box behind the clothes dryer?

"Done your homework?" Bunky's father asked with that disinterested tone the boy had come to recognize.

"Did it at school," he answered with an equal lack of enthusiasm, his thoughts on the bird.

"I don't want you foolin' with that goddamned bird anymore tonight," he commanded, not looking up from his dinner plate and barely pausing between mouthfuls of meatloaf to get the words out.

Bunky was not a happy boy when he went to bed that night.

The next morning, he got up extra early and ran, clad only in his underwear, to the garage. But before he even reached the clothes dryer, he noticed something: the bird wasn't squawking. And when he looked into the shoe box, he saw that it wasn't shivering either. He picked it up and was immediately saddened to find that it was cold and stiff. He didn't have to examine it further to know it was dead.

His first thought was of what his father would say. Then the boy was overwhelmed by a burning sense of guilt. Maybe if he'd left the chick on the sidewalk, its parents might have been able to save it. But that was crazy, he thought. Where would they have taken the baby bird? And how would they have picked it up? So many troubled thoughts flitted in and out of the boy's head, but it was what his father would say that bothered him the most.

In his father's eyes, Bunky could never seem to do anything right. The boy didn't like sports. He was too shy. He preferred to read books and daydream rather than get out in the neighborhood and *mix it up with the boys*. It seemed that everything his father wanted him to be, Bunky wasn't. Maybe that was why his father hardly ever looked at him when they talked. It was as though Bunky was only a shadow of a real boy. At least that's what he thought his father believed. He felt he wasn't the kind of son his father wanted. And Bunky thought this business with the bird would make for at least a week of lecturing on how inept the youngster was. Bunky wanted so much for his father to be proud of him for something. *Anything*. Instead, he had, at least to his way of thinking, failed again. He had let the baby bird die. And he was certain his dad would interpret the situation that way.

He knew he could never let his father see the dead bird. He didn't want him to know. He had to put the entire episode to rest as quickly and quietly as possible. It was then that he remembered the small, square screen in the back of the house, down near the ground. It was the opening to a crawl space accessing the house's plumbing, which snaked its way under the first floor. The house itself was set up off the ground about two feet and the space between the ground and the underside of the floor was empty, except for the plumbing and some machinery which made the floor heater work. He'd first become aware of the crawl space when his father squeezed into it one summer day to replace a pipe.

Though neither of his parents was up at that early hour, Bunky ran from the garage, cupping the lifeless little form in both hands, so no one would see what he was carrying. He found the screen which led to the crawl space, pried it loose, then tossed the stiff, tiny body into the opening. It landed a few feet away, rolling over a couple of times before coming to a stop. Its featherless wings clung close to its skinny body as though it was still trying to keep itself warm. The eyes were open, and Bunky imagined they were looking at him accusingly. One of the eyeballs was covered with dirt, and he thought to crawl in and wipe it off, but he stopped, realizing the bird was now dead, and it didn't matter if there was dirt on the eyeball. Still, as he looked at it one last time, he wished that somehow it would blink the dirt away.

He replaced the screen as quietly and quickly as possible, then ran inside the house to the bathroom, where he washed his hands for a long time. There was soft, cold dirt on his hands. He was lost in thought as he watched the dirt flow into the sink from his long, brown fingers in circles which formed a tiny whirlpool near the drain before it disappeared from sight. Soon, there was no sign of dirt, only clean, white porcelain gleaming like a giant, sparkling tooth in a toothpaste ad. He left for school early that day, hoping to avoid seeing his father and running the risk of having to explain about the bird. It seemed Bunky was always trying to avoid his father.

It hadn't always been this way. He remembered a time when he was very little and his mother was pregnant. His father had been different then. He'd been happy and laughed a lot. He'd been nice to Bunky then. He'd pick him up and carry the boy on his shoulders and they'd go for long walks through the neighborhood. Oh, he teased Bunky a lot about being a bookworm and a less than ideal all-around boy, but what the hell, his father reasoned, there'd be other kids. Then something happened to his wife and she lost the baby she'd been carrying. It was then that his father changed. The parents argued nights in their bedroom and Bunky could hear them, even though he pulled the covers tight over his head. His mother cried a lot and kept apologizing to her husband because she'd been told by the doctor she could never have another baby. Bunky didn't know why she couldn't. He just knew that it was terrible and made them all unhappy.

Not long afterward, his father stopped looking into their faces when he talked to them. And he got mad a lot. Real mad. And he started drinking. He even talked to the TV as if it were a person. Of course, the people on the TV never answered him, but he talked to them anyway. They were, after all, if not sympathetic, at least non-argumentative.

So his father continued his drunken tirades with the TV, going on about how his dead son would have been different from Bunky, had he lived. He'd have been big and played football. They'd have done *manly* things together. His other son, he lamented to the always agreeable TV set, wouldn't have been skinny and studious. He wouldn't have been at all like Bunky.

It made the boy sad to hear his father talking to the TV like that. How he wished the baby hadn't died. Maybe then his father would have been happy. He prayed the doctors would fix his mother's body so she could have another baby. Maybe then his father would laugh again and stop being mean to him and his mother. But she never did become pregnant again. Mostly, she sat in her room after dinner and read her Bible. Sometimes she cried softly, quietly to herself, unaware that sympathetic little ears listened intently on the other side of her bedroom wall.

Bunky and his parents lived in the Baldwin Hills section of Los Angeles. It's a decidedly middle to upper-middle class neighborhood comprised mostly of professional blacks. The homes are roomy and expensive and those families who are really *in* live in what for decades have been referred to as the *Dons*—streets whose names begin with the word *Don:* Don Lorenzo, Don Felipe, Don Timateo, Don Luis, Don Zarembo, etc. Bunky's house was on Don Felipe Drive. Even though the families in this hilly Los Angeles suburb have traditionally been bourgeois, their kids sometimes acted a bit rowdy once out of their parents' sight.

No one was more aware of that fact than Bunky, who, at age nine, simply didn't fit in with his chronological peers. He was awkward when he tried to play basketball, or even walk. His clothes never seemed to fit right.

His pants were often bunched up at the waist and seemed to be pulled up high, almost under his bony elbows. One of his socks was forever slipping down into the heel of his shoe. His curly, black hair seemed always to be in desperate need of a comb and more often than not, his shirt was forever creeping out of his pants. He was the kind of kid who was always chosen last for any team during physical education class. It wasn't that Bunky didn't try. He tried with all his heart. It was just that he simply wasn't cut out for sports. He was so terribly, laughably uncoordinated. No matter which sport he attempted, he undoubtedly wound up injuring himself, if not someone else.

It was easy to see why the other boys teased him. Actually, they often did more than just tease. Sometimes, when they were bored, they'd rough him up on the way home from school. They'd take his backpack containing his books or push him to the ground and take his belt off so his pants would fall when he got up and tried to run away. They called him names. Mostly they called him a sissy.

He hated walking home. Sometimes he stayed after school until everyone else had left so he could avoid the bullies. Once he fell asleep in his classroom coat closet and when he awoke, it was dark. He panicked, fearing he'd have to spend the night there, but the night watchman let him out. He ran all the way home, fearing what his father would do. As it turned out, his punishment was unexpectedly easy: bed without supper after he lied and said he'd forgotten about a late choir practice. His father would never have understood the truth.

On the afternoon of the day Bunky hid the dead bird beneath his house, he was walking slowly home from school, preoccupied with thoughts of the little chick. He looked down at the sidewalk as he inched his way home, lost in thought. What he *wasn't* thinking about were those bullies. He kept seeing flashes of the bird staring at him from under the house, dirt still clouding one open eyeball. But he believed his secret was safe from the rest of the world. He was so deeply involved in his thoughts that he failed to notice some of his unrelenting nemeses from school were catching up with him as he approached the small park located half way between school and his house.

He wasn't paying attention and didn't see the four boys waiting behind the park restrooms. Just as he was passing the corner of the building which housed the restrooms, they snatched him off the sidewalk and started pushing him toward the swings, teasing him and pulling at his ill-fitting clothes all the while. It was a familiar routine. Whenever things got particularly dull, they'd enliven their day by picking on Bunky.

Today they were unusually rough on their young peer. One of the boys punched him squarely in the stomach. They didn't really hate Bunky, it's just that the school day had been boring, and they knew they could always have a few moments of fun rousting the skinny kid who seldom fought back. He was easy prey.

But this day was to be different.

Children often fail to realize just how much pain they can inflict when they hit another person, either with their fists or some inanimate object. As a result, they sometimes inflict more damage on each other than they perhaps intend. The blow to Bunky's stomach was a perfect example. It's doubtful the boy really intended to hit Bunky hard enough to make him throw up his lunch, but that's exactly what happened. Of course, this only gave the other three boys something more to jeer at, intensifying their determination to beat the shit out of Bunky.

It was a classic example of the primeval animal instinct to go for the throat once a weakness is exposed. Bunky recognized one of the boys. He was Stink Pot's older brother. He also remembered that Stink Pot was the one who suggested feeding the baby birds to Mama Cat. At that point, something in Bunky's young mind snapped. He was tired of getting his ass kicked. The older boys realized something was different about Bunky. For one, he resisted their efforts at pinning him down on the ground with far more energy than ever before. They were surprised. His legs and arms were flailing in every direction and in the fraction of a second it took them to regroup, Bunky was up and off like a chicken freshly escaped from the butcher's block, but the boys were right behind him.

They caught up with him at the swings. There was a little girl about two years old sitting in one of the swings kicking her little legs in a futile effort to propel herself. Bunky's attackers lunged at him and all of the boys, Bunky included, hurled themselves into the swings, knocking the little girl face down into the sand under the swings. She righted herself, her tiny face caked with sand, arms outstretched, screaming at top pitch for her mother, who wasn't close at hand.

The boys ignored the little girl totally, concentrating, instead, on subduing Bunky, whose adrenaline was raising him to new heights. He pushed away first one boy, then another, amazing even himself as he conjured up strength he'd never known before. And the more he fought, the better he felt. It took the combined efforts of all four of the other boys to finally pin Bunky down on his back in the sand, but he was far from giving up. He pushed hard against the boy holding his left arm, causing the boy to lose his balance and fall down, bringing his face close to Bunky's. Since the only thing Bunky could move at this point was his head, he moved his face forward with a quick motion, bringing his mouth close enough to the boy's head so he could take a bite out of his left ear. He clamped his teeth down on the kid's ear so hard he could feel the gristle separating under the pressure of his jaws.

The boy screamed as though he was being murdered, but there was no getting loose from Bunky. The youngster was in such genuine pain that he instantly let go of Bunky's arm, but it wasn't until Bunky started choking on the stream of blood which now flowed from his opponent's ripped ear that he finally released his toothy grip, using his now free hand to wipe most of the warm, sticky blood from his mouth.

The realization of what he'd done sickened Bunky, but only momentarily. Now that his one hand was free, he reached around desperately for something, *anything,* he could use as a weapon. The usually shy, timid little bookworm had simply been pushed to the proverbial wall and there was no turning back all the rage that had been building up inside him for all his nine years of life; rage against his father, against the school bullies, against everyone who had misinterpreted his kind, sweet nature for weakness. He was insane with hurt and guilt and loneliness, and today he was not getting his ass kicked.

While the one hapless boy ran screaming across the park with part of his ear dangling from threads of bloody flesh, the other three continued with their increasingly difficult effort to do some physical damage to this sissy-turned-tornado. At least they'd always thought he was a sissy. Now they were having second thoughts. One of the boys got in a couple of good licks to Bunky's face, causing him to turn his head to one side and close his eyes against the blows. But he continued to grope in the sand with his free hand, searching for a stick, a rock, anything at all he could use as a weapon.

Finally, he touched something. It was hard and long and rusty, with a kind of point at one end. It was an old railroad spike which had been used to nail down the wooden beams which surrounded the sand pile, keeping the sand in one area. It had apparently fallen loose and become half buried in the sand.

The boys' mood was no longer merely mischievous. They weren't going to be satisfied with merely roughing Bunky up. They were a few years older than he and were seriously intent upon teaching him what they felt was a well-deserved lesson. How dare this puny little sissy lay into them this way, they thought. Their blows took on a new intensity, which caused Bunky to swing his free arm with even more desperation and determination. He wielded the railroad spike through the air like an old, crusty knife which had lain undiscovered all this time, waiting for this moment to fulfill itself.

Finally, the spike found its mark. Bunky still had his eyes closed against the flying sand and fists, but he felt the slender piece of rusted metal sink into what he instinctively knew was flesh. One of the boys screamed and suddenly everything stopped. The three remaining attackers and Bunky were motionless, except for their labored breathing and the quietly crunching sound of the sand as they began to separate themselves from one another. The little girl still sat not far away, crying and wiping sand from her mouth and eyes.

When Bunky finally opened his eyes, he was horrified at what he saw. One of the boys, obviously the one he had stuck with the spike, was facing Bunky on his knees. Bunky and the other two boys stared at the injured youngster in shocked disbelief. His youthful, cherubic face was streaked with blood. His right eye dangled from its socket, still connected to his face, but only by what appeared to be veins and arteries attached to the back of the eyeball itself.

It was a gory sight: the eyeball hanging there, looking at nothing, lying against the smooth, innocent cheek, the eyelid drooping grotesquely over the now sunken space where the eye had been. The injured boy got up, then began running around in disconcerted circles, moving more on impulse than with any preconceived sense of direction. The other two youngsters took off as fast as their legs would carry them and didn't look back once.

A crowd soon gathered around the blood-spattered boy and the little girl's mother finally arrived, ignoring her own offspring to attend to the boy, who was by now in shock. She screamed for someone to call an ambulance. Bunky watched the scene and it seemed to play itself out before him in slow motion, like the slowed down instant replays during the televised football games his father watched on Monday nights.

He walked home very slowly that afternoon. His head was spinning as he recalled all that had happened. What a curious assortment of emotions he felt: revulsion at the memory of the boy's eye and the taste of warm blood from the other kid's dismembered earlobe, pride over how he had defended himself, fear of what his father would do when he found out what happened. He took a longer time than usual getting home that day.

He wasn't sorry about what had taken place in the park. He was just glad it was over. The one feeling which dominated all others was that of new-found self-esteem. Bunky felt, perhaps for the first time in his life, that he didn't have to live at the mercy of anyone ever again. Not the bullies. Not even his dad. He was going to stop being afraid. He wasn't a sissy. He could defend himself. They'd have to find someone else to pick on from now on.

His thoughts switched to one of his cute classmates, a girl whom he'd admired for a long time, but to whom he'd never spoken, fearing rejection, plus the inevitable teasing he knew would come from the other boys. But that would be different now, he thought proudly. Once the story of the day's events made its way through the student body, he figured he'd emerge a hero of sorts. Maybe now he could talk to that pretty girl, whom he imagined had been glancing at him from the corners of her eyes.

He knew that what he'd done to the boy in the park was horrible. There was no denying that. But he felt so damned good! He kept thinking to himself that he really wasn't a sissy. He was just as much a boy as were the other guys. He felt taller, bigger, better than he'd ever felt about himself. And no one was going to cheat him of this moment. *No one*.

When he arrived home, he went immediately to the bathroom and washed the caked, dried blood from his hands and face. His blood. The boy's blood. It was all intermingled on his face and hands and clothes. The blood was dark and dry until the water in the sink diluted it. As he stood there cleaning himself, he remembered having washed his hands after the bird died and how the dirt had formed a little brown whirlpool as it made its way down the drain. This time there was another whirlpool, only it was red. The dark color faded to pink, then clear, as the water continued to cleanse him of the day's bizarre experience.

Then, finally, as before, the color was gone and all that remained was the glistening whiteness of the sparkling porcelain sink and the shiny silver drain hole which gleamed under the bathroom light. Bunky felt cleaner than he'd ever felt in his entire young life. Clean in body, and more importantly, in spirit. He stood back and looked at the new boy in the mirror and savored the strange, new happiness he felt.

Bunky had taken his clothes off and was stuffing his dirty pants and shirt into the laundry bag in his closet when the doorbell rang. It was still early afternoon and his parents weren't due home for at least another three hours. Besides, they wouldn't ring the bell anyway. He figured it was probably someone he knew at school. Perhaps even someone who had heard about what happened in the park.

He stood behind the door as he opened it, sticking only his head around to see who was there. He was shocked to see 'ol Cat Eyes standing there with his arms folded. Seeing Bunky, the corners of the reverend's mouth went into that familiar mechanical smile position, while the mismatched eyes locked in on Bunky's face. Instinctively, the boy started to close the door, slowly, even before the man spoke.

"Your parents home, boy?"

"No, sir," Bunky answered, pointing his face toward the floor to avoid looking into those eyes.

If the boy hadn't been so terrified of the older man, he might have pointed out that it was only a little past 3:30 pm and his parents were still at work. But the reverend already knew that.

"Well, I'm gonna talk with them about you and your school friends. You kids can't be runnin' wild through this neighborhood."

"No, sir," the boy mumbled almost inaudibly, still looking at the floor.

"I don't mean to say you're like them," Cat Eyes continued, softening his tone a bit.

Without looking up, Bunky began to slowly close the door, but he was stopped by the grownup's big, hairy hand as he grasped the door by its edge and pushed it open, revealing Bunky's slim body, nearly nude, except for his underpants. The boy was extremely uncomfortable standing before 'ol Cat Eyes this way, but he was frozen with fear into his position, his eyes still downcast. The reverend looked down at Bunky for a long, contemplative moment.

Bunky wanted to force the door closed and bolt both the locks, but he couldn't move. Even though he was looking at the floor, he could nonetheless feel the eyes, stretched wide open so that areas of white shone all 'round the pupils, staring at his naked, brown body. He felt himself blushing, though it wasn't visible through his dark coloring. He was grateful the Reverend couldn't tell he was flushed with both embarrassment and stark terror.

"I'll come back later when your parents get home," the Reverend said in barely audible tones.

His mouth was saying the words, but his concentration was on Bunky's small body with its firm, pre-adolescent butt straining against his Fruit-of-the-Loom briefs.

Bunky was so relieved: Reverend Cleaver was leaving. He was going to come back later. Thank God! He continued to gaze at the floor nervously.

"Yes, sir," he answered without looking up.

Then, as Bunky started ever so slowly to close the door again, he was aware of an opposing pressure to open it wider. Cat Eyes was pushing against him and the boy's terror mounted.

He didn't know exactly why he feared the reverend so. The man was, after all, an adult, to be respected and obeyed. But it wasn't the usual chastisement from a grownup that Bunky feared. He always paid attention to what adults said. He'd been taught by his parents that grown people were wiser and that they looked out for the best interests of children. If a kid did something wrong and one of the neighborhood adults walloped him on the butt or even yelled at him, that kid knew he was going to catch additional hell from his own parents once the grownup told on the child. The adults were definitely in charge, collectively, and Lord help the kid stupid enough to defy one of them.

So it wasn't the normal adult/child relationship that Bunky feared whenever he was in the Reverend Cleaver's presence. What, then, was it that scared the boy so about this big, freckled-faced man with the mismatched eyes? Well, the eyes themselves were certainly part of it. Bunky had never before in his entire life seen any human with eyes that were two different colors. It was weird. Even on Mama Cat it was weird. It was even worse on a human. In Bunky's mind, it made the reverend more animal-like. But at the particular moment he confronted the man at the front door, Bunky felt in a creepy way that what he had always feared in his nightmare was about to happen: 'ol Cat Eyes was about to catch him at the end of that chase.

Bunky was surprised at himself for daring to push the door shut against the reverend, but it was a futile effort. 'Ol Cat Eyes didn't even have to try hard to keep it open. Bunky's heart was pounding so loudly in his ears he was certain the reverend could hear it, too. The door was finally wide enough for the large man to pass into the living room.

"While I'm down here, I'm sure your parents wouldn't mind if I used your bathroom."

"Well . . ."

But he was already inside.

"I'm sure it'll be alright."

"But my mother said . . ."

'Ol Cat Eyes placed his hand firmly on Bunky's shoulder.

"Just show me where it is, son. I won't be a minute."

Bunky walked slightly ahead of Reverend Cleaver toward the bathroom. His feet felt as if they were cast iron and it was difficult placing one in front of the other. When they reached the bathroom, the boy tried to step aside and let the grown man pass, but the reverend only hardened his grip. He was now hurting the boy.

"Ow!"

"Come on in here. I need you to help me."

Bunky's feeling of terror was at its greatest now. He had no idea of what was going to happen to him in that bathroom, but he knew it was going to be horrible. He lost all pretense of composure and began to struggle against the reverend's grip, but it was useless. He might as well have been a toy doll and the older man a huge gorilla. The reverend snatched him inside and locked the door. The boy reverted totally to being the frightened, innocent child he was and began crying uncontrollably. 'Ol Cat Eyes spun him around and slapped him hard across the face. Bunky stopped crying and looked up at Reverend Cleaver, terrified, not knowing what to expect, wishing his parents would come home early, wondering what he had done to this man to deserve this. He searched his memory, but could recall nothing he had done.

Reverend Cleaver kept his left hand on Bunky's shoulder, as if the boy were going to run away, but he couldn't have run even if the thought had occurred to him. He was so confused by what was happening that he didn't think of running, or anything else for that matter. He simply reacted to each moment, each bizarre new event, as it happened.

The older man never took his left hand off the trembling boy. With his right hand, he began to nervously unzip his pants. This done, he fumbled around inside his pants, through the opening in his boxer shorts, for his penis. He trembled, as though he couldn't get past these preliminaries quickly enough.

Then Bunky noticed something odd, almost funny, if it hadn't been for the absolute seriousness of the situation. It was the reverend's undershorts. They had little red hearts on them! The child was able to detach himself from the gravity of his circumstances for the briefest of moments and at one point he almost smiled at how ridiculously funny the hearts looked.

But he was snatched back to the horrible reality of the moment when the reverend's hard, fat penis plopped through the opening in the middle of all the little hearts. Bunky's mouth dropped open when he saw the penis. He looked away quickly, as though looking at it was bad. He turned his head away as far as he could and closed his eyes.

'Ol Cat Eyes used his left hand, still on the boy's shoulder, to force Bunky slowly down on his knees. As he did this, he turned his body so that his huge penis was now sticking out through his underwear on a level with Bunky's face. He still hadn't released his trembling grip on the boy's shoulder, and he used his right hand to try and force Bunky's face to come in contact with his now stone-hard penis. As he moved it toward the child's face, Bunky couldn't pull away, but he did manage to turn his head so that the penis, surrounded by scraggly, reddish and white hairs, slapped against his cheek, smelling of that special, rancid odor that occurs only beneath the foreskins of uncircumcised males.

What happened after that was fuzzy in the young boy's mind when he tried to recall it during the days and months that followed. But if the experience was anything, it was certainly his most horrifying nightmare come to life, only he never imagined anything quite this terrible could actually happen in real life. In his dreams, he was always running from the reverend, but the man never caught him. Sometimes, when he awoke in a hot, feverish sweat, breathing hard like he'd been running his heart out, he would laugh quietly to himself, feeling proud that he'd once again cheated 'ol Cat Eyes of his prize. He would lie there on his bed, gazing through the thin curtains at the moon-lit backyard and try to imagine what would happen, *in his dream,* if the reverend ever did manage to catch him. But even his wildest imaginings failed to equal this incredible, horrible reality.

At some point, the reverend forced Bunky to lie face down on the shaggy white rug which lay in the middle of the bathroom floor. The boy was held in place there by the fat, hairy left hand which had still never left the boy's body. With his right hand, the minister was able to pull Bunky's underpants down from his small butt just enough so the man could place his bulging penis against the boy's slim, brown body.

Bunky was trembling all the while. Not a violent thrashing about, but a constant, all-consuming shaking accompanied by a quiet whimpering. Tears flowed slowly down his face onto the rug. The minister spat onto the fingers of his right hand, then slapped the spittle onto the boy's smooth butt. Then the man was half lying, half perched on his right hand, which was braced on the rug, for his full weight would surely have smothered the small boy, literally crushing the life from him. As it was, Bunky could barely breathe and the minister's face was so close to his own that the boy could smell his foul breath and feel the dampness of the salty sweat which dripped profusely from the man's face onto the boy's neck and back. Bunky was frightened, but in his child's mind, the reverend was still an adult and as such, the boy didn't feel, even in the midst of such unspeakable humiliation, that the grown man would really hurt him. But that belief was shattered when, accompanied by a loud groaning and increased sweating, Reverend Cleaver plunged his big penis into the boy's anus.

Bunky's trust in adults ended at that moment. The intensity of the pain was beyond the child's imagination. It shot through his body, reaching instantly into the farthest extremities. He felt it in his legs, his feet, even behind his eyeballs. He wanted desperately to move away from the hard, intruding penis, but there was no space between his body and the rug on which he lay. Again and again Reverend Cleaver stabbed the boy's now bloody buttocks with his unrelenting sex organ. After a while, the pain passed into numbness and the blood became a macabre sort of lubricant. Then the reverend screamed and pushed himself into the boy's body one final time and ejaculated. Afterward, he fell onto Bunky as though he were having a heart attack. Bunky was barely conscious, but he thought that something had happened to the reverend.

There were no tears now. The child simply waited to see what each new moment would bring and submitted to it, hoping it would all end soon.

The large man was panting heavily as his sweaty body nearly crushed the breath from the boy's small, thin frame. Then he lifted himself off the child and as he pulled his penis out of Bunky's anus, a new wave of pain sliced through him. His skinny, wrecked little torso twitched violently, reacting to the intense pain. Still, there were no tears. The reverend got up, still breathing hard, still perspiring, still trembling, his putrid stench filling the small room with an odor Bunky would never, ever forget.

Reverend Cleaver was a mess. His nappy, red hair was in desperate need of combing. His pants were down around his knees, traces of semen evident around the opening in his underwear, staining some of the little red hearts. He slowly got himself together, looked around as if finally realizing where he was and what he'd done. He looked down at the boy, lying so unnaturally still on the blood-stained white shag rug, and smiled a demonic smile. Bunky didn't move. He simply lay there, his eyes closed against this ghastly reality. He was determined not to open them again until the minister was gone. He was so ashamed. Surely, he thought, something must be wrong with him for him to have attracted the reverend in this manner.

"You'll be alright," 'ol Cat Eyes said as he fastened his belt.

Bunky still didn't move. He tried not to breathe. At this moment, he wanted more than anything not to exist.

"An' I know you're not goin' to say anything to nobody. I know that, 'cause you're smarter than them other kids. You'll be alright. You're a good boy."

Then he left.

Bunky lay there for what seemed to be a long time, but he knew he had to get cleaned up before his parents came home. He had to get rid of every trace of what had happened so his father wouldn't find out. His father would be furious if he knew what happened. He already thought of Bunky as being a little sissy. He'd probably think his son *encouraged* the reverend. All these thoughts flashed through Bunky's mind as he forced himself to begin cleaning up the bathroom, and himself.

First, he put the rug in the bathtub and ran water over it 'til the blood was rinsed out. Then he took off his bloody underwear and stepped into the tub, pulling out the knob that released the water through the shower nozzle. He watched the water flow down his body, washing away the minister's smell and the blood and the sweat. The warm water stung as it spattered against his bruised buttocks. His anus had been torn a bit and the salt in the reverend's perspiration burned a little before it was washed away. He dried himself off, then wrung out the rug and hung it over the side of the tub as his mother had trained him to do following his daily showers.

Then the boy, still dazed, put on a pair of jeans and returned to the bathroom to rinse the blood from his underwear. He placed the stained briefs in the sink and turned on the water. The sink was soon filled with redness as the blood separated from the fabric. He let the water run for a long time, but he couldn't get all of the blood out. He certainly couldn't put his drawers in the dirty clothes hamper like that. His mother would surely ask him how they got bloody. He decided to get rid of them. But where? Under the house! Where the bird was.

He slipped on his tennis shoes, went to the opening at the crawl space, pried off the screen, then tossed the soiled underpants into the opening. They landed next to the now dusty body of the bird, still staring blankly into the near darkness under the house through dirt-speckled eyes. He replaced the screen, then returned to the bathroom to make certain the sink was clean. There were still traces of blood near the drain. He ran the water a while longer, but even after all the blood was gone, he could still see it there in his mind. The sight would continue to flash into his consciousness for years afterward whenever he turned on the water in the sink.

His father never did learn of the horrible events of that day. At least not those centered around what the reverend did. He found out about the fight Bunky had in the park. He even went to the school and met with the principal about it and, to Bunky's surprise, he actually defended his son's actions. It had clearly been a case of self defense and eventually all the excited talk about the event passed into legend. Best of all, the older boys didn't bother Bunky after that. They could sense that he was somehow different now. And it wasn't just that he'd stood up to them. It was more than that. It was the new look in his eyes. He was different in a way they couldn't understand.

Bunky would feel guilt over the incident surrounding the minister for many years, well into his adulthood. It would be years before he'd be able to convince himself that he hadn't caused what happened. The timid, shy, introverted little boy experienced rites of passage that day in the bathroom and in the park. He left innocence and trust behind and turned his feelings increasingly inward.

What an emotional day it had been. The fight, followed by its momentary elation. Then the disgusting business with Reverend Cleaver. An incredible, horrible day for any nine-year-old boy, but especially for Bunky. These psychologically and physically painful rites of passage had come early for him.

And the pathetic vestiges of the briefest of childhoods lay in dusty secrecy under his parents' house.

Hector and the Madrina

LEONARD TIRADO

Wind whipped off the river like a slap across his face. He didn't mind. It woke him and was almost a relief. To feel the welcomed smack of cold reality, something he'd have bitched about any other day, seemed to ground him. And he needed something solid, it seemed, to stand on. Last night had been too fuckin' much . . .

He had half-wanted to bolt out of that room, but stayed, somehow attracted by more than just curiosity. Like it was a way of getting back at his old man or something, he reflected now on the pier. But I shoulda' stopped playin' along with her long ago. Then none of last night's crazy crap would've happened.

"Stupido spics, actin' like they still back on the island." Internally he grinned with NueYorican smugness, lifting his head back to catch an updraft of air off the choppy waves out and in front of him. The otherwise smooth and shiny light brown skin of his face crinkled around his eyes, the creases being made giving the impression of the most intense pleasure being experienced. "Shit," he thought, "somebody walkin' by will think I'm cummin'."

He laughed quietly to himself at this. Not now, save it for the maricons, was the flash-thought he had without even filling out the words in his head. Stifling a satisfied guffaw, he lowered his head, shaking it back and forth mirthfully, opening his eyes slowly, savoring his humor. It was mid-afternoon on the west side piers, the sky dirty gray and streaked with cheap-looking, torn clouds. They looked like the tufts of cotton you yank out of aspirin bottles, the kind his crazy old jibaro grandma kept leaving 'round her house across the hall from his parents' apartment.

"Fuck, listen to me. I talk like I hadn't grown up there off the Grand Concourse." He shook his head, the humor turning sour. "That should tell you somethin'," he thought, to no one in particular. "I don't even think of it as my crib no more. You'd think the folks would get the message when I'm not in the Bronx often enough for them to have to piss and moan about my staying out all kinds of hours.

"But my grandmami's ok. A little crazy. But then the whole family's fuckin' nuts. Grandpapi, a stone cold, old time Puertoriqueno all his life. Scared of only three things. Priests and fuckin' white cops were two. The third was grandma. Sometimes I think the old man said the rosaries to ward her off. When they called her a madrina I didn't know those bugged NeuYoriquenos meant she was some sorta barrio priestess.

Grandpapi had been more citified, worked in San Juan, and was one hundred percent Catholica. He'd returned to San Germain, met his future wife and married, emigrating to the states just after the war. He knew she was of peasant stock, blood mixed more of Taino and Caribe Indian lines, laced with a lot of Yoruba African, than his.

Grandma's folk were hill people, and they were certainly wilder than the relatively tame town folk his grandpa came from. The only noticeable craziness was in the preponderance of missing fingers and thumbs among townsmen. He had noticed it when his grandparents, parents and he had returned to the Island for a reunion with all the relatives left behind. It was something needed then since his grandparents were aging and might not see their kin again.

In that mixed up combination of pride and fatalism which the boy noticed was common to older Puerto Rican men uncomfortable with as-similation, grandpa had explained this tendency towards digit-deficiency among his townsmen. It was due to machete brawls fueled by Ron Rico. When rummed up, the workers would take these banana, pineapple and coconut harvesting tools to each other in fights over women.

He'd spent the rest of the vacation just staring, somehow with awe and trepidation at those missing thumbs and fingers seemingly everywhere he went. Their absence became a paradoxical lack which seemed an asset, an overwhelming "plus." It intimidated the gnawing inferiority his father had begun to verbally and physically pound into him just as he entered adolescence. It resonated with the mano lesserness he felt whenever his father's ire lit upon him.

Papa had long since made it a habit to deride the boy's competency at every turn, even to the point of challenging his paternity of him to his face. His father had done this out of spite, during an argument with his mother. As in any other emotion-loaded exchange between them, he had quickly deadened himself to the word's intent. He had immediately stifled self-awareness of the pain and disorientation thudding in and out of him. The entire living room—the cheap Woolworth's curtains on the window, the floor's olivey linoleum, the plaster Santa Barbara and its votive candle glow on the corner wallmount—all dulled imperceptibly. This was his survival mode, and all it allowed the boy to see and hear was a vague, watery, far off image and echo of his mami's plaintive protest over this man's shoulder.

Eventually, beneath the weight of it all, this was what he finally came to see his father as: that man. He lived with a stranger, and for a while he had scanned framed pictures and scrapbook snapshots for some remembrance of the parent he dimly recalled once having. But he got tired of that, and tired of living under that man's roof, another victim like his mother.

It had culminated on that trip to Puerto Rico. It had fallen into place, his feeling of being nowhere, out of it. They had come for the holidays, but he spent Christmas and Three King's Day and the New Year's looking at that man's relatives, staring blankly and being hugged by strangers, being a stranger to himself.

The only one who noticed something wrong was his grandma. His father avoided any confrontation at all with this wiry and pointed-jawed, high-yellow old woman. Esperanza was her name, and she was his paternal grandma, but the authority she exercised always struck her grandson as being more than just mother-right alone. In what would otherwise be a man-defined family hierarchy, she appeared as an abiding, status-unto-herself presence.

It was more than influence, it was power. A kind of power that seemed to come from some place back in beginnings before there was a Bronx, before being Puerto Rican even, but somehow innate to it.

Her craziness amounted to something after all. It kept her daughter-in-law from becoming a husband's punching bag. Yet his mother expressed caution in the reserved gratitude she expressed to Esperanza. Like her husband and her father-in-law his mother displayed a wary deference to the old woman's authority.

During the Puerto Rico trip Esperanza had noticed her grandson's increasing distance, so had drawn him closer to her. More than just love and concern were involved. It was as if she was unilaterally rearranging relations within the family, literally excising him from his mother and father's orbit and into hers.

He had felt the beginning tugs of that movement when he had fled next door to her apartment whenever relations between he and his father were most strained. It was there he had noticed the mermaid statue.

Like any Puertoriqueno household, his grandparents' apartment had its share of icons Catholica. Santo Antonio, Our Lady, Santa Therese, Santo Isidro and others, as plaster images and framed pictures, looked on three of the four rooms of the small apartment. But in a fourth room, in the rear, away from the plastic covered sofa and reclining seats common to old folk, was a different atmosphere. It was as if the apartment's territory of jurisdiction abruptly altered. Catholicism seemed as left behind as the noisy arguing between his papi y mami.

This fourth room was off the kitchen at the left, and was about the same size as her grandson's bedroom across the hall. He came to look at this similarly, as his grandma's room was where she could get away, even if she still slept with and shared the marriage bedroom with her spouse. Therefore, it didn't take too long before her grandson saw this, too, as an additional retreat and shelter for himself.

He had seen the mermaid in his grandmama's room on the top shelf of a large, four-shelved cabinet attached to the furthermost wall from the doorway. There were other figurines on these shelves, prominent among them a lithe, robust, gold becrowned black man, bejewelled and broad-grinned with a large single-hoop earring through his left ear. In a plate alongside, a lit cigar would sometimes tracingly smoke the room's sunlit air.

This room was the brightest in his grandparents' apartment. And it was off-limits to his grandfather. Not that the old man begrudged his wife this. He scrupulously seemed to avoid the room, only surreptitiously giving it a glance, even when giving assent in any conversation Esperanza might initiate about it. The room's presence and its contents was evidence of a long-arranged truce consequent to Esperanza's betrothal to him on the Island.

When Esperanza wasn't housecleaning or shopping, she could be found in this room puttering, it seemed initially to the boy when he first chanced upon his grandmother there. His grandparents had moved up to the Bronx from off of East 115th in Manhattan. There appeared to have been some complaint about this from the boy's father—something about Esperanza's meddling in his familia. Esperanza's spouse had half-heartedly tried asserting patriarchal authority, but could not dissuade her from what was obviously a unilateral decision. And grandpapi was of no mind to jeopardize an apparent long-standing truce, even for the sake of honor or appearances.

Far back as he could remember Esperanza seemed to especially favor her grandson. Sometimes the boy wondered if that was part of the growing animosity he felt from his father, a confused, hapless, frustrated combination of envy and resentment, as if he viewed Esperanza's attention to his own son with jealousy and a rage of betrayal upon the boy's part.

Sometimes her always eyin' me could be a grande pain en mi culo, he recalled, half-derisively, but then weighed in again the next moment in her defense. Esperanza had also saved that same culo plenty of times, too! He shook his head to a beat only he could hear, there on the pier as another gust of jagged wind buffeted him.

He'd been little then, this being a good eight years before their trip to Puerto Rico. He'd run into his grandparents' to hide from his pop who'd come upstairs from a particularly nasty street-brawl. This was the earliest memory of his father: blood-matted hair, blood streaking his creased brow and scowling face yowling in Hispanol, his mother screaming, "Arnaldo! Arnaldo!" Her brittle-nailed fingers were gesticulating vaguely for some sort of aid as pop scoured their kitchen for a baseball bat, too busy seeing red to notice her.

That shift had been too much, he recalled, for a five-year-old not knowin' what the fuck's goin' on. He'd taken off for his grandparents' in terror. Blindly, out of habit, he had burst from his apartment over to next door on spindly, half-stumbling legs.

Esperanza had literally caught him on the rebound from the unnerving commotion of his parents. Blindly he had bounced into her slim, bony frame as she was exiting from this room off her kitchen. His grandparents were still unpacking stuff at the time, and corrugated boxes, empty and still packed, begged off the A&P, had made the apartment area an obstacle course. But the boy's disorientation and shock seemed to provide him a radar that averted his colliding with anything as he scrambled zig-zag to the apartment's rear.

"Hector . . . Hector . . .!" Esperanza's exclamation was a simultaneous command and coax, calming the boy with its authority and comfort as he bounced off, then clung to her. His grandmami hurriedly wiped her hands on her apron so she could hold him. The noise next door had obviously caught her ear and had interrupted her own doings. As she stooped her short frame and gave him an assuring hug, the boy noticed five strands of differently colored beads around her birdlike throat. They were nothing like the usual Catholic rosaries he'd occasionally seen around the throat of other women like his mother.

So she had escorted him into her special room where he had seen the statue of the black man, some sort of African king with the name Chango. Jesus, all them statues had mother fuckin' names, and Esperanza talked to them like they were all alive. It was ok when he was a kid, kinda' like havin' dolls or imaginary friends, but he never let on to his father about it. Remembering the ol' man from that night in the kitchen was warning enough that it wouldn't go over too big with him.

But the mermaid was something else. She caught and held his anxious eye that day he accompanied his grandmother into special room. In the background the boy heard the slam and shout, complaint and consolation of his parents through the walls of both apartments. But the noise was distant, muffled, fading away as he looked at the mermaid, first out of surprise and curiosity, then deepening interest.

The mermaid was a slightly chub-faced, beige beauty with wavy black hair falling to her rounded and bare shoulders. On her tresses the mermaid wore a gossamer silver hair-net, and together they fell across naked maternal breasts and a torso that ended in an aquamarine fishtail. The statue, including its pedestal, stood a good ten inches in the top place of prominence on what Esperanza called her Canastillero, or altar. Draped over the mermaid was a string of alternating blue and white pearls.

"Never mind them," his grandmother told him, dismissing the faded commotion with a brush of her hand, and an extra close hug. "Dona Jainana has been waiting for you." She ushered him from the kitchen strewn with boxes to the side room.

The mermaid had a name, and some connection with him it seemed, for Esperanza added, ". . . Like she waits for all her omodere," and turned and crouched before him, looking at his questioning face closely. "And omo-mi, you are indeed one of her children. I've seen it more and more every day. It's why I told grandpapi we were moving here!"

Esperanza scrutinized her grandson's momentarily blank look, as if drawing something up from it. And he did feel a strange, warm stirring, like the slow turnover of ocean waves.

He was never to feel anything like it again until that trip to Puerto Rico, on that side-drive to Arecibo. Upon that cliff-side of tall grass, the lush and lazy crash of actual waves sounding from rocks below, adrift in the hot midday sun, the pressure of his cousin's hard palms upon his shoulders . . . And the damp of sea-salt and beginning sweat upon the groin being pressed into his face.

Memories had suddenly crisscrossed in his head, the first summoning up the second. He quickly brushed the latter from his mind. He was 17 now, and had been trying to distance himself from Esperanza. He realized his grandmother was probably crazy with all her half-Spanish, half-African— Yoruba she called it—bullshit. It was scary, and he had enough to worry about on these streets without bein' spooked by bohio shit that belonged back on the Island.

It had started back then in the old lady's altar room. Esperanza saying she was going to ask the mermaid's ache, the thing's power and blessing for him. "Since your birth Yemaya has been watching over you, Hector, and it's time to acknowledge your elada with gratitude . . ."

She had placed one hand on the back of her grandson's head, the other on his forehead, tilting it back. He hadn't known what to do next, especially when his grandmother began to hum and rock back and forth. And when these words seemed to emerge from a secret, depthless place within her body and into the sunlit room . . .

Acherererere Iya milateo, Yemaya asayabico Olokum,
ibutagara dedeguato Olokum, Ocobayireo
Arabaibulaomi,
Cofieddeno Iya-mi Ayuba . . .

He had played along with his grandmother, being obliged to the old lady for standing up for him so often. What's more, Esperanza was a source of extra cash those times he didn't feel like making the walk, when the faces of the same johns every night were getting on his nerves. He liked the pro mano image he'd earned on the streets early on in his hustling, but he felt that somehow the steady faces of his regulars were clinging to him now, dragging at his consciousness like Esperanza hanging onto his shirt- sleeve last night.

Esperanza had talked him into attending some party she'd been talking about months before. He'd been especially sick of the walk lately. He prided himself on his outlaw status. Hustling 'cause some of his homies had tipped him to the easy coin it garnered, he fast made a king's rep. Owing no one anything, he'd kept it clean, not turning into a champion ripping off his tricks to maintain a jones.

Trouble was, the crank and crack heads and P Funkers were stumble- bumming downtown to the Village, and scaring off the more reliable johns, leaving only the freakier doggers around. Money was getting tighter be- cause uptown burnouts were less likely to keep the belt on in order to up the ante. Wave enough vials, and any of these mother fuckers became two way bargains with no pretenses of just bosin' it. A fuckin' shame 'cause he liked the Village.

So it hadn't taken his grandmother much to talk him into accompanying her back to Harlem. Babbling some shit about his asiento, she had sat him down on the plastic-covered sofa, telling about what had been a busy day for her.

Straight-backed and serious she had looked him pointedly in the eye there on the couch. "Listen, Hector, I had an audience with the Babalawo, Don Tito, about you." Her grandson knew who she referred to: another crazy jibaro, a Puerta back on the Island who emigrated same time as she. Instead of the ex-sugar cane cutter he'd been, everybody treated him like the pope or something.

Fuck! Summertime, old Don Tito sat on his trusty orange crate on the sidewalk outside his building sipping his Ballantine from under the brim of the pava he'd wore over from PR, even though he was a retired assembly line worker form a corrugated paper box factory in Jersey. The mother fucker was even crazier than his grandma!

Esperanza eyed her grandson with her black crow's eyes. "The padrino has been my confidant since our kariocha together back in Arecibo. We had been childhood playmates, so your grandpapa had no reason to be jealous, especially since grandpa is an aleyo, an unbeliever. Anyway, I've been telling him about you, Hector."

"Telling what about me?" had been her grandson's irritated response. He didn't like his business spread about 'cause sooner or later it'd get back to his pops, and there'd be renewed hassles. Besides, how much did Esperanza know about him anyway to fuel her gossip back in the old barrio?

"That you're one of Yamaya-Olukun's chosen, omo-mi," his grandmother reminded him. His mind flashed to the mermaid on her altar, which he still occasionally glanced at, as if it still held hidden significance for him. He shivered.

"Only a Babalawo like Tito can toss the Dilloggun, what's needed to be done before I could be certain it was she who is your ocha. As the Italero of our Ile-Orisha he consults the cowrie sea shells which divine these things. Only then could I be sure enough to have these made . . ." Esperanza had bent down to her large purse crumpled on the thin rug by her couch seat. From it she fetched a hand-sized white-ribboned mass of aquamarine tissue paper.

His grandmother gently, gravely placed the hand-wrapped tissue upon her lap. Only then had he noticed she was wearing the white lace dress and shawl worn only for rare special occasions, times he had watched his grandfather almost powerlessly just frown and oblige her unexplained exit from their apartment.

"Now I can give you them," Esperanza had told her grandson, slowly untying the ribbon, unwrapping the tissue, the cadence and tone of her voice calm and low. Laying there in the open crumple of paper were five bead necklaces. "Here are your colares," she explained, adding, "Hector, let me put them on you . . ."

He had just sat there as she placed each one gingerly, yet increasingly joyously, around his neck. His grandmother counted them off one by one with a significance he didn't understand. "Here is the eleke of Obatala," she said first, putting a string of all white beads 'round him. "Of Oshun," she said next, this strand being all yellow. Esperanza uttered, "Chango," and followed this with a string of beads that alternated six white to six red. Inexplicably her grandson felt his mouth thickening with anxiety, suddenly overwhelmed by wonder about what next to expect. Esperanza went on. "Eleggua," she said, stringing a necklace of alternating reds and blacks, three to a color, around him. Her grandson's throat tightened, his mouth dry all of a sudden as she almost whispered, "And Yemaya" with a slight emotional tremble. She reverently touched the rug and kissed whatever dust there might be from her used fingertips.

This last necklace was identical to that strung across the mermaid statue; seven white beads alternated with seven blue, then a single white and single blue bead for each complete cycle up to seven for a finished strand. For a moment the necklaces weighed upon his throat, then a numbness, a lightness to him seemed to spread from there throughout his body.

This lightness had sunk through his legs into his feet, allowing his grandmother to quickly hurry him out the house and onto the subway without protest. The ride seemed a flush of dull, vaguely outlined blurs of colors. Nothing and nobody stood out in his mind except Esperanza. Her presence was more felt than seen sometimes during the ride. He had had sense enough to hurriedly button his shirt and bundle his heavy coat to conceal the necklaces. But, unseen by others, their weight against his chest poised an uncanny centeredness past which the wash of everything else seemed to go.

The subway's dull roar seemed unending, yet, when it sounded most so was when it abruptly burst. They rose into blurred, yellowy Spanish Harlem streets that jumbled past his eyes and ears like he was caught up in a waterlike flood of Autumn night. Then they flashed by a neighborhood botanica. Passersby and exiting customers who were strangers to her grandson seemed to doff hats and bow to Esperanza.

The sharp, sudden turn of the street . . . his grandparents' old tenement apartment building . . . up the squat stoop . . . through a mouthlike dingy lobby . . . down a once familiar main floor corridor that now seemed a winding, downward slanted tunnel to his dazed and dull eyes. Overhead, like snakes slithering quickly by, basement ceiling pipes steamed and hissed.

Then the thick slap and pounding of bata drums—the three of them: Iya, Itoleye, and Okonkolo—exploded in his ears. They were the kind he sometimes saw NueYorican homies play at the park. The sight and scent and brushed-by feel of dozens of Puertoriquenos flooded around him. He was in some unknown never even guessed at room beneath Esperanza's old building, surrounded by white clad dancers of all the barrio's colors and sexes and ages.

They writhed and swirled around him, seemingly oblivious to him, yet he still felt somehow to be the center of their attention. His feet were unsteady, he blinked uncomprehendingly, reeled, but maintained his footing. He felt awash as dancers swept 'round him, like he had stepped off some beach into an incoming human wave. The dancers whirled, blurred, their outlines less and less distinct, he becoming immersed in body heat and flecks of sweat.

The interweaving drumming became distant. Like a bird cry over an ocean's noise he thought he had heard Esperanza's voice in the crazy language of hers, over and over . . .

He Yemaya Lorde Aboko Hae Aboko Lariote Lari Ote
Ote Ote Yemaya Lorde Lari Ote Lario Lario Lari Ote Lari
Ote Ote Ote Lario Lario Ote . . .

The patches of white and blue black, the octaroon and maroon, beige and olive—the people swirling around him—seemed to acquire birdlike shapes, as if accompanying Esperanza's more and more birdlike cry. He had blinked, swayed, and in his mind's eye had flashed back to that Arecibo cliff and the hotness radiating off the shimmering beach below. Overhead, sea gulls—gaviotas, his grandmama had called them—arced and sliced across the azure, but he hadn't been noticing the sky. The gaviotas' shrill cries had come to his ears, heightening the new yet frightening excitement he'd discovered at his cousin's sweat-beaded crotch.

His mouth had gone wet at the recollection of the taste of salt to his cousin's pubic curls. The brushing of his cousin's thickening and lengthening cock upon his cheeks and chin, the prod and gradual push of it between his inexperienced lips. The pressure of moving hands upon his thirteen-year-old head, fingers snaring themselves in his hair, the quickening pace of penis into gulping mouth . . .

Fuck, no! He yelled at himself or no one in particular. Fuck this shit! I'm the mother fucker who bags it . . . it's them who pay for it. As out of a bad dream, he seemed to wake and panicked. Sweat-drenched he looked quickly 'round, then bolted. Out of that fuckin' nuthouse, away from those crazy jibaros . . .

The sudden shriek brought him to the present. He glanced up and saw a seagull wheeling around close to the river waves. His eyes went red. He pushed himself away from the pier-rail, spitting. Backing away, he picked up a chunk of busted pavement and heaved it at the bird. Fuck You! Fuck You! Get the fuck away. . . .

Walking away, he looked around, seeing if any johns were around. It's them who want it . . . it's them who pay for it. . . . He stopped short. And saw her.

She had come up on him unheard, unseen. This tall statuesque black woman, skin a deep chocolate, eyes a lunar white in which were set shiny ebony pupils. Her thick hair braided in cornrows over which hung a gossamer veil with milky pearls woven in. He stopped short. A sea smell wafted to his nostrils. He eyed her closely, not knowing what to expect.

He saw the oval ripeness of her breasts straining against the turquoise waistcoat she wore, but his eyes widened at the strand of pearls hanging loosely from her throat. It was of the same alternating blue and white order as the beaded necklace draped upon his grandma's mermaid statue. His hand felt for the necklaces around his throat as he remembered.

He looked from her chest down to her matched miniskirt. His breath intaked on itself and choked slightly. He had thought her a stray street hooker, but saw the barely restrained bulge of cock outlined against the skirt's tightness. The Transvestite whore extended an open palm in inquiry, "How much?"

"Get lost, Ioca," he tried sneering, but for some reason fumbling to back it up with any meanness. "I don't do queens," he added, feebly, as if in apology, awkwardly feeling the seventeen years he was, for a kind of power emanated from her eyes, reminding him of the sparkling heat reflected off those Arecibo waves and beach. The TV whore stepped towards him and opened her purse. She tossed him a hundred dollar bill.

"We have unfinished business, Hector," she told him. It was crazy, but he didn't ask how she knew him. He just watched the uncreased C note flutter to the ground like a seagull circling around a spied fish in the sea. He didn't say anything, just nodded his head to an abandoned garage nearby.

He wasn't even aware of their even walking over there. They seemed to have floated. Through the rusted, half-pushed-aside garage doors, past broken windows, across the garbage, discarded rubbers and needles and pipe screens. The sound of flapping wings, the cries of the gaviotas and the sea-scent returned on the sound of drums pulsing in his ears.

He looked over his shoulder. They were deep inside the wrecked building. The TV whore imperiously unbuttoned and removed her waist-coat. Brown nipples poked out as she lifted her blouse, breasts bouncing heavily free. He felt a free hand of hers push him gently to the floor. He didn't know why he was letting her get away with this shit. Hector was on his knees there amidst the crumpled newspapers and thrown away and ripped old porn mags.

Yet he didn't do a damn thing. He heard the sound of the skirt being pulled down, the slide and snap of undies being flung. He waited on all fours, like some fuckin' bitch, he told himself, trying to get angry enough to resist and slap this maricon into place.

Yet he did nothing but feel the playfully rough tug of his denims from his flanks and down his behind. His buttocks' short hairs were brushed by a breeze from a nearby broken window. The TV whore's long forefinger traced the curve of his rump with its lacquered fingernail. Then she swept both her hands up and down his ass, kneading each buttock. She spaced his bent legs further apart, nudged the rest of him close to the garage floor.

He felt one of her hands spread his ass open, the other slowly insert phallic hardness into him. The drums and gull cries rushed to his forehead with beads of sweat: he had suddenly thought of the pain of being fucked. But the TV whore's cock eased into him, deep inside, gradually, awakening him to sensations and feelings he'd pushed away before. "Omo-Yemaya, subirse el orisha a su caballo," the queen whispered huskily into his ear as she pressed her chest against his back and her cheek along his half-turned face.

As the TV whore rocked in and out of him, he finally realized his grandmother had been right about who and what he was.

October 1979

JAMES L. WHITE

October 8, 1979   **I** don't know how to begin this or even if I want
to begin, the story of my life, because I'm a failure and a very unhappy
person. That means a lot of the words would whine a great deal, but I think
life is unusual because it's full of romantic deception upon which I've
acted. That makes it unusual; the romantic deception. Through most of my
young life I was on drugs of one sort or another which made the romance
seem real enough. Because I was (and am) mentally ill, it all seemed real to
me. So I lived a fiction as I do now. I was a half-rate ballet corps dancer, a
soldier, a poet of some small merit, a wanderer of the earth, and a self-hater.
But how does one begin all this . . . a little house simple enough on the
prairie, humble origins where the basic virtues of honesty and forthright-
ness bored me . . . no. My origins were humble enough; I never rose from
them. Today, at 43, I had to count all the pennies in a jar because it's Columbus
Day and the banks are closed. I came up with six bucks and some change. I want
enough to go to the bathhouse this afternoon.

Again, the origins; because so much of my life is out of touch with
reality or perhaps because I perceive it in a different way, it's hard for me to
describe it clearly. I lived in a yellow house in Indianapolis with a mother
who always seemed old to me and mostly without joy, though she remains
in my life, as with most homosexual men, the most constant and strongest

figure. I had a father who seemed no more than a shadow. He worked nights as a gateman for the gasworks and would leave me a small present in his smoking stand in the morning, an orange or a little toy.

That's about all I remember of him, until I was eleven and my family forced me to go to the hospital and see him. It seemed he was lying on a table in General Hospital, nearly naked, a sheet over his middle and glass tubes seemed to protrude from him in all directions. The white sheet seemed so white in the gray room of the city charity hospital. My father seemed so removed, as though he'd gone elsewhere the way the dying often do, that he didn't seem himself. Later, I was to see a photo of Spain's great bullfighter, Manolete, taken directly at his death. He was on a strange makeshift operating table, completely covered with a white sheet save for his head. Because the camera was old, the white of the sheet burned the photo so it seemed to glow. The men about Manolete, all in black suits and bowlers, were posed before the camera. Posed! They were grinning, or staring directly into the lens of the camera. Every one of them posed; not one looked at Manolete—the great flower of Spain—who had already gone out, who had the grace in death not to pose, who seemed to me luminous in his death as he was luminous in his life.

But my father seemed removed too. I didn't really know him there on the table, so thinned by the disease, having been in a coma for days. But I didn't know him in life either. He was a large shadow that I feared. The only images that stay with me are the summer nights on weekends when he'd be home sitting on the front porch smoking his cigar, the sound of the porch swing when we lived on Winter Avenue and the glider when we lived on rural Street, how he'd not say much; just the glow of the cigar, the yellow bug light on the porch and the moths.

He and my mother were never married which made him more of a stranger. My mother bore me. She'd had three children by another man who left her, so she raised them herself. Then she met my father who was married to an invalid, so he could never really marry my mother. But these are legends and half-lies and I'm not sure of the truths of the occasions because they were extracted from an alcoholic cousin of mine for a few drinks I'd given her. All I know is he was a shadow and silent, and his world was ruled by women. And they must have been women who hated him, or hated men in general: my mother to this day hates men, I believe. She must have.

All she could remember was their cruelty and strength against which she must have felt helpless. Her maiden name was Baley and she lived with her mother and father on Irish Hill, the very poor laboring part of Indianapolis. She was English blood living among the Irish laborers. My grandfather, who I never met, who was another shadow in my life, was a brick layer and house painter and a drunk. So there were always strange drunk men around the house, and my mother would say sometimes, "They'd try to get dirty with me," and she'd have to throw them out.

But all this is shadow again, not the real truth. The real truth is locked in our bones, in the history of our bodies and is never spoken. The real truth about the story of our lives is so far locked down in us that it has no words, and that is the most honest history. Not that my father was a stranger and smoked his cigar and looked long out into the night nor that my mother hated men and said two days after we buried my father, "It's a terrible thing to say, Jim, but we're better off without him," nor the night he died when she put his pillow in the closet and slept from then on in the middle of the bed. This is recordable history. What we all feel and never say is the honest truth.

I am this history. Forty-three, dying of a bad heart, a moderately good, moderately known poet. But all that lies too. You ask me who I am and I say, "I'm a man something like my father, always looking away, looking hard out into the long night. I am my mother, working hard as any man to keep the two of us alive after his death and hating the struggle and hating the males who caused the struggle. No, this isn't who I am either: I am the result of these emotions. The nameless, the voiceless and soundless built me, where there was no father to become, no mirror in which to look, only the need to call "father" into every street, every bar, every desperate hour of my life. Who has the right to call any man "father?" That is burden indeed, and yet what son doesn't want to call that name as though someone could help or understand.

Again, this becomes a lie. When it's voiced, it's a lie.

My father would disappear for long hours on weekends. He'd walk downtown. He must have been very lonely. He must have wanted desperately to talk to someone. He was, to my knowledge, totally severed from his family, his origins. I don't even know where he came from. Only his real name wasn't White. It was Broadell, Roscoe Broadell, which means "the fastest horse of the broad valley." When we buried him, we buried him under the name White or god-knows-what. There were so many lies in my family or, more correctly, there were so many truths to choose from, and each had part of the truth in it. But generally what was silent was the larger part of the truth, the larger history of myself.

I wondered where my father went when he disappeared. I'm a very sexual man and I always dreamed that he sought flesh in some way. Even the flesh of the burlesque house. That would be a mysterious connection with my father, for I've spent a large part of my life seeking every conceivable sexual act with men but somewhere in my stomach it is known that it was never the right man. My father was never dead enough, so I tried to find him through other men, and of course it was never the right man. As the psalm says, "Like the hart desireth the waterbrook, so longeth my soul after thee. . . ." To say villain of my father is easy enough, that he was a bastard, that I am his bastard. Those are simple ways to define a person, but to say he is a part of my loneliness and that I must have been a living part of his despair is to say it more clearly. From here, I don't think we're so good or bad. I think we're simply led astray by what we believe as the truth.

(I think it must be important to get rid of what I think is literary about my life and to write beyond that surface to the marrow which is not literary but more beautiful. I stare right now at a white wall that won't let me get by with anything because it is myself again, without frill, without mysticism, without the useful lies that have kept me going all these years.)

There are such strong pictures I remember of my mother after my father died. An old woman in a black coat chopping wood for the fire stove. In summer, an old woman lopping chicken's heads off as they flew around in great bloody circles up toward the blinding sun then down to the ground. She seemed to have all the strength in the world to do that—but she must have all the anger necessary in the world to do that. To put her fat body in a girdle and then into a cheap black dress, to carefully count bus tokens, have her lunch in a brown paper bag. She worked first as a seamstress, then as a salesperson for a Jewish credit store on South Illinois where the Jews treated the workers like shit, even in the '40s when we were just getting news of Hitler's camps. I was glad in my young way that the Jews were being mistreated because my mother would come home at night, beaten and tired from the day, and say, "Damn Jews." So I knew they were people who made my life unhappy.

And even today, now that I am a civilized and educated man, when Jewish friends do something that annoys me, I'll think, "Goddam Jews," and feel better. But there was a time when I was more ill and didn't allow those thoughts to surface; I had heart failure instead. So there are times when "fuckin' Niggers" will do nicely. It seems odd: once I allow myself to voice those things I feel free of them and I feel free with Black people or Jewish people . . . but underneath it all, I don't care one hoot or a damn about either group.

I have always had the ability to look straight at you and tell you exactly what you want to hear. It's one of the ways I have, one of the ways homosexual people learn to survive, by giving the illusion of reality.

October 9, 1979

Wall, I wonder why I don't want to write poetry anymore. It's because I've gone as far as I want to go with it at the moment. I feel I'm as good as I'm going to get for a while, that the language and metaphor of poetry will no longer do to say what I have to say. I'm very tired from my last book . . . too tired, I think, for into it went most of my dying and I want relief from the intuitive takes that come from writing poetry. I want to use my intellect a little more closely. Writing poetry, one must write too much from the body and see too much from the stomach. I need a break from that. Plus, and this is a very large concern: I want to see if my book's going to sell on the big time. The big time's very important to me . . . has been . . . will always be.

Why remember? What has my life got to remember? That I grew up out of a strange mind. I can't say life is childhood, adulthood, middle age. For me, it's always been backwards and forwards. I could never see my place in the family. I knew I was with people who were adults and I was very small, but I didn't know why they were connected to me. I didn't know what "mother" meant because my sister Mary took care of me a lot. I didn't know what "father" meant because he worked at night and slept during the day.

He seemed angry all the time. All the men of my childhood seemed angry. Drunk and angry. I think it was because the women were so strong. Irish women can endure anything and what most of them have to endure is men who drink too much and stay out late drinking with other men. It's an odd vantage point writing this as a homosexual because what I see as I look back at the men of my family is that they were more comfortable with men. The women must have frightened them. They were like naughty boys with their drinking, and I wonder if in some way they weren't homosexual. They seemed to be with women out of a sense of duty and obligation. Even now I seldom find a "ladies' man," a man who enjoys the company of a woman rather than another male. I enjoy it when I meet one, but most of the men I know are husbands, "good men" and hubbies. They've gone from a childhood with their mommies into manhood with their mommies again. They have their male friends for fun and play (and I'm not speaking of homosexuality). But I believe both men and women are responsible for this phenomenon of mommies and little boys. The roles are comfortable for both, but how boring they become to me.

I remember very little about the yellow house on Winter Avenue. I remember a dairy that had a silver tower and railroad tracks. All through my childhood I remember railroads because we lived so close to them. They thrilled my childhood because those great, beautiful, loud, clanging, steaming, black things were going somewhere . . . somewhere that I would never know. I'd look at those trains going down the tracks and my heart would long for the distance those train drivers must have known, those grand old fellas who always waved. And late at night (in another house when I was older and we lived by the coal yard) the trains came very close and would shake the house, would shake the window panes, and again would shake my heart, wake me from my sleep with the most warm comfort, their whistles like something searching the night. The train whistles calling out became me. Something about them would stay forever though I knew life would not. My father talking softly in the bedroom wouldn't last. My world of things wouldn't last.Only trains and the end of the world, the two inevitable elements of life. The beautiful great trains and the flaming balls of fire which would destroy the world before I was grown.

I would ask my mother if the end of the world would really happen. She would pause and say, "Yes." She really believed it would happen and it always terrified me because it happened from sin, my sin, and the sin of those around me. There was nothing to be done about it. I would sit on the back steps with my dog Jerry, in the very late day and think, "This is the time it'll happen, when the sky is nearly red." I would look at the conveyor belts and machines in the coal yard that looked like gigantic praying mantises or prehistoric dinosaurs and think, "This is the way the world will end, these strange shapes taking form, the world in flame, my mother and father and sisters and brother dying in flame, everything going up in flame because we are alive and to live means to sin." I would sit on the back porch steps and cry with my dog and think about this often, would talk to my young friends about it. Now I realize we were experiencing the first atomic bomb blast in our psyches five or six years before its happening.

But I was brought up during WWII so flame and destruction were a part of my nature. The newsreels were full of it. But it was death I related to myself. It was death I was somehow responsible for. I wonder even now if I can carry with me a yellow figure, running and burning in the night. Where fiery chemicals are made by companies with benevolent names like Dow. I carry these things with me as we all indeed must.

Last summer I saw a very great Nagouchi show at the Walker Art Center. A man my age, Japanese-American. He had one room, full of scale models of unfinished projects, projects that were never funded. One of them was a proposed tower filled with the bones of the Hiroshima dead to be placed on a mountaintop where the wind would play songs through them. Terrible songs, not like the haunting and lovely train whistles of my childhood, but songs that could only be played from death. The idea of the tower haunted me. One Sunday I woke up and thought, "If the wind would play these songs, what would the words be?" I tried to write them but couldn't, knowing silence and wind are better and greater than what could be said. Later that Sunday I found out it was the anniversary of the Hiroshima bombing. Psychic? Of course not, but I think the gesture of destroying so many people with our technology is something that has been put into our bloodstream. All of us! I believe I cried for the dead when I was a little boy worrying about the end of the world.

I think we have all had to carry this with us. But what I carried more, looking back on it all, was fear. That's what we lived with in the forties. When I was seven or eight I knew there was a war someplace and that my brother was gone and the people to hate were Germans and Japanese, but it was a vague something that I never fully understood . . . it was something out there.

There was a paint company across the street from my house. Very late in the war, German POWs were employed there. They stayed at Camp Attabery and were brought in by trucks, had little brown paper bags just like school kids. The first day they were there we were coming home from school and saw them. We were little school kids and we all picked up rocks to throw at them, calling them Nazis and Krauts and Huns. Al Moody, the owner of the plant, came out and said if he caught us doing that again, he'd call the police and have our fathers put in jail. That stopped us.

But I would sit by the fence staring at them for hours. They were young men like my brother and spoke German which amazed me enough. But they were not what I had been told they were: they were human! One man in particular always smiled at me when I came out of the house and sat by the fence. I think I must have loved him. He seemed beautiful . . . I think now he had blond hair. I remember the sun and cold fall mornings, him by the paint-tanks smiling at me, how I hated every German in the world but him. But if you make the exception, your argument's shot forever.

I have often seen gay men and straight women have very warm and full relationships. I've questioned why that is and one element is that they are both free of sexuality. The woman is not pursued and the man doesn't pursue. The air is clear of demands and the games of sex. Some of the closest friends in my life have been women. We seem to experience a sense of relief almost.

My sexuality was beginning to waken about the time of the German POWs, and terrible pictures of the concentration camps were being made public. There were also sexual undertones to all of that. The "girly magazines" picked up on it right away, and at Pillman's Drugstore there were always drawings of men beaten, tied and beaten, their chests exposed, large bleeding muscles. The women always wore leather and a swastika; she was in power. I always had sexual feelings for the GI who was being beaten. I'm not trying to make a case for sexual masochism or sadism but more to say that there was always more than what met the eye. Even my brother, to the family's amazement, came home and married a school teacher, second generation German, named Stellmach.

October 10, 1979

As a young girl, my mother worked in a bird cage factory twisting wire into exotic designs, "You had to go as fast as your fingers could go," she'd say, "and if they bled, you kept right on going." I remember as a little boy how terrible I felt, that I should like to have done something to stop what it was my mother had gone through—the bird cage factory, the drunken men in her father's house. Even now she has a recurring dream of having lost some money in a stream and her father, angry with her, knows this and is coming after her. Her hands are buried under water looking for the money and she's afraid.

There's nothing romantic or even novelesque about poverty. I've always hated it. I've always been frightened of it. I inherited the fear of it from my mother. But I believe I inherited fear of life in general from her. Her life was painful and full of huge controls she didn't understand. The control of men, the control of money, the control of "the Jews." And she fought back with real anger and hatred, some of which carried to me.

I remember the day after my father's burial my mother sitting at the kitchen table trying to collect herself, which meant biting her lip and looking out the window, saying, "I don't know quite how we're going to make it," and then she cried. And the next day she went down and found the job at Rite's Clothing and Jewelry, Easy Terms. My mother and I to this day have a private joke about "easy terms." Whenever something is obviously crooked or impossible, we look at each other and say, "easy terms."

That period of my life in Indianapolis was rather fantastic, or seemed to me fantastic. Rite's Clothing was right across the street from the Mutual Burlesque House which had a second floor stairway that led right into the bar next door called "The Stage Door." A fantastic enough place. There are rumors that late at night James Whitcombe Riley would view the women of the Mutual Burlesque and then drink himself into oblivion at The Stage Door. But the burlesques fascinated me. It was naughty and forbidden, but my mother always had stories of the strippers who would come to the store to buy clothes "on terms" and how they seemed decent enough though they were still cheap.

I look back on the period and think of it with real excitement. I never knew we were poor. It never occurred to me. "Nigger kids" that lived way down on Rural Street were poor, but my clothes were clean, I got lots of presents at Christmas, and on my birthday we always had lots of food . . . so what was poor?

On Saturdays I'd stay at my brother's house and we'd pick Mom up after work. She'd usually have bought four big ham sandwiches on egg rolls and potato salad at the bar. We'd go home and eat. My god, the food back then! You can't imagine how good the food was, and cheap, too. There was a place called The Phildelia Oyster House which was so dirty-looking it could crawl. Old winos always worked there. There were three things you could eat: oyster stew, raw oysters, and steamed shrimp . . . lovely shrimp boiled in water with a little bay leaf and melted butter. Businessmen went there at noon. Oh God, it was elegant. And there was Wess Deli, I'm talking about the old one. Thick ham sandwiches and big egg rolls and great potato salad or baked beans, or the city market with everything you could imagine, foreigners running the booths and the best food you could buy. The Jews and Italians and Greeks all bought their stuff there, and there was a real Chinaman who sold tea. He wore a little gray jacket, chain-smoked, wore a little black silk hat, spoke almost no English and sold the most exotic teas, the finest, from wonderful red tins.

Oh, God, those people were beautiful, were so utterly who they were, and what they sold was pure. It was class! We were poor, and when we bought there we knew it was good. Now, in 1979, I think a true poverty has settled into people's lives because they often don't know what the really fine is—not the expensive, but the fine. There's no place for the young people to learn it. It's not around much. To not have is one thing, but to not know is a terrible thing.

We would pick our mother up in front of Rite's in the snow, and the iron bars would be slowly closing in front of the windows. My mother was in her salesperson black dress. And the snow and all the Christmas things glittering, the streets and the burlesque with a star billed in front, her tits being slowly covered over with snow. "Evelyn West, and her fifty-thousand-dollar treasure chest." My mother would talk about some of the "stars" coming into the store: "My God, she was every bit as old as I am, and bleached hair so stiff it looked like a haystack! But she seemed nice though. Just as easy to talk to as anyone you'd want to know."

My mother too has always had an air of acceptance about her, a kind of liberal spirit hidden to most of the family. I don't know if that's because in the past she decided things weren't quite as proper as people carry on about, or because she felt her son is homosexual, or because she went against the grain of what must have been a pretty Victorian society, not marrying, having an illegitimate son. She was never too condemning of the bizarre. I think it's because we were a bit bizarre. Even now for some odd reason, she lives on a street in Indianapolis that is inhabited by lesbian couples. She is very accepting of them, is involved in being their friend. I don't say that as a grand statement but more as another example of how with her (as well as with the rest of the family), the truth of something may be there as long as it's never voiced.

My older sister Gert lived with a drunken man for thirty years and never cried out for help until finally her heart nearly exploded from grief at not saying what she wanted to say. She was in a spin all those years, and my heart has done the same. In writing about these drunken men, I too look at the men in my life. Three-fourths of those I've loved have been either drunks or drug-dependent. And part of my love process has been to take care of them just like the women in my family have had to take care of drunken men, pull their shoes off, listen to them wail the sorrows of their plight, tend their anger. It's as if the women enjoyed the men being like children so they could do what was most familiar—offer solace.

One of the things that so frightened me when I drank (and if I drink now) is that I rage in my sleep. I roar, and I've done so since I was a young boy. The underneath in me is terrible—the three-quarters below the iceberg, fearful and dark and large. Yet on the surface I've appeared a gentle and kind man. That's one of the useful lies of my life. I think that's one of the useful lies of being homosexual: we appear to be what we are not and our terrible anger is masked. Don't be confused when you see a swishy homosexual man being campy and outrageous. You are observing anger, anger and outrage he himself is often not aware of. His feelings of violence and frustration are taken out against the society by breaking the icons. All minority groups have their hidden angers: the slow "shufflin'" black (though that has almost disappeared), the stoic calm Indian who goes out and drinks himself into oblivion and suicide, the grotesquely comic gay man, drunk and popping pills. It is all an inappropriate acting out of anger, emotion that is inverted and eventually destroys the angry person, destroys the homosexual, and I think of course that's what the society wants: America has always been good at giving minorities enough rope to hang themselves. With the Indian it was government aid through the Bureau of Indian Affairs, with the Black it was the attempt at turning them into poor reflections of whites by keeping them on programs that allowed them to stay poor, and with homosexual people it's a building up of public hatred. The most liberal person can still comfortably hate gay and lesbian people; it is still an accepted hatred. As the joke goes: "A faggot is a homosexual gentleman who just left the room."

I saw such a structure once when I was in the Army, stationed in

Germany. I had taken a German tour to Paris. On the way back we stopped at the WWI battleground of Verdun where thousands upon thousands of white crosses were on well-cared-for green lawns. A large chapel had sun pouring through the stained glass onto the shrine-like graves of the French officers. Below was a round, glass-like structure where the bones of a million, million, million men were housed, as many as on resurrection day, as many as depicted on terrible medieval wood blocks of dancing skeletons going toward hell. All the bones of the unidentified dead placed in this great sphere.

It was Sunday, late. Vesper bells were chiming someplace. The German bus driver was leaning against the door having a cigarette—he'd seen all this before. Old French women in black were tending the graves.

Is this the eternal job of women?—I ask this as I write it—tending the drunks, tending the dead, tending the sick? I've heard women in my own house say, "He was a good man but he liked his booze," "He was a good man but he could never hold a job," "He was a good man but he had that temper." The women seem to endure. Until having found this new freedom, it seemed as though my plight was to endure the grandiosity of male egos because I have tended, as the women of my family have tended, as I have learned from them to do. To tend, to wait, but no more.

October 11, 1979

I watched the city of Indianapolis change from a soldier's town during WWII back into the mild and ominously conservative . . . yeah, unimaginative place that it is today. But during both WWII and the Korean War there was a carelessness and ease that made it a comfortable place to live in. Anyone as drawn to sin as myself found the whole atmosphere of a downtown area dedicated to taking the money of transient troops "for a little French fun" their cup of tea. For me it was not so much "my cup of tea" as relief from the tight and closed atmosphere of my house and my mother. It was dark in a way that I'm sure has marked my entire life.

My mother was in a great deal of pain. She must have felt enormous rage and abandonment at having been left alone to raise a small boy. She wanted me to know how hard life was, how difficult it was for us, how men had caused all this, so from her I developed this fear. And this attraction.

But the time during the wars was great in the city. Indianapolis had a strip on Illinois street that I've seldom seen equalled. Perhaps I was simply young and it was my first such experience, but on a Saturday night it lit up the sky like a zircon ring bought at a pawn shop. For some reason, everyone called the strip "the Levee," just a section of bars, the bus station, cheap hotels, a great cheap chili parlour called Blacker's Chili Parlour. If you could stand eating the food and didn't throw up, you would realize it was great food . . . great chili, great tamales. Perhaps this was a foreshadowing of my love for the Southwest and its great food.

But the strip represented a kind of freedom for everyone. The servicemen had that ease that came from being transient, also that fear of not knowing what lay ahead. So they were a doomed and cavalier and casual lot, and the whores on the street were, by and large, an easy-going group. But there was about the strip a feeling, too, of danger, a feeling that one had to force a lot into those weekend nights. For the servicemen, it must have been their wanting to stay with a girl one more time before something happened to them that they had no control over. There were a lot of beds squeakin' in the hotels up and down the levee. For the women there was easy money to be made quickly, for the cheap nightclubs it was "lettin' the good times roll." It was a desperate moment in all our lives that everyone took advantage of. That damn old cheap midwestern town and everyone in it was trying to say good-bye to those young men, those sweet flowers and it seems the only way we knew how to do it, from the time of year one, was to get a troop drunk and fucked and roll-him-if-you-can before his ass is shipped to Germany, or Japan, or Korea, or Vietnam. It's a terrible way to say good-bye to those we love. It's a terrible way to deal with our own fear.

Looking back on it, I wish I'd had the courage not to have gone to the Army, to have gone to jail, but I was afraid because I was gay, and for me, saying I was gay was something you didn't do in the fifties. But I've lived long enough to have a few wars under my belts. To have seen the green rubber bags filled with men sent home and to see how large power corrupts, and to see how large power and money buys us all. I think now of the young men who have gone to jail or defected to Canada rather than going into battle, and I believe history will view them in later days as war heroes, too. I have lived to see non-violence viewed also as heroism. Perhaps some of the men who didn't go into the war were cowards; that seems a perfectly valid reason for not going. I went during peacetime and I'm quite sure I'd have been a physical coward had I to face a real war and combat. But I can't condemn those who fought in war. I have known too many sweet sweet men, and like so many of us, we can become easily confused by those very large and grandiose ideas such as patriotism, duty and honor, and find ourselves dying for causes we don't understand. But I find it changing somewhat. I find young people more willing to live for what they believe than die, and that seems a very positive change.

There were nights I spent on troop ships crowded and packed with seasick soldiers after I'd finished basic training and was being sent to Germany. I'd wonder if I was a coward and I'd always answer, "Yes." I remember something very wonderful about my trip over. We all were to sleep on berths that were stacked high and so close that you couldn't turn over. You had to strap yourself in, and there was another troop that slept right next to you. They made sure we slept head to head, not head to foot. I'm sure I would have sucked this guy's cock if the latter had been so. We didn't know each other, barely spoke. I can't even remember what he looked like now. He seemed attractive. In the night, after I'd get off guard duty on the late watch, I'd crawl into my bunk and hear him sleeping heavily. The large area where we all slept was very dark except for an occasional red exit light so we were all cast in shadows. We heard the pound of the sea, and the cast of the ship was felt deeply in us. I'd crawl into my berth and strap myself in. About the third night out I'd gotten off watch, went to my berth and I noticed the troop I slept next to was losing his blanket. I pulled it up around his shoulders and we woke the next morning holding hands. And we held hands or shoulders or touched in some way until the voyage was finished. There in the night we touched, and I wondered if I was a coward and I knew in my bones I must have been, but I knew in my bones that we all must have been, and I loved him in the dark in some small way as he must have loved me. Was he homosexual, too? I don't know. I don't think so. I think he was simply afraid like myself, afraid of what lay ahead. And somehow, touching made us less afraid.

I know this about straight men: I found it out in the Army and in other places throughout my life, they too have a wonderful way of making love to each other. There is a lie that has seemed to have gotten credence lately that males don't know how to love each other. I don't believe this is so. I was very well loved my time in the Army, and I felt full from it. If we are willing to look just a little bit below the surface, we can often find the wonderful opposite of what's being said to be true. But I think that takes a lot of very careful listening.

Looking back on it, we were afraid of the night, the men on the ship, the men of my life, myself: afraid of what the large and dark night would bring. All of us breathing in the great ship, being taken to places we'd never heard of. I wonder now if that isn't sometimes the connection or one of the connections that all men have in common, that we are afraid of the dark. Even the man who slept next to me. We slept as close as lovers all the way across the ocean and very late at night we would hold each other in some fear of the dark. I never spoke to the man during the day, but it was as though our hands could offer some small solace against the unknown that lay ahead. I see no reason now why men or women should go through that terrible fear that is brought on by large institutions we do not understand: war, the government, a great duty to country.

I had never seen the ocean before. One of the great miracles of my life happened as we left the docks in Brooklyn. It was towards evening and the ship began to pull out and I began to feel her dig deep into the water, rocking as the sea spray and wind of October was all about me. In my head, as sure as a radio being turned on, I heard music. I heard Tchaikovsky's *Italian Symphony* clearly, every note, as the ship moved slowly to the great ocean. I felt as though experiencing some great mothering woman, the rock was the same lull of a rocking chair when I was a baby and my mother's hill-woman voice sang those nameless lullabies that she must have heard her own mother singing; I felt all this was locked in me and I felt a great joy. Even now, it seems fitting that ships are called "she" and we, the men in them, are called brave. But under our bravery is the great motion of women. I wonder if men are not always with some element of mother-women, and if the same must be true of women, that they find us still in some small way a part of their fathers. These are things I can't answer, only think about. It is a way that I've always had of sensing life.

Ninety percent of the men on ship were terribly seasick. They were the color of Palmolive soap and vomited faithfully for fourteen days without eating. I felt wonderful and gained weight. My curse. When I feel wonderful, I gain weight. The sea air and the constant rush of the sea with its great changes made me happy, and I was to hear the *Italian Symphony* almost constantly while I went over. The difficulty was that I didn't like the *Italian Symphony*, so I was sick to death of it by the time we arrived. The same thing happened when I flew for the first time. So I'm stuck with the same music. Is it possible that someone in charge of music someplace in the universe pulled the wrong card on me? And I'm destined at every great moment of my life to hear something I don't like? Life goes that way.

Ruby's Red Slippers

ISAAC JACKSON

"**I**n the old days, you could buy a car for what they're asking for a month's rent nowadays in Manhattan.".

I loved it when Ruby reminisced. The summer was over and so was my latest love affair. The flame of this fling burned so brightly and so quickly that I was permanently blinded to men for at least the next few months. I resigned myself to hibernate for the winter and lick my wounds. With Ruby's laughter I could forget my mistakes.

"Play me that old Alberta Hunter record again," I said.

"Oh, her? Sure, child, she was so much better back then." Ruby turned on the turntable. An old fifties job, and the room is filled with the sounds of the young, vibrant Hunter.

"I tell you, you young people will never know. After she made her big comeback doing those television talk shows, she was never as good as when she made these records."

Ruby leaned over. To this day, I swear that wig was Ruby's hair. The old queen never lacked her looks, even if her large rambling apartment was dust-filled and going slowly downhill.

"It wasn't her fault though," Ruby continued, "the back-up musicians these days can't play. She can't get the arrangements she used to."

Ruby leaned back while stretching her arms over her head. She moved like a cat. Only the slightly flagging biceps revealed her age and gender.

The way she dressed. Her attitude. Being called "she" and "her." It was all part of Alberta Hunter's generation as well as Ruby's.

"Oh well, after rock and roll came in, nobody wanted to practice anymore," she sighed grandly, as if this was a final important statement on the subject. "Electricity hides everybody's mistakes."

Within view were two pianos, numerous antique piano stools, boxes of old 78s, sheet music and lamps of every conceivable height; all crowded together to great effect. Like the oriental rugs beneath them, these objects from flea markets long-gone seemed unmovable. And so they have been. Ruby has been in that apartment for over thirty years and so has much of the furniture. That's from before I was born.

I never understood why old people like Ruby try and keep the daylight out of their apartments. Maybe they think the sun will age them. I've been too embarrassed to ask Ruby exactly why she does this, not that she looks a day over 45.

The 78 was over. Ruby got up, flipped it and sat back down. She offered me some tea, but I refuse, "but I would like to see your photo album," I told her.

As part of the ritual, Ruby must say no at first, demurring: "Why would you want to see a bunch of old black drags nobody even remembers?"

"Because it's my roots. My history."

"Well, I always have said one should dye one's roots if they is turning silver." She laughed, and I insist once more. Then she "gave in" and got up to blow the dust off the photo album.

"Here I am with the Red Slippers. We were a female and male imper-sonators vaudeville act. We sang blues numbers and ragtime. We did ok, couldn't compete with the movies, though. When the war broke out a lot of them went 'straight' making training films for the armed forces."

"What happened after that, Ruby?"

"I went solo. I toured for over ten years doing every nightclub between here and the west coast. In the fifties the money was good. Especially the resorts."

Then it stopped. I wanted to hear more about her past, but Ruby didn't want to encourage the "importance" of it all, yet I know that these stories are as special to her as they are to me.

A few days later, my phone rang at home. It was my mother. She asked me to come home and visit my grandmother who was not recovering very well from a recent stroke.

"I fear it may be one of her last months, Brandy. You won't like yourself if you don't come out now, while she's conscious."

"Oh Ma, you're so melodramatic." But it did the trick. The next day I was driving on the Long Island Expressway to their suburban home. It was a weird day. I could feel it in my bones. There had been a hail storm earlier in the day, unusual weather for this time of year.

Everything seemed normal when I got to my parents' house. "Grandma is waiting for you, dear," said my mother as soon as I pulled my coat off. "Tell me what you think of her room. I hired a housekeeper to come and help her keep it clean. I also put in some new carpeting to help cheer her up."

"Ok, Ma, I'll go see her right away."

The part of the house where my grandmother lived was sort of a wing off by itself. Originally intended as a guest room, it now served as an out-patient hospital room. If it wasn't for her poor health, the old lady would not have been living with them.

I was nice to her anyway. I understood her feeling like a stranger in this house, if not her more immediate painful paralysis. I didn't grow up in this house either, and I certainly wouldn't want to die here. She nodded her pained face in recognition. I looked back, asking myself why hadn't we ever been close to one another.

I knew the answer: my mother always hated her. As a child, I was taught to anticipate the arrival of my grandmother the way one prepares for a visit from a witch. It's not that I didn't like my poor grandmother. It's just that I never got a chance to like her.

"When are you getting married? I don't think you're ever going to get married. How is that friend of yours . . . ?" I was shocked to hear my grandmother, apparently on her death bed, try and reach out and touch my life.

"I don't know who you mean," I responded, although I knew perfectly well. She was probably referring to a friend I brought by the house once when she was visiting. I would never have brought home one of my lovers to see my family. It should have occurred to me sooner that they were already expecting to meet them.

"How are you surviving these days?" she asked.

"I'm in real estate now. I'm making a pretty good living at it. I want to buy a brownstone soon. I'm just waiting for the right one in Harlem to come on the market."

"You want to live up in Harlem? Why, child?"

"Grandma, Harlem has some wonderful buildings. You used to live there, didn't you?"

"Oh yes, I raised your father up there. Right there on Convent Avenue, near the college. That's where we were."

"That's prime real estate now. What was Harlem like back then?"

"Oh, it was real different than now. There used to be lots of things to do up in Harlem; lots of places to go. Musicians. Clubs. Didn't have to go downtown. All the nightlife was in walking distance. And the people were so nice and friendly. Didn't have the crime we have today. On a hot summer's Saturday night you could have a party start by itself in five minutes. Back then, you could walk home by yourself at 2, 3 o'clock in the morning, and as a woman, I could walk up the stairs to my apartment alone and not have a single fear. That ain't the way it is now, is it? Why you want to move on back there now, boy?"

"Oh, searching for my roots, I guess. Tell me, did you ever see Alberta Hunter back then?"

"Yes, I saw her when I was a girl. I always loved the singers. Bessie. All of them."

We both laughed. It was the first genuine laugh we'd had together that I could remember.

My mother was happy I spent so much time talking to Grandma. She thought it was because of the new carpeting and the work of the new housekeeper that I stayed longer than usual in her room.

"I rescued your grandmother, and y'know Brandy, your father doesn't even thank me for it. She *could* have been in a nursing home. But black folks aren't like that. Our old ones are going to be comfortable and clean in their last years."

My mother moved toward the bay windows to draw the shades. The deep, sky blue pile carpet absorbed her every step, leaving no footprints, no traces. I thought of the living, and the dead. My grandmother, Ruby and rugs.

"Mother, when was the last time you went shopping at a flea market?"

"Right after you were born and we had no money, before your father got the business off the ground. Why?"

"Because I think we should go and buy something for Grandma at one. I think she'll appreciate it."

"The idea. I won't have anything of the sort in my house. She doesn't need old, faded things. She needs to look at bright things . . ."

"That robs her of her dignity. New things just remind her that she is old and useless. I know an old, uh, woman . . . who lives completely surrounded by her memories and she has twice the energy of Grandma." I, of course, was thinking of Ruby.

My mother laughed mockingly, and sniffed, "I didn't think you knew any women at all."

The conversation crashed down on me. I was cut off and said no more.

A month later when I learned of my grandmother's death, it was that day I conjured up to feel the blankness in my heart. I could have learned so much from her. I suddenly had urgent reasons to document Ruby's life. In the week following the funeral, I told Ruby of my plans.

"I want you to get me the names as soon as possible," I told her.

"Child, have you gone mad?" asked Ruby.

"No, I'm quite serious. I already have a space for you all to rehearse."

"I'm not sure if half those Queens will be able to, let alone want to, get back up on the stage again."

"Wouldn't you jump at the chance?"

"Why, sure, every offer is only as good as the next one. If you really want to put us back together again, I'll help you, 'cos you're my special kid."

"Look at *La Cage Aux Folles*. Get your costumes out of the mothballs and get ready for the all-new 'Ruby's Red Slippers Review.' I've always wanted to see you singing again. Let's start calling up all the old Queens."

Now the review is into its third year Off-Broadway. My mother stayed away until the *New York Times* said it was "spellbinding." Now she calls me every day for free tickets. The hardest part of all this is trying to explain why the show is dedicated to my grandmother. It's not the kind of thing you can put into a press release.

Sex and Love

PETER McGEHEE

Meet this kid on the subway. Spot him at Wellesley, but don't meet him till Bloor. Train breaks down, which never happens on the TTC, but it stalls or something. Car's full. Everybody looks at everybody else. I smile. He smiles back. Scoots down in his seat. Twists his T-shirt in his fingers. Scrapes his beat-up Stan Smiths against the floor. Sexy. And young. Too young. Not my bag, that.

We're almost to an I-see-what-you-see grin when he bunches up his jacket. Puts it between his head and the window. Leans against it and shuts his eyes. Should've been my shoulder. Should've gone right over there.

I look out the window. Can only see the tunnel. I think about the good-old days when you'd meet someone on the subway, have a drink, go home, fuck, maybe get something to eat, then fuck again. I just can't seem to get with it.

What with "safe sex" I'm inhibited. Especially with strangers. I mean, there you are in the throes of lust and you've got to stop and have this discussion about condoms, health history, and how deep are you gonna kiss me. So I've just about decided to give up on it. Sex, that is. I've got some good memories. I've even got a lover. Had him over seven years. Our sex life is pretty routine. I keep suggesting we expand our repertoire. Like last week I mentioned investing in a double-headed dildo, something we could do together. But David just makes a face. He says he doesn't need that. I say it isn't a matter of need, maybe it'd be fun. He just shakes his head. David makes a lot of friends on the side. He adores safe sex. Has no problem with it. Even wears a Condoms-Are-Fun button. I say, "Sorry. I'm just not as lucky as you." Then I get a lecture: "It has nothing to do with luck." He tells me to relax more. He says plenty of people are attracted to me, I just don't notice it. "Yeah, people who don't attract me." He says, "Sex comes from emotion. Anyone I like enough I can have fun with." Well maybe, goddamnit, but sex is physical. How can you pretend PHYSI-CALITY doesn't have all the world to do with sex? David says he loves me. I say I love him too. Then I wonder if it's true. I tell myself, of course it's true. But why do I fantasize so much about leaving? Why do I windowshop for things I'd buy for an apartment of my own? And what about David? Why doesn't any of this ever get to him? He's so happy and well-adjusted it drives me crazy. But it's exactly why I married him. When we met, he was exactly what I was looking for. Exactly.

Train starts moving again. Kid sits up. Looks at me. Smiles this big grin that gets bigger and bigger. I know this look.

I'm fifteen and go over to the scoutmaster's assistant's to get some help on a merit badge. His wife is just leaving to do the Saturday shopping. She's gorgeous. So's he. He gives me a Coke, shows me some *Playboys*. Then he shows me a magazine with just guys. Rocky and Bullwinkle are on TV. He says he wants to show me something in the attic. He's got this mattress and an old sleeping bag up there. He wrestles me down. Towers over me with his hands on his hips and a great big hard-on in his pants. I'm sort of trembling. He gives me this look so I put my hand on his crotch. Pop that sucker out of his jeans like a jack-in-the-box. We take off our clothes. Make out like crazy. I've always dreamt of this happening and each time I touch him, each time I feel his erection brush against my skin, I have to pinch myself to see if I'm really there. He's massaging my butt. He slips a finger into my ass. It hurts. He whispers, "Relax." He whispers about my prostate gland and asks me if I can feel what he's talking about. I begin to get the idea. He lubricates his penis. It shines like something newborn. He sets my legs up on his shoulders. Enters me slowly. It hurts again for a minute, but as he moves inside of me, he stirs up another sensation altogether. It's like I'm a pinball machine and the jackpot lights up; it's better than anything I've ever felt. He's masturbating me and I come. Five minutes later I come again. Then he grins. Grunts. Shoots up my insides like magic and hell.

The kid's still smiling like he knows what I'm thinking. I look at him like he's the most precious thing in the world right then.

Go over there, I say to myself. I stand up just as the train pulls into

Bloor. I'm suddenly immobilized. Almost get myself pushed out with the exit crowd. The kid looks at me with his eyebrows cocked like question marks. I don't know what to say. He saves me the trouble. "Where you going?" he asks.

"No place really."

"Just riding the subway?"

"That's right."

"What's your name?"

"Kevin. What's yours?"

"Kid." He pats the seat next to him. I swallow. Sit. Stomach's doing a tango. I feel his leg next to mine.

He says, "Wanta come over for lunch?"

"Where?"

"My place."

"You got your own place?"

"My parents, but they're at work."

I'm in the thirty-third floor men's room of the Toronto Dominion Building, locked in a stall, having a good cry about my life. I look at my pants down around my ankles. My white legs. The spots where the hairs have fallen out over the winter. I've just turned thirty. I hate my job. My brilliant career is as far off as it ever was. And I still don't know what to do about David. Lately, we've been talking about a move to the West Coast. Together. But I don't want to be any more together than we already are. Or do I? I ought to move back to New York is what I ought to do. David wouldn't follow me there; he hates the States. Christ, any minute I'll be covered in herpes.

Enter Drew Edwards. Flawless, handsome Drew. Twenty-eight and an associate in the firm where I'm a word processor. I've imagined him seducing me one night when we're working late. I've imagined watching him shower after a good game of racquetball. I've imagined what he thinks about when he masturbates.

I watch him through the crack as he sidles up to the urinal. See him unzip. See his happy face, happy penis, happy pee flowing freely, fingers subconsciously massaging it along, fingers that could have been anybody's, mine even. He finishes, zips himself up, flushes, farts. He washes his hands in the sink, smiles at himself in the mirror. He knows it's me in the cubicle by my pony-fur shoes. He says sarcastically, "Gonna stay in there all day? I've gotta have my Project K by two, don't forget." He leaves.

I cry some more. For how ordinary my dilemma is. How unspecial I've managed to make myself.

In comes the maintenance man with his cleaning cart. He fills the paper towel dispensers. Puts fresh toilet paper in the stall next to mine. Pulls at the door to the one I'm in. It puzzles him to find it locked. He knocks. "Anyone in there?"

I don't answer. He gets down on all fours and looks up at me. "You deaf or something?"

I still ignore him.

He goes into the next stall, climbs up on the toilet seat, and gestures wildly, "Hey! You!" He throws in a roll of toilet paper. It hits me on my head.

I jump off the john, hitch up my pants, and throw open the latch with the intention of killing that bastard.

I end up in the computer room. My supervisor sees I'm in a state and sits me down in her office. She did a doctoral degree in psychology and asks me a few psychiatric-type questions. Then she deduces, "You couldn't be more normal. Happiness is just a chemical reaction between vitamins, pride and inventiveness." She smiles. "All you need's a good nutritionist."

Train pulls into Eglinton. "This is us," Kid says. He dodges up the escalator two steps at a time. Past the newsstand. Past the candy kiosk. Hurrying me out to the bus ramp.

The bus is waiting. The driver seems to know Kid. Probably sees him every day. Eyes me suspiciously, so I say, "Fine, thank you, and you?" He looks at me like I'm crazy.

At the back of the bus, Kid sinks into his seat with his spine curved into a perfect 'C.' He stretches his legs out in the aisle, his hands to either side of him, one under my thigh. The bus starts moving. He leans over, paves a sidewalk on my neck with his tongue. Mr. Penis fills with blood. Makes me squirm. Kid enjoys this. Sinks even lower into his 'C' to show me his.

I won't tell David about today. He'll say how was work and I'll say just fine. I can just see his face. Feel his five o'clock kiss and soft hello suffocate me. Then we'll have a drink like any two reasonable people. Eat dinner. Maybe watch *Dynasty*.

Dynasty always puts me in a vicious mood. I'll ask David, in an insinuating tone, if he's seen of his "friends" lately. He won't say anything. Just his leg will twitch.

All David's friends have one-syllable names. Bob, Rich, Tom, Brad, Jim, Joe. I love it when they call and David's not home. I know it's one of them by the way they ask for him, hesitating slightly because they know it's me, the lover.

I'm very friendly. "May I take a message?" I ask. They give me their one-syllable name. I write it down. "And your number?"

"Oh, he has it." This is where they start to get smug. Little do they realize how many Bobs, Richs, Toms, Brads, Jims, and Joes David knows! I repeat their name with great vigor, then hang up.

When David gets home, I tell him who's called. He says, "Oh really?" I listen for a trace of guilt, but David never feels guilty. He says, "You know I only see them when I can't see you." I hate that.

Before I go to sleep, I'll manage to blame my depression on the weather. I'll remind myself leaving would be expensive. And who's to say I wouldn't regret it?

Bus turns into an old neighborhood. Big lawns and a mishmash of comfortable old houses. Kid pulls the bus bell. Walks to the door and hops off. People are staring. He says, "Crazy, huh?"

As we walk down the street I see some of his neighbors pacing inside picture windows. They're probably watching some game show. Maybe they're about to win a million dollars. Maybe they're spies and on to me. Maybe they'll call up Kid's mom or dad. Search out my identity. Look me up in the phone book. Come over to my place and put an end to my nonsense once and for all. "How old did you say you were?"

"Don't give me that age trip," Kid says, peeling out in front of me.

I watch his butt. Looks like the butt I caught my first VD from, an airbrush artist I met hitchhiking in San Francisco. I felt like I'd finally arrived as I stood in the VD clinic taking my handful of penicillin. A real homosexual.

The airbrush artist died recently. Of AIDS. I haven't known as many people as some, but I've known enough. I spend a lot of time thinking about it and thinking how glad I am it's not me or David, and what if it is?

I've got a friend who's in the hospital right now. He originally went in because he was losing his vision. Turned out his eyes were full of Cytomegalovirus. They gave him an experimental antibiotic intravenously, twenty-four hours a day for two weeks. The virus only stabilized. When he got out of the hospital, he was thirty pounds underweight. He was back in two weeks later with the same virus plus Kaposi's lesions were beginning to appear in his mouth and on his legs. He got out in another two weeks. He went back again with pneumonia. The latest is that the Cytomegalovirus has moved to his brain.

I visit. We talk about how he feels. How his family's doing. How great all his friends have been. His lover. And thank god for the health care system in Canada. If he'd been in New York, he'd be dead by now.

He lights up a cigarette. "The only thing I haven't managed to quit." He laughs. He's got all these books stacked by his bed about macrobiotics and mysticism. He tells me he's gonna use voodoo to get rid of the Kaposi's. He says, "To think of all those hours I spent in school on things like math and chemistry when I could've been learning how to grow my leg back —"

I find I'm crying. He says, "Hey, I'm OK. Listen, I don't want you worrying about me." He doesn't understand. It's not his illness. It's his guts. It's that I love and I'm afraid to say it. Afraid he will think it false.

The AIDS Committee is holding a twilight vigil in Cawthra Park. I don't really want to go, but at the same time, I don't want to miss it. They seem to have a talent for picking the whiniest, most uninspired speakers, and god could we use some inspiration. The Committee's president looks like he hasn't had a bath in weeks. To lend effect to his funding plea, I suppose. The sister of a guy who died recently reads a prayer. Divine Will and love. She stumbles over the words. A local chiropractor, in the pink of health, sings an original folk song in a very original key. He tries to get everyone to sing along, but no one does. A rock 'n roller in a high-rise hollers down, "Faggots!" The crowd acts deaf. Only a few heads turn to see who's said it. If I were an AIDS ghost, I would've pissed on them all.

Finally we are instructed to light the candles we've bought for a dollar's donation. As the crowd disperses, people stick them into the ground. The wind blows them out instantaneously.

I spot David. He's come from a meeting and is standing with some of his political cronies. He seems as depressed as I am.

I try to imagine a vigil worthy of the people I've known. I see something at Radio City Music Hall. Thousands of AIDS patients. In a chorus line. Sick and skinny. Can-canning across that great stage. They're outfitted like the Rockettes and have long, flowing wigs. They stop. Face the audience. Sing a choral version of the aria Tosca sang to God: "I lived for art, I lived for love/never did I harm a living creature. . . ./Ever in pure faith my prayers rose/Ever in pure faith. . . ./Why doest thou repay me thus?" It raises the roof, literally. Out they fly, one by one. A million Peter Pans, free at last.

Kid unlocks his door. "Don't steal anything, OK?" A portrait of a much younger him hangs in the hallway.

"Haven't changed much, have you?"

"It's my mom." He takes my coat. "Let's go upstairs."

The walls are lined with pictures from his birthdays, piano recitals, and various school trips. His room's a mess, clothes piled in the only chair. There's an autographed poster of Domaso Garcia thumbtacked to the wall.

"Baseball fan?"

"Sometimes."

He plops down on his bed, kicks off his Stan Smiths. Hooks his thumbs in my belt loops. Presses against my crotch. Blows through the material, hot enough to feel. Mr. Penis is in bondage. I reach in to make an adjustment. Kid leans back on his elbows and presses Mr. Penis with his foot. Size 8.

I pull off his socks. White cotton scented slightly with his sneakers. Lick his toes. He giggles and grabs for me. I dodge him. Lick the arch of his foot. The sole. The heel. His skin is like cream, and my hands glide beneath the cuffs of his jeans to see if all of it feels the same or if the quality changes with the hair on his legs, but no. I lick his fingers. Wish he were an octopus. Wish for more appendages to devour. More of him to wrap around me as I descend. Hand in his shirt. The smoothness of his back. Hand slipping down. Beneath the waistband of his jeans. Unbuckling them. Peeling off his underwear. Pale pink Calvin Kleins. His cock, so full. So sweet to kiss and sweet to swallow. He'll be catalogued with all the great genitals I've known. To be called upon when I'm alone and need them most.

"Stop," Kid whispers, tongue in my ear, freezing. "Too close." Wants a kiss is all.

He dives under the covers. Works his way up my length. To my crotch. Lifts my legs. Outlines my ass. Spits on his fingers. Gives me one. Gives me two. Sees my eyes roll. Gives me three.

He kisses me like crazy. I pull him on top of me. Slap his butt. Tug his nipples. Eat the vein along his neck. His penis, against my thigh, springs between my legs.

David and I are in a restaurant having dinner. I wanted to go to a different one but he insisted we try this. The lights are too bright, fluorescent. The food is too dull and costs too much. Too many people are smoking. I hate the way David's looking at me. As if I'm supposed to supply some feeling or dialogue to make the evening a good one. I hate the way he eats.

We walk down the street together. Get on the subway together. Get cruised together. Get off together. Go across the parking lot to our building together. Ride up the elevator together. Walk into our apartment together. Listen to the messages on our answering machine together. Kill cockroaches together. Brush our teeth together. Get in bed together.

I pick a fight for no good reason just before he falls asleep, then get furious with him for letting me do it.

I lie there trying to remember a movie or play where two characters are stuck in the how-it'll-probably-be-again-but-isn't-now sort of thing. But all I can remember is new romance. Adventure, fire, sex, meetings on the sly. Or breakups, the more violent the better. Or Gina Rowlands going off to the loony bin. Or kids on the subway. Or scoutmasters' assistants. But never what really happens between people. I mean, who cares about that?

Best not to know anyone too well. When you do you just have the same boring problems you always have.

Kid rips open a condom pack with his teeth. Kneels in front of me. Pulls it on without the least bit of fumbling. Grins from the tickle of the lube.

"You're quite adept at that."

"Learned it from a friend of my uncle's."

Love the whites of his eyes. His kiss getting vicious. His hands digging into my shoulders. The spit on his teeth. The smile that breaks on his breath. The cum that fills the rubber that should be filling me.

I look deeply into his eyes. He lets me. We fall in love for about five minutes.

He says, "Nice."

"Yeah."

He rolls over. Sighs. Feels like he has to say, "This friend of my uncle's" — he pushes his hair out of his eyes — "we're kind of involved."

"Listen, don't worry. I've already got a lover."

David and I are kissing passionately in our sleep. When we wake up, we stop. Our breath is sour. We look at each other like strangers. The room is full of a shadowy half-light. "I love you," I finally say, "don't you know that?"

"Let me make you a sandwich," Kid says, slipping on a pair of gym shorts. He goes into the bathroom and comes back with his father's robe. He hands it to me.

In the breakfast nook he tells me he has to write a paper for his physics class. That he was supposed to work on it this afternoon and'll probably be up all night. Then he says, "I'd like to get together again sometime, if you would."

"Sure, whenever. You could even come by my place."

"What about your lover?"

"He's out of town a lot."

"Live anywhere near Jarvis Collegiate?"

"Two blocks." I grin.

He leans back in his chair, holding onto the edge of the table for balance. "The nature of infinity," he says, rocking.

"I beg your pardon?"

"The paper I've got to write. The universe going on forever. From way off in outer space right down to the tiniest dot on your fingernail."

"Sounds complicated."

"It's not."

The sandwich is finished. Our plates are in the sink. Kid undoes his father's robe. Slips it off my shoulders. Stands in front of me just short of touching, yet I can feel his temperature, the tips of his toes, and his penis again getting hard.

We go into the bathroom. Get in the shower. Keep soaping up until the smell of cum makes us dizzier than even the steam.

"My parents'll be home soon," he says as we dry.

We stand in the entrance hall. He's written his phone number on a slip of paper. He folds it in half and tucks it in my pocket. "Call. OK?"

I'm back on the subway. David and I are coming home from a dinner party. We're slightly drunk and having a jolly old time talking about who was there.

We get into our apartment. I put on some show music. The overture swells and we begin to dance, dancing a little dance that only we know the steps to.

Despair

DAVID B. FEINBERG

My anxiety level was high and it was time to do something about it. I had reached a particular level of anxiety that corresponded to the resonant frequency of my brain: one more day in this state and it would explode. I needed to either elevate it to a frequency that only dogs hear, or decrease it to a reasonable level, so I could focus my anxiety on things like nuclear war, famine, torture in Third World countries, Beirut, Afghanistan, Lebanon, the West Bank, crack, the homeless, and my relationship with my mother. In short, it was time to take the Test.

I decided to take the Test after I discovered that two former sexual partners of mine had AIDS by reading articles in the *New York Times*. The first article dealt with AIDS in the workplace. "Why, look! There's Ralph," I said to myself, coughing up breakfast and several unrelated meals from the past two weeks. The second was a human interest story about AZT in action. "Gee, didn't know Mark was on AZT these days," I commented from a supine position on the floor, having just fainted.

I decided to take the Test after reading an article in the *New York Times* where the New York City Health Commissioner said that all those with the virus were doomed. The prevailing figures I had been reading stated that approximately fifteen percent of those exposed to the virus come down with AIDS within five years of infection. I figured I could wait it out: if I stayed well for five years, I'd be home free. I neglected to consider that at the time the epidemic had only been tracked for five years, and the esti- mates stopped at five years simply because there were no further data. And now it turned out that by seven years' incubation of the virus, the incidence rose sharply.

I decided to take the Test after reading seventeen well-meaning liberal heterosexual columns in seventeen well-meaning liberal heterosexual peri- odicals where seventeen well-meaning liberal heterosexual people described how they each underwent their own personal well-meaning liberal hetero- sexual hell by taking the Test: their fear and trepidation, their casual doubts and anxieties, along with their awkward self-reassurances that it would be extremely unlikely to get a positive antibody result, although they may have had more than three sexual experiences with more than two partners in the past seventeen years and it's conceivable that one of the partners was a hemophiliac bisexual who did intravenous drugs in between weekly blood transfusions, and it's conceivable that they were inoculated with a tetanus vaccine using a needle that had just been used on a hemophiliac bisexual who did intravenous drugs in between weekly blood transfusions when they were twelve and stepped on a rusty nail at Day Camp Mohonka in the Catskills, and it's conceivable that their mother could actually be Haitian and there could have been a mix-up at the hospital or the midwife's, and it's conceivable that the blood transfusion from the heart-lung-kidney- and-thyroid transplant by Doctor Christian Barnaard had contained some tainted blood from a hemophiliac bisexual who did intravenous drugs in between weekly blood donations. I mean, I appreciated reading the first article where a well-meaning liberal heterosexual columnist described the trials and tribulations of taking the Test; and even five articles of well- meaning liberal heterosexual columnists would have been within the bounds of propriety and taste; but *seventeen* of those abominable articles made me want to scream. I had it up to here with these well-meaning liberal hetero- sexual assholes so far removed from the crisis that they could be living on Jupiter. You see, these well-meaning liberal heterosexual columns all ended exactly the same way, with the results sheepishly revealed in the final sentence, almost casually, nonchalantly: Oh, by the way, I was nega- tive. What was this, I thought, some fucking dating service?

I decided to take the Test even though I had not had the mean amount of one thousand five hundred and twenty-three sexual partners in the past ten years that the papers reported from the initial group of AIDS patients (I was rather shy for my age); even though I had not undergone what was coyly referred to in the press as traumatic sex (although in some sense all sex is traumatic) in certain downtown clubs in the presence of a large audience; even though I had never been considered what was coyly referred to in the company of my friends as a "slut" (which is undeniably a relative term).

I decided to take the Test even though it wasn't necessarily the politically correct thing to do, and certain radical gay columnists in certain radical gay periodicals were predicting the most unbelievable repercussions: mandatory testing of the HIV antibody; discrimination in insurance, housing, and employment of those who tested positive; closing the borders to aliens who tested positive and at the same time other countries closing the borders to Americans who tested positive; internment camps for those who tested positive. As time passed, a significant portion of the above alarmist predictions became realities.

I decided to take the Test even though the local gay paper insisted, virulently, that HTLV-III was *not* the cause (although the virus had been renamed HIV two years earlier by an international committee in an effort to solve a dispute about who had discovered the virus first, an American scientist who discovered the virus in 1984 or a French scientist who discovered the virus in 1983) and the local gay paper was backing the African Swine Fever Virus theory, or the Tertiary Syphilis theory, or Chronic Epstein-Barr Virus theory, or the Cytomegalovirus theory, or the Track Lighting and Industrial Gray Carpeting and Quiche theory, or the Immune System Overload theory, or the Amyl and Butyl Nitrate theory, or a variation of the Legionnaire's Disease theory in which some contaminant got into the air-conditioning system of the Saint discotheque, or perhaps a new noise virus at a certain frequency had gotten into the sound system, or the government Germ Warfare theory where some experiment had leaked, not to be confused with the Government Genocide theory where the government deliberately distributed contaminated K-Y lubricant at homosexual gatherings and contaminated needles at shooting galleries, or the Airborne Mosquito theory, or the Toilet Seat theory, or the No Gag Response theory where male homosexuals as a consequence swallow vast quantities of as-yet unidentified toxins. The local gay paper offered a new and improved conspiracy theory each and every month, and I suppose it was just my problem that I couldn't keep up with all of these new trends and fashions in disease consciousness; I mean, I guess I was being pigheaded and stupid to accept a parsimonious explanation that had been offered by our admittedly mendacious government, and maybe I was just too irritable and lazy not to make a concerted effort to keep track of each new crackpot theory (based on a somewhat-justifiable paranoia) which more or less ignored all scientific research to date and was generally so incredibly stupid that were the theory to be rated on the Stanford-Binet test of general intelligence I doubt it would be able to tie its own shoelaces unassisted or balance a checkbook or cross the street without being run over by a Mack truck.

I decided to take the Test because I was from a rational background and I decided that it wouldn't kill me to know, even though a friend who had AIDS told me that if I found out I was positive, this would create additional stress which would in turn weaken my immune system thus allowing the virus to replicate, a sort of Heisenberg effect where the knowledge of a situation affects that situation, so in fact, it *could* kill me a little faster than otherwise, and what would the benefits be of finding out if I were positive because there wasn't a cure and why would it help to know my status if it wouldn't change my behavior because I would continue having safe sex and getting enough rest and eating right and exercising and taking Geritol, I mean vitamins, either way? I told him that if I turned out positive, I would brood and contemplate suicide and lose perspective and quit my job and go to Italy and finally learn how to deal with my mother and stop transferring money to my Individual Retirement Account and move it into an insurance policy and only renew magazines by the year and would insist on being paid in a lump sum if I won a lottery as opposed to a twenty-year payment scheme because I would probably be dead in twenty years and the tax benefits would be outweighed by the world-wide cruise through whatever countries still allow HIV positives to travel and maybe I would take one of those fancy new placebos that everyone is talking about like active lipids or naltrexone or dextran sulfate or wheat grass juice or maybe I would see a nutritionist and stop eating sugar and become macrobiotic and then die a lot faster from not eating enough protein or maybe I would start meditating or maybe I would finally achieve a sense of spirituality and meaning in my life as it neared the end and drop this worn cloak of cynicism for crystals or Gurdjieff or reincarnation or God or free parking or maybe I would start writing like Anthony Burgess who when mis-diagnosed with a brain tumor wrote four novels in a year, or maybe I would have some cosmic revelation earlier because I was ready for it, or maybe I would join a bowling league or maybe I would just give up. I mean, I operated under the basic premise that ignorance is *not* bliss and why should I stick my head in the sand when I should perfectly well be able to stick the gun in my mouth instead? And then, of course, there was the extremely slim chance that I was, in fact, HIV antibody negative. Maybe, who knows? I could actually relax for a few minutes. I mean, Rome wasn't built in a day. I'm sure it's nothing that fifteen years of intense psychotherapy couldn't get to the bottom of.

I decided to take the Test because, although I generally don't believe in predestination as opposed to free will, from a logical standpoint, we are all born with certain finite constraints: None of us is immortal; hence, none of us has an unlimited number of heartbeats left. Women are born with a finite number of ova, ready to plop down the Fallopian tubes at the rate of one every four weeks, from puberty to menopause; similarly, we are each born with a finite number of orgasms to experience, cigarettes to smoke, and lovers to betray. Knowing whether I tested positive or negative could help me determine more precisely what these numbers were. I was just moderately curious to find out what would be a reasonable number of cocktails, nightmares, Lean Cuisines, boyfriends, vacations, apartments, breaths, jobs, and bowel movements to expect in this lifetime. Perhaps if I knew I only had a few sexual relations left, I would avoid intercourse in order to stretch things out.

I decided to take the Test because I had reached the point where I believed that it was a fundamentally irrational act *not* to take the HIV antibody test and after all I *did* graduate from Northwestern University several eons ago, majoring in mathematics and minoring in philosophy, and consequently I still felt a responsibility to behave rationally.

So, nervous like when I was seventeen and in college and still a virgin and went to a drugstore and spent hours studying depilatories and decongestants and diuretics before finally asking the kindly pharmacist for condoms in a cracked voice, I picked up the phone and dialed the city AIDS hotline and made an appointment to take the test at the earliest available time slot, six weeks later. Like a secret agent, I was identified by a numeric code only.

During the next six weeks I did the usual things: made a will, sold my co-op, changed my job, upped my insurance, reconciled with my family, wrote a novel, worked out at the gym seven times a day, had sixteen failed romances, tried to volunteer as an astronaut at NASA so I could experience the relativistic effects of traveling at high speeds (time contracts when approaching the speed of light, thus the six weeks wait would seem less interminable).

The six weeks wait was an eternity.

That morning ("There's still time to chicken out," said my friend Dennis), I woke up early and took the bus. I had scheduled my appointment for 8:30, when the clinic opened, so I could take the Test, vomit, and then casually waltz into work fashionably late, as usual.

There was no time for breakfast; I didn't want to be late. I took the bus down Ninth Avenue. I had to stand until Forty-Second Street. I couldn't concentrate on the *Times*. The bus let me off right in front of the Chelsea Clinic. I hadn't been there since 1980 to get treated for a venereal disease.

Outside several homeless people were sleeping on benches. A man swept debris from the concrete with a broom. The clinic was next to an elementary school, with a jungle gym outside. It was 8:15. The building was closed.

I circled the block. On the sidewalk several sexually responsive individuals had thoughtfully left their used condoms. It reminded me of the first time I ever set foot in a gay bar, back when I was nineteen in Pasadena, California. I had circled the street seventy-two times before gathering enough courage to enter. I was shy; I wasn't ready to make a lifestyle commitment at that point in time, and I thought entering a gay bar would be an irrevocable step. I mean, they'd all think I was a homosexual.

I had a quick bite to eat at an awful deli on Tenth, surrounded by the harsh accents of the outer boroughs: the snide voices, the know-it-alls, the jokers. "How could they joke at a time like this?" I wondered. I returned to the clinic, ten minutes late for my 8:30 appointment. Two people were already in front of me. I was given an interesting and informative booklet to read. Why did the print fade the harder I tried to concentrate? The woman at the desk asked for my number and then asked me to make up a new one, tossing the first away. I signed a release form by copying a statement instead of signing: with no signature, no identifying marks were left. Then, I had a brief counseling session with a therapist, a woman with dark hair cut butch, a warm and sympathetic lesbian.

"How do you think you were exposed?" she asked.

"I may have forgot to use a condom five or six thousand times back in 1982, before there were rules and regulations to follow."

"Why are you taking the test? What will this knowledge do for you?"

"I thought," I thought, this was a test, and the right answer would be judicious and thoughtful and beneficial to humanity, "that I might be able to help further the cause of science and medical research by becoming an experimental subject, should I test positive."

"I wouldn't if I were you," she counseled. "They have double-blind experiments. For all you know you could be eating sugar pills. And what's worse, you may be on some toxic drug. Suppose you're in a study and they find out another more promising drug. You can't switch." Then she told me about macrobiotic diets and stress reduction and home-made AL721.

"That's a bit drastic for me. I mean, should I give up meat just to live another six months?" There was this trade-off between sex and life, between red meat and a few more years. Why should I have to be making these choices?

"For the next two weeks, I want you to act as if you have already tested positive," she advised. "Prepare yourself." Did she know something that I didn't know? Why couldn't I enjoy my last few possibly blissful and relatively stress-free weeks (although by this time my anxiety meter reading was off the scale)? I made an appointment for two weeks later to get my results.

The Indian medical assistant looked up from his textbook and put on two pairs of red plastic gloves. "Give me your arm," he instructed. Carefully, he stuck me with the needle and filled a test tube with my blood, then wrapped the gloves around the sample for safety. I wondered how he could do this all day. How can he stand it?

That night I found out that Gordon had died in the afternoon. My first reaction was, "See what you get for taking the test?" I eventually convinced myself there was no cause-and-effect relationship between the two events, still, I felt it was not a good sign.

"You can always just take it and not bother getting the results," said my friend Dennis. "You can back out at any time."

The next day I called Richard in California.

"If it turns out I'm positive, I'm going to take the next plane out of here and get a cab to your apartment and knock on your door and you'll answer and I'll say, 'Thanks,' and pull out my pearl-handled revolver from my purse and shoot you dead."

"Come on, Benjamin, I didn't necessarily infect you; it could be any one of thousands."

"I know it would be you. Who else fucked me with such relish and regularity? Who else do I know with lymphadenopathy from 1982? Besides, it's easier for me to deal with when I can pinpoint the blame on someone else."

"You should be here in San Francisco. We're so specialized here, we even have groups for people who are waiting to find out whether they tested positive or negative."

"Two-week groups?"

"That's right."

"If only they came out with the safe sex regulations two months earlier, I'd still be alive."

"You *are* alive, Benjamin."

"You know what I mean." Was it better to have loved and gotten infected than never to have loved at all? Was I even capable of love? Who knows?

Instead of San Francisco, I went to Provincetown, the only gay mecca to which I hadn't yet made a pilgrimage (I had already been to Key West and West Hollywood). I had another disastrous safe-sex romance, and then I got too much sun and not enough sleep because there was sand in my weekend lover's bed, and being the Jewish American Princess that I am, it felt just like a pea; I mean, the pull-out mattress hadn't been turned since the War Between the States, so I tossed and turned and created my own forcefield of anxiety, and so my face decided to punish me with a minor outbreak of herpes which, in turn, got infected with impetigo which, in turn, increased my level of anxiety so the herpes got worse and worse and by the time it had reached its nadir I looked more or less like Jeff Goldblum in the remake of *The Fly,* and this was not during the first half-hour of this picture, this was *serious* skin disorder. So I went to my doctor, who had fled the city that January because of burn-out from the AIDS crisis, and saw his cruel replacement, a cold and inefficient reptile who misdiagnosed me with shingles, a disease that typically affects only half of the face, whereas my face was a *complete* disaster area. And then this lizard had the tact to tell me that I should definitely take the HIV antibody test because shingles was one of those opportunistic infections that tends to strike people with lowered immunities and he said that he felt there was a ninety percent chance that I would be positive. At which point I told my own personal nominee for Mister Compassion and Tact of 1987 that I had already taken the test and as a matter of fact was expecting my results the following day.

I went back to the Chelsea Clinic for my results, looking like the Creature from the Black Lagoon. Guess what? Unlike the seventeen well-meaning liberal heterosexual columnists in the seventeen well-meaning liberal heterosexual periodicals, I turned out to be positive. Hold the presses! This had to be front-page news. If I wrote a column, I'd make the *Guiness Book of World Records*, the cover of *Time, Esquire,* and *Woman's Wear Daily,* as the first columnist to turn out positive in the history of civilization, and parlay this into immediate financial gain, a guest spot on the *Hollywood Squares*, a bit part in *Miami Vice,* when I realized I would be dead before the residuals came because my life expectancy wasn't quite so long as it was even a week ago. You know, here I was, thinking like an actuary. I decided it was time to get a television set, something I had been struggling successfully against acquiring for the past ten years, along with a VCR so when my apartment was converted into a sanatorium I'd be able to amuse myself. But I didn't go whole-hog: cable would have to wait.

And oddly enough I fell into this deep funk.

I had a friend who was nice and supportive and after I took the test and got the results, he got really mad at me because I was depressed because what did I expect? and didn't I realize the likelihood of being positive? and what difference did it make anyway? and I told him it was the doom, the absolute doom that got to me, and he said didn't you know about that before, you imbecile? and I said this is the sort of thing you can't really figure out what your reaction will be until you do it, and I tried to explain to him about the Heisenberg principle but he had math anxiety in a bad way so he stuffed his fingers into his ears and said, I don't want to listen. And of course a couple of months later he took the test anyway, on the advice of his doctor who told him that if he had high blood pressure wouldn't he want to know if he was at risk of a heart attack? even if it was only a ten percent chance. And he was negative. And another friend who had moved to Japan three years ago to evade the AIDS crisis and the Reagan administration and also because something snapped in his brain when he turned thirty and he — with no prior warning — became a wizened and depraved rice queen who had traveled nine thousand miles just to get laid; well, he took the test and he was negative too. And then another friend who had according to conservative estimates sucked every Negro penis in the tri-state area between the ages of sixteen and forty-five in subway tearooms, trucks, changing rooms, and in the back seat of cars; well, he took the test, and he was negative too. And part of me, since misery loves company, wanted just one close friend to be positive too, but the sensible part of me, you know, the part that still has occasional communication with my cerebral cortex said, "Thank God they're negative," using the expletive for effect since thank god my experience had not changed me so profoundly that I was no longer an atheist.

So this is what I do: I go on with my life. I go to ACT-UP activist meetings, never saying a word, and end up more stressed-out than I was before; I go to demonstrations and scream myself hoarse and then visit my new primary health-care practitioner who, unlike the lizard, gives me hugs and prescribes medication for my sore throat and my various and sundry female disorders; I get my T-cell count taken every three months; I go to a few Body Positive meetings and attend a group rap session that is headed by a psychopath and shortly thereafter drop out because once again my stress-level has tripled during the course of the meeting; and I want to end the AIDS crisis and stop the government log-jam of red tape and paperwork and there should be some sort of cure in the near future and the only thing is will I still be alive; and I'm wary of the macrobiotic diets and crystals and lipids and other untested and unverified treatments but at the same time I'm afraid to do absolutely nothing, maybe I'm paralyzed by inertia and fear, I don't know, and I don't want to take AZT when the T-cell count drops below 200 because it's highly toxic but at the same time I know it can't be all bad because some more insane people at the local gay paper want to charge all doctors with malpractice for prescribing it. And I take acyclovir for my herpes twice daily to prevent recurrences because herpes is particularly bad for the immune system and I'm avoiding the sun: this summer I'm going to be a porcelain goddess, a pale creature of the night. And sex: what about sex? When I see a guy I've been flirting with for the past four years, what do I say? What are the rules? Should this be broadcast? Are there any tactful ways of telling the relatives? How can I have sex with someone without telling? Does it matter if the sex is absolutely safe? What do I say when I meet someone new: would you like to have sex with someone who may or may not have a fatal disease?

And now I never sleep through the night; I always wake up at three or four, tense, filled with anxiety. Like Dorothy in the Wizard of Oz, I sit, watching helplessly as my T-cell count drops every three months, the sands of time running out.

Once I awoke from a wet dream, swimming in a sea of infected sperm; I leapt out of the bed to wipe it all up, quickly (how does one stem the tide, the flow?). And one day I was sitting at a coffeeshop and my nose began to bleed spontaneously. I hadn't had a nosebleed in years. The blood dripped bright red onto the plate, onto the napkin. All I could think of was infection and disease. All I could think of was the virus that was coursing through my blood. I blotted it out with the napkin and sat there ashamed, frightened, in despair.

Remembering

for Jonathan Ned Katz

JAMES TUSHINSKI

Dear Paul, someone had written on the piece of paper.

Nothing else. *Dear Paul.*

The piece of paper lies on the desk against the wall. I am in a room, standing in the middle where they left me, looking at the walls, the bed, the desk, the piece of paper. *Dear Paul.*

Is this my room? I imagine it is, though my thoughts won't focus, don't connect. Clothes hang in the closet. Pictures and clippings are tacked to the walls. The place looks lived in, personalized by someone. Me, I guess. Did I leave in a hurry? Was I in the middle of something? A pen lies near the piece of paper. Was I writing a letter?

I sit at the desk, not aware of how I got there, unable to recall walking across the room, pulling out the chair. The piece of paper is too white, the ink too blue.

Dear Paul, it says. I pick up the pen. Underneath the words I write: *Who are you?*

I write it slowly, printing it in careful imitation of the preceding line. The pen seems connected to my hand, as if the ink flows from my veins.

I'm in this room. Your name is written here on this piece of paper. If this is my room then I wrote your name. I must know who you are.

I look up. The window is high in the opposite wall, covered on the outside with a grid of iron bars. The door has a window as well. The glass there is embedded with wire.

Before I was in this room, before I sat at this desk and wrote the words on this piece of paper, I was walking down a corridor. I heard noises, people talking, things being moved around, but the noises didn't come to me all at once. They came individually, selectively, weaving in and out of importance, balancing, then contrasting each other. It was pleasant in a way. I wanted to cry.

Next to me, a large man in white held my arm. I realized then I walked very slowly, almost shuffling, and the man was there to help me. That made sense. I leaned against the man, who was warm and hairy.

And before I was walking down the corridor, I remember being someplace else. Another room, bigger than the room with the desk and the piece of paper. I was on a bed, a hard bed with white, white sheets and railings on the side. A man leaned over me, shaving my face with an electric razor. Was this the same man who helped me down the corridor? I couldn't be sure. The man shaved me with the razor and I thought, *why does this man have to shave me? Why can't I do it myself? And why can't I move my arms and legs? Where am I? What am I doing here?* The man stopped shaving me long enough to take a tissue and wipe away the saliva that suddenly ran out of my open mouth.

All around me in this larger room I could feel other people in other beds just like mine. I couldn't see them because I couldn't turn, but I could feel them and I could hear them thrashing around, moaning or pulling on restraining straps. I remember the sound of leather stretched by their beating and pulling. Someone screamed, not in this room, but in another room close by. The scream sounded like one long cry, as if all the air had been forced from someone's lungs. An involuntary scream it was. Without fear, without meaning.

Another scream overlapped the first, coming from a room even farther away. Then another scream, and another, one close, one not.

There was a pause and the chorus of screams began again.

I look at myself in my mirror. My mirror. My room. They've left me here long enough for me to assume as much. I'm wearing a white gown tied at the back. My hair is matted, cropped close. My eyes are glassy. Every so often I have to force myself to close my mouth. I soon forget, though, as I stare at my face. My mouth falls open again.

I mustn't be very old, I think. *That's not why I'm here. This isn't an old folks home. I'm younger than the man who brought me down the corridor. I'm a young man, really only a boy.*

Looking at the room reflected in the mirror makes me dizzy all of a sudden. I take a step backwards.

I'm here because I did something wrong. The thought comes out of nowhere, but I know it's right. An image comes along with the thought. A woman stands in front of me, her face both sad and furious, a strand of hair falling into her eyes. She holds something for me to see, accusing me silently. I've seen her before.

I start to cry.

I did something wrong, that's why I'm here.

Back at the desk, beneath what I just wrote on the piece of paper, I carefully print on a separate line, as if I'm making a list.

I have done something wrong.

They gave me a shot which made me drowsy. As they helped me walk into the room full of buzzing equipment and laid me down on a table, I kept thinking I was going down a long, narrow corridor with alternating black and white stripes on the floor. I wanted to step on the stripes in some definite order, but as I tried to remember what the order might be, I heard the buzzing and saw I was lying on the table. They rubbed some salve on my temples. I didn't remember anything after that.

It was always that way after the shock. I had to go through the confusion each time. Each time I lost the memory of ever having had the shock before. Each time it took a few days until I remembered where I was, what my name was.

Sometimes, though, I did remember going through it. My mind cleared up briefly and I remembered the shot and being laid on the table and I remembered not remembering anything else. I asked a nurse how many times I'd had the treatment.

"I'm not sure," the nurse said. "I'll have to look it up."

Later, when the nurse came back and told me, "Twenty," I couldn't remember what I'd asked. So I smiled and nodded instead.

There are so many people in this place. They walk along the corridors with a dead, washed-out look on their faces or they sit and chatter with animation. Doctors and nurses walk past me. They sometimes smile and ask how I'm doing, but mostly they seemed preoccupied. The orderlies never ask me anything. When they're not around, I hug whoever is near me. I'm not sure why. I seem to remember someone I hugged and touched and kissed, someone special. Was that in this place or somewhere else? I hug a man standing stiffly against the wall. He doesn't move, continues staring straight ahead. I don't think he's moved for days.

My periods of clear thinking frustrate and encourage me, and there are times I can remember the day they came to take me away.

"We can't tell you anything," they said. "You have to come with us."

There were two of them. Two big men who put me in the back seat of a station wagon. My hands were tied behind me somehow. With string? Maybe I'm imagining that part. Maybe my hands weren't tied at all. It's all pretty unclear. The sign over the gateway said HOSPITAL and I remember thinking, *she's gone and done it, just like she said she would.*

Music went through my head sometimes—chords, arrangements of notes—and my fingers twitched rhythmically in time. I would stop whatever I was doing, whatever I was in the middle of saying, and listen, knowing I'd heard these notes somewhere before. They started out clear, distinct, each note making a finger move, but soon the notes would jumble together, overlap, finally stopping abruptly, then starting again, as if someone were turning the dial on a radio in my head. Soon it all faded away. My fingers stopped moving.

In my room there is a big calendar so I can always tell what month, day, year it is. Most of the time that's helpful because I forget so easily. The calendar says December 1970, which makes sense because the hospital is decorated for Christmas. I remember making a brightly colored paper chain for the tree. Then they give me a shot and they take me into the room full of buzzing equipment and the next time I think of the Christmas tree, it's gone. The calendar says 1971.

The doctor asks me to sit down. I'm not sure if I've seen him before. Fat. Red face. Chain smoker.

"How are you today?"

"Fine," I say, confused. My mind feels like it's expanding outward, drifting away like smoke.

"Do you know who I am?"

"Doctor . . ." I say. I can't continue. My voice trails off and I wave my hand. The hand seems to speak to me. It says, "Doctor . . ."

"Good. Now, do you know who you are? Do you know your name?"

"Yes," I say, defensively. It's a lie, of course. I try to make a connection. I try to pull my thoughts together and concentrate.

The doctor smiles. "Then what is it?"

I strain a bit; my face twitches slightly. *This is important,* I'm thinking. An unfocused, desperate feeling comes over me, a physical feeling coming up from inside me, from the center of my body, from some organ near my heart. I want to cry but worry that would make me look crazy. I bite my lip. I open my mouth. Nothing. I close my mouth and bite my lip again.

"Take your time," the doctor says. "Cigarette?" he says, offering.

I strain again, letting a little gasp of air escape, then a word comes out of my mouth.

"Mike," I say, and laugh. I *have* seen this doctor before. I take the cigarette but am afraid to ask for a light. I hold it and try to make it feel comfortable in my hand. The doctor puts the pack away, doesn't take a cigarette or offer me a match. He doesn't mention the cigarette again. Is this a test?

"Very good." He writes something on his yellow pad of paper. "Now, tell me . . . do you know why you're here?"

I inhale tentatively. "They told me to come . . . they told me . . . that you wanted to see me."

"That's right, I did want to see you. But I meant do you know why you're at St. Catherine's? Do you know why you were sent here?"

I shake my head. *Perhaps you should stop smiling. Maybe he thinks you can't understand what he's saying. Don't watch his mouth so closely.*

"If I say the word 'homosexual,' what's the first thing that comes into your head?"

You've got to listen. He said something to you, and you forgot to listen. The room seems to elongate for a moment, the doctor's voice gets very far away, then everything snaps back and the light from the window becomes a little more silver than just a second before. My eyes drift to the floor where a little circle of sunlight swirls with motes.

The doctor waits patiently. I shrug with an embarrassed smile.

"Homosexual," the doctor says again, separating the syllables. "The first thing that comes to mind."

"Doctor, I . . ."

"Don't think about it, just say a word . . . any word at all. Homosexual . . ." His voice turns upward and leaves the word hanging. I see it, know it'll have to be brought down. With my own voice I capture it, hold it for a moment and then offer it to the doctor, dropping it onto his lap like a small stone.

" . . . sunlight," I say, for the circle on the floor is turning whitish now, reflecting all color.

The doctor looks disappointed and writes something hastily on his pad.

"You know that before you came here you were a homosexual," he says, a little impatient.

"Yes," I say. The doctor tells me this so plainly that it must be true, though I really can't remember if I have been or whether being homosexual is good or not.

Mother. Wait.

My mother. I see her holding an envelope addressed to me and a letter. She shakes it in my face. I remember that. *What kind of a man writes to another man . . . it's so very hard to behave . . . the beaches here are filled with such pretty men . . .? What kind of a man writes that to you?*

I have done something wrong, I think. I feel the doctor looking at me, but I can't take my eyes off the circle of light. Little colored specks twirl from it now, and the doctor's voice is so very far away.

"And how do you feel about that?"

Then the sunlight is gone and when I look up to see where it went, the doctor is quite clear, sitting in front of me, all curves and angles, all fat, red, smoky angles and curves.

"I don't think . . ." I say, smiling again, "I don't think I understand . . ." I can't remember what he just said to me. "It's the question . . . I don't understand it." I'm sweating. Water is dripping off my forehead and the cigarette is damp now. I drop it. Did he notice? Can I stop my hand from shaking?

"It's quite simple." The doctor's voice snaps. "Do you or do you not feel it's abnormal to sexually desire another man? What's your opinion on that?"

A pair of transparent yellow cellophane shades covered the music store's front windows, cutting out the afternoon sunlight and washing the room gold. The image flashes in front of me, then something else follows it—an anger and a fear, unfocused, but suddenly familiar, rising up in the golden light of the music store then drifting away. Everything is hazy now. The doctor is near me but I'm not sure where. It doesn't really matter. I've lost interest.

"No," I reply very calmly, for all the world like that is the answer I know the doctor wants.

His face reddens even more. I'm pretty sure we've had this conversation before, perhaps many times.

"Why do you persist with this?" the doctor asks, his voice tired, his face annoyed. "We've gone over this again and again and, frankly, I'm beginning to think you're wasting my time. You're not putting any effort into this. None at all. I don't just wave some magic wand and cure you, you know. That's not how this works."

I look at him, wanting to appear clear-headed. It's best when I can follow a tone of voice, when I know what's being said without having to concentrate on the words. The doctor speaks so seriously to me, his impatience becoming something like compassion, I think. He's trying to help me but I'm not sure what I'm supposed to do. His words start to echo and I know I'm slipping away again. He's losing me. A chord of music plays in my mind, a chord struck on a faraway piano. I cock my head to listen to it. My fingers twitch. The doctor says something but the chords block it out. Just for a moment. Then I'm back.

"I'm sorry?" I say.

"Home. I'm sending you home. That will be for the best. Help you put things in perspective."

A feeling rises from inside me again, rushing up like a panic of bile not stinging, but burning like vomit. It passes all through me and leaves me aching and frightened and empty. A tear falls on my hospital gown.

"Look . . . doctor . . ." I lose my thought, clutch at it, bring it back, watch it evaporate before me.

"You'll be back among familiar people, back with your family. You can help around the house." He flips through some papers clipped to a manila folder sitting on the desk.

"You . . . play the piano I understand?"

"Yes," I say, simply because the doctor looked it up in his files. I don't remember ever playing the piano before. "Doctor . . ." I feel like I'm confessing, determined to tell the truth, almost anxious to receive whatever punishment the doctors thinks is necessary. Instead of fighting the confusion, I plunge into it. "I can't remember anything . . . I can't go anywhere . . . I don't think you understand. I don't remember *anything* . . . please don't send me away."

"Home," he says, as if the word means something to me, as if I'm supposed to know what's waiting for me there. "I'm sending you home."

"Home," I say, nodding, and wipe the tears off my face with the back of my hand. I wonder if I should get hysterical, if I should scream and tear at my hair. Home, yes. I must have had one. I must have had a mother and father and a sister and a brother. Or maybe I'm an only child. No. There's a sister and a brother and no father, but how I know or who they are is lost to me. And yet I'm alone, it seems. I can't keep up the energy for hysteria, am suddenly indifferent to my past's disappearance. My face must go blank at times like this. Moments must go by while I sit, unaware, my mind chasing a thought as simple as *I must have a home* and watching it change into a series of shapes, the words diagraming themselves, losing meaning, bogging me down in the verb-ness of *have* and the noun-ness of *home*.

The doctor sees my face. He knows what's going on. ". . . told you about the treatment before," he says when I come back, as quickly as I left. "It temporarily rearranges your memory banks. Cleans them out. Helps you start all over again from scratch. Of course it's a little confusing at first, but that's to be expected. You'll forget things. Simple things like your phone number or your middle name. But that's all part of your mind putting itself back together. But when you haven't had a treatment for a while you may find yourself panicking for no reason. That's normal, too. So I'm going to prescribe tranquilizers for you. Four times a day. I'll tell your mother. She'll see you remember."

"My mother . . ." I say. The word makes me feel a little less indifferent, though I can't say why.

"*And* you'll be meeting with me. You and your mother. Regular group therapy sessions. My group meets every Wednesday." He watches me while I finish crying, then hands me a handkerchief. "That's enough of that," he says, not unkindly. "You'll soon be back among familiar surroundings. You'll be fine. You trust me, don't you?"

I moved into the reception area just like I was floating a few inches above the floor. It wasn't really a pleasant feeling because I had so little control over myself. Pushed around, but tethered like a balloon. The tranquilizers kicked in while I sat waiting in my room and now the air looks cloudy. People had halos of light around them that looked like headaches made visible. The halos throbbed rhythmically if I looked at them too long. If I looked at the people. At the halos, too. Through the hazy air, I saw a woman in a heavy wool coat. A tired, uncomfortable-looking woman. Her halo was gray, though I could see underneath the gray some wisps of ash blonde. She wore glasses with big, light blue frames that helped round her thin face. She smiled.

I knew it was my mother. People and things came back to me in no particular order and just as quickly left me, but she didn't need to remind me who she was.

"The doctor says there's no reason to keep you here anymore," my mother told me as we sat in the car. It was cold. I didn't remember walking out the hospital door or across the parking lot. I didn't remember opening the car door. But I could see the hospital from where I sat. I could breathe on the window and watch my breath condense. A gray layer of hardened snow lay on the ground. The other windows started fogging up. "He says with the pills and that therapy you'll be fine." She pushed a lever, sliding it toward me, and a loud noise filled the car, followed by a stale jet of air. The windows melted before my eyes.

"I know, Mother." It's almost funny that I was able to speak coherently through this tranquilizer haze. The windows were gone and I could see the hospital again, a dark old building made of dark and sweating stones. I thought about laughing, thought about reaching out to see if the windows might still be there. Then I thought about the act of laughing and the idea of the window. The air got warmer in the car. "The doctor told me that, too," I said.

She looked at me.

"I did this for your own good," she said, her voice trembling a little. "We all did. You needed help. You'll see. It was all for the best."

I wasn't sure how to respond, so I said nothing.

"You resent us, no doubt, for . . . for what's happened to you. Try to see it from our perspective, though, Michael, and don't hate us. Give it some time."

"I don't hate you, Mother. Can we go now?"

She pulled another lever, stepped on a pedal slowly. The car moved.

"You don't look so good, Mikey. Did they treat you all right? If they didn't, you'd tell me, wouldn't you? Did they feed you at all? You look so skinny. I'll bet I know what you want. I made some of your favorite coffee cake for tomorrow morning. You just need some of your mother's cooking, don't you? All your favorite food. Whatever you want."

"I'm just tired," I said, but the act of forming the words through the haze didn't seem funny any more. It would be frightening, almost monstrous, if the chemicals in my blood hadn't made me so calm, if the words didn't just fall out of my mouth and land gently all around me in the stuffy air. "I'm really tired."

The layout of my mother's house is unfamiliar. I try to concentrate and remember it but I soon give up. It's easier to pretend, though at first I ask questions. I don't know which room I'm supposed to stay in, so I ask. My mother turns away and starts to cry.

So I learn how to pretend.

Sometimes, as the days pass, I *do* remember things, though. Where the broom is kept, how to push on the upstairs bedroom door to open it when it sticks, who the man is in the faded sepia photograph on the mantel (my grandfather). When these memories leave me, as they always do, I panic. I look around as if I might see them go, see them fade away like a taunting ghost, and a fear grips me, telling me the memories will never come back again. None of them will. Everything leaves me, my name, where I am, what I'm doing. Gone. The tranquilizers don't help, not really. I'm still scared. I'm still blank and scared by my emptiness, but my panic takes hold in slow motion. I can't scream. All I have the energy for is crying. But then, just when the despair is at its greatest, the memories come back. They always find me again. I just haven't learned to wait for them. I always forget that part. The patience. I forget about patience.

But in my mother's house some things still elude me. Even when I think everything is starting to connect, I know there are gaps. At least, there are some I'm aware of and probably just as many I haven't thought about. First, there's the homosexual part. I know it must be true. I know it always had been true, though I can't remember many details. The letter my mother found, there's that. But who was it from? Did I love someone, a man? Do men even fall in love with each other? What do they do? I can't remember that part at all.

And there's the music shop where they came and took me away. Had I worked there? Did I have a job? Am I a musician? The doctor said I played the piano, and that could explain the chords and notes in my head, my twitching fingers, but I don't see any piano in my mother's house. How could I be a piano player when we don't even have a piano?

A few days after I came home, my brother and sister arrived for dinner. At least that was who my mother said they were. Their faces looked familiar, but I couldn't be sure. They bustled into the hallway carrying several brightly wrapped packages, and I guessed that the woman clinging to my brother's arm had to be his wife. Or was she his girlfriend? My mother hadn't mentioned her. My sister looked at me strangely.

"We brought your Christmas presents," she said. "A little late." She shrugged and lit a cigarette.

"You look wonderful," the other woman said. "So rested."

Before we all sit down for dinner, I slip upstairs to take more tranquilizers. The pills are large and go down with difficulty, leaving me coughing and flushed. I sit on the edge of the bathtub, close my eyes. My breathing grows steady. *Remember,* I think, *remember, remember, remember. If you could just remember something about these people you wouldn't be so afraid of going to dinner. Do you get along with them? Are they older or younger? Something. Anything.* I feel the panic slowly rising inside me, demanding that I scream, but just as suddenly the edge of my pain softens and fades away. Is it the tranquilizers working so quickly or just my anticipation of them?

"Are you coming?" my mother calls.

Throughout the meal I heard the conversation from a great distance, realizing I was being addressed directly only when the pauses between the sentences became too long. No one else seemed to notice the amount of time between a question and my answer. Maybe for them it was like no time passed at all. I saw long minutes of silence become solid, materializing like wooden blocks around the table. When my mother got up to retrieve something from the kitchen, my brother leaned over and poured me some wine.

"Drink up," he said.

"Is that a good idea?" his girlfriend-wife asked. "Isn't he on medication?"

"A little wine won't hurt you, Mike. Isn't that right?"

My brother's voice moved upward. A question. I nodded. He leaned closer, spoke low in my ear.

"I want you to know," he said, "that I didn't realize she would really go through with it. I signed the papers but I thought she'd chicken out. She always had before. I want you to believe me, Mikey."

The voice in my ear sent a shock through me, making the little hairs on my neck stand up. My brother was close enough to hug. Should I kiss him? Should I kiss him on the mouth? Instead, I reached for the wine and took a sip. I lowered the glass, everything happening in slow motion, and watched my panic start to grow again as if I were detached form it. The liquid slid down my throat, burning.

"Yes," I said in a whisper, putting my lips almost on my brother's ear.

"You two stop that," my mother said, coming into the room with a large box. "Always telling secrets." She seemed happy, relieved, as if I'd done something I was supposed to do. I leaned toward my brother again, wanting to make my mother smile, but ended up losing my balance instead and knocked my jaw hard against his shoulder.

"Did you give him wine?" my mother demanded.

The box is in front of me on the table. Inside are a number of smaller boxes, beautifully wrapped, and many envelopes with cards inside. The box is big. I *know* this, but now it seems so small and far away. The air begins to fill with haze again. My family glows slightly.

"We didn't know you had so many friends in the city!" my mother says. "The packages and letters just keep coming."

I smile, a little frightened, and drain my wine glass.

"You shouldn't be drinking, Mikey," she says. "Not with your pills." Then to my brother: "Don't you give him anymore."

"Open ours first," my brother says.

My sister stares at me from across the table.

I reach for the box my sister-in-law holds out, but it doesn't seem to have any solidity to it. My fingers pass right through and I watch it drop onto the table, upsetting the salt and pepper shakers.

"Goodness!" my sister-in-law exclaims. She picks up the package and looks confused, watching me.

"I don't think he even knows he dropped it," my sister says in disgust.

Pushing up through the haze, I take the present, slowly, deliberately. I try to untie the ribbon and peel off the paper but my fingers won't move in the right way. They feel thick—bloated and soft. A string of saliva hangs in the air and drops onto the package. It takes me a long time to understand that it came from my own mouth. I try to move my jaw, to stop the string of drool. With an effort, I succeed.

"Jesus," my sister says.

And now I start to cry. My words come out in an angry slur.

"I'm not taking any more pills."

"Mikey," my mother says, "the doctor told you . . ."

"I'm not taking any more pills!"

The silence around the table takes an oval shape, stunned and watching. My sister-in-law looks down at her plate, then gently takes the present and unwraps it. When she finishes, she sets it down in front of me. Inside is a small music box. She lifts the lid and a tune starts playing. A tinny, unrecognizable melody.

"It's your favorite song," my brother says, halfhearted.

I stand up violently, knocking my chair backwards and surprising myself. I'm not sure where the energy comes from or why this anger makes it up through the haze. Why do these people make me so mad? A scream sits inside me, waiting.

My mother looks terrified and beaten. She moves her hands about, clutches the table cloth, covers her mouth, reaches out to me.

"Mikey, please . . ." she says. "Please . . ."

"Just calm down," my brother says, touching me. "Take it easy." Then he turns to my mother and asks, "Does he need some pills or something?"

"All these presents from your friends," my mother says, trying to divert my attention. "Let's open them. Would you like that? Would that make you feel better? We didn't know you had so many friends in the city. We thought you were so lonely. You didn't tell us."

"I don't know what you're talking about." I try to pronounce the words clearly, with anger and poison, but they bleed from my mouth. "I don't know who those people are. What city? What the hell are you talking about?"

"Mikey, don't say that . . . all your friends . . ." My mother is crying now. Then she shouts at me. "You're doing this on purpose, aren't you? You're trying to make me crazy, too!"

"Those people are gone. They've been erased. Aren't you happy? Isn't that what you wanted?" I try to say these things, but the words turn into one long moan. My thoughts click on and off like circuit breakers. I see the black-and-white-striped corridor before me and I take a step. A note sounds. It rings in the air and is joined by another note as I take another step. They're harsh and discordant together. I've got the order wrong. I stumble and fall forward.

A blanket is pulled up around my neck. I lie in a bedroom. It's dark. The clock says 2:15. My head is clear, as if a large space exists there, an open window with a breeze blowing the curtains inward. A blue sky. No clouds.

I sit up.

I don't hear any movement, no sounds except the ticking of many clocks and a distant hum.

Suddenly I panic.

Where am I? What's my name? How did I get here?

I get out of bed. The fear fills me up instantaneously. Like a drop of oil on a clean white cloth, it saturates me.

Where am I? What's my name?

I walk to the hallway, grabbing onto the door frame to steady myself. Nothing looks familiar.

How did I get here? What's my goddamn name?

As I move down the hall, I notice a bathroom to my left. I go in. Close the door. Sit on the toilet in the dark.

And I breathe.

And breathe. Rapidly at first, then forcing myself to go slower, slower. Taking air in, feeling it fill my lungs, pushing the panic out. Slowly, slowly. As suddenly as the fear comes on, it vanishes, leaving behind the house, the bathroom, my name. I stand up and turn on the light. Inside the medicine cabinet are my tranquilizers. I remove the top and hold the bottle upside down over the toilet.

Downstairs I find the letters and cards. I take them up to my room and read them. Most of them don't make much sense. Names I don't recognize. Get well soon. Merry Christmas. Mention of parties. Nothing very personal, except for several letters, all from someone named Paul. They're different, wonderfully different. From these letters, I assume Paul and I shared a lot, more than just an apartment or similar interests. Some of the gaps fill in. I read the letters and a story unfolds before me: "The Story of Mike." But I don't remember much of it. It sounds like some episodes from a TV show—something dramatic, something dark. It might keep your interest for a while, but it isn't happening to you so you can turn it off when it gets too strange.

I was a graduate student in music. During summer vacation, I went home to work a job my mother had arranged, teaching piano in a local music shop. That was the last anyone heard of me. Paul is in love with me.

My mother and I went to group therapy once a week. The group met in the basement of an Episcopal church and consisted of four other patients and their parents. I dreaded going. It was too large a group, and I never said anything unless the fat, red-faced doctor spoke to me directly. Unless Dr. McCutchen spoke to me directly. I tried to remember these things. Names. Addresses. People's faces. My mother on the other hand, liked to talk.

"I know Michael blames me," she would say.

"Why don't you tell Michael that," Dr. McCutchen would reply. "He's right here."

But she couldn't stop talking long enough to look at me.

"When a mother sees her child ruining his life, turning away from what's right," she might continue. The other parents would nod. They understood, even if the first three weeks my mother couldn't bring herself to explain what my problem was, how I had turned away. It didn't seem to matter to the parents. They didn't need to know the specifics.

I pretended to pay attention but I found myself sneaking glances at the others in the group. A bony girl with a bad complexion always sat in the same position, her ankles crossed, her hands fumbling with the ruffle on her skirt or the gauzy scarf she sometimes wore. Her name was Karen and she never looked at anyone directly. Instead she kept her chin tucked in and her head cocked uncomfortably to the side and then glanced right up at the ceiling as she spoke, explaining and re-explaining why she hadn't worn the same dress she'd worn the day before. Karen's father accompanied her, looking rather embarrassed and conservative. He wore a dark blue suit, though the tie was always different.

Each patient moved to the same spot every week, some willfully and others looking rather helpless. Karen had to sit by the door. Next to her father sat Scott, a boy I liked the look of until he scowled at me. His father, so short and round and without much of a family resemblance, scowled at me, too. Scott had tried to slit his wrists. He excused himself from Thanksgiving dinner, went into the bathroom and gashed himself with a steak knife.

Marguerite sat next to me.

"She smiles too much," my mother said, but I couldn't see anything wrong with that. Her mother always combed Marguerite's hair before the session began, yanking a brush through the long, dull, brown hair. Marguerite would just wince. Her mother claimed Marguerite didn't eat. On the other side of the room, a pasty-skinned boy named Alvin sat with his mother, who was just as pale. She never seemed to use words longer than two or three syllables and would shrug a lot. Alvin cried at least once a session. I felt in league with these four people, all close to my own age, but at the same time I felt different from them. I couldn't bring myself to say that, but the doctor . . . but Dr. McCutchen knew.

"How are you doing this week, Mike?" he would ask, greeting me informally before the session. Or he would ask, "Feel like talking tonight?"

Finally about halfway through the fourth session, after Scott tried to explain why he slit his wrists, there was a pause. No one seemed willing to speak, so Dr. McCutchen turned to me.

"I think it's important for the group to know that Mike was hospitalized for homosexuality."

A look of shock crossed the parents' faces. Scott scowled again. The others, for the most part, didn't react much and I thought that maybe their own problems seemed a lot more interesting to them.

"Mikey's better now," my mother said. I could see she was mortified, almost struck dumb, flushed and blubbering and torn between hating the doctor and knowing he was somehow right to do what he did. She looked at me, as if it were my responsibility, as if I had planned all this and then tried to save face. "But Doctor, he won't take his pills . . . he threw them away . . ." She was getting even with me. I made her promise not to tell about the pills.

"I think it's important for Mike to talk," Dr. McCutchen said. "I think it's time for Mike to tell the group about this. Don't you, Mike?"

"No," I said.

The doctor smiled. "Do you feel hostile?"

"Yes," I said.

"And why is that Mike? What do you think is causing this feeling?"

A scream sat inside of me, waiting. I knew I'd have to appear calm or seem crazy. And I wasn't crazy. At least not at that moment I wasn't. That much I knew. I spoke slowly, quietly, but I couldn't keep my voice from shaking.

"I wish," I said, pushing the scream back down, "I wish you would understand. But even if you don't understand, which you don't, I want you to know that this isn't any of your business. But if you really want to hear what I think, I'll tell you. I think there's nothing wrong with me except I can't remember things. But I wasn't like that before you got ahold of me. Everything else is fine. That's what I think."

My mother looked sick and furious. My hands shook.

The members of the group were silent. I don't think they were shocked at what I said but at what I had done. I broke one of their rules of etiquette.

I hadn't shouted or cried or condemned myself. The doctor still smiled, a frozen, ridiculous smile.

"I can see," he said, "that we still have some work ahead of us."

We are both silent during the drive home. My mother's jaw is stiff and I can see she isn't planning on crying. Not this time. She's angry. My heart beats too fast. The scream inside me didn't go away.

"I just don't understand you," she finally says.

I don't say anything for a moment, then reply, "I'm not going back to that group."

"Michael," her voice becomes shrill, "a doctor has prescribed this for you, just like he prescribed the pills. You can't go against a doctor's orders. He knows what will make you well. You're acting like a stubborn little boy, and I won't have it. Not while you're in my house."

"There's nothing wrong with me!" I say.

She pulls the car over the side of the road suddenly and turns off the engine.

"Nothing?" she shouts and hits me weakly with her fists. "Four thousand dollars for *nothing*? Nothing is *right* because you haven't changed a bit!" The scream starts to slip out. I can feel it. My body gets rigid, trying to hold the scream in, but without warning my hand jerks and strikes my mother. We sit in silence for a while, surprised. *I've hit my mother,* I'm thinking. But I struck at something else, too, something that is and is not my mother, something above and around her. It is the scream, breaking out of me. The silence between us elongates and I feel little memories slipping away.

"Those doctors are stupid!" my mother hisses at last. "They don't know what they're doing." She hits me again. "And you! It serves you right with your stubbornness. I wanted to help you. I wanted you to lead a normal life. But oh, no, not you. Mr. Know-it-all. Mr. Free-thinker. Mr. Pervert! Go ahead! Be miserable and lonely the rest of your life, you stubborn ox!" She can't keep herself from crying, now. She tries, but the tears, once they start, form continuous streams, cutting through her dusting of makeup. "You're my son," she says very quietly. "I love you. Why are you doing this to me?"

I look at her. The scream is gone, leaving a space behind inside me. I'm looking at her from some great distance, watching names and faces and numbers lose their meaning for me as though I reached into my pocket, pulled out my handkerchief, and scattered thoughts like coins.

"Shut up," I say. My voice is toneless, tired, uninterested. That space inside me makes me feel light. I float above the car, watching. "Shut up and drive us home."

I changed trains twice, finally arriving in the city, where Paul agreed to meet me at the station. I didn't know what Paul would look like, so I just stood at the gate and waited. A stocky young man with short blond hair and powerful, large hands came up to me before long, looking nervous, relieved. The man kept making a move to touch my arm as we walked out of the station, to take my hand, but would draw back, catching himself.

"I missed you so much," Paul whispered to me in the cab.

We went to Paul's apartment. *Our apartment,* I reminded myself. We stood in the hallway looking at each other until finally Paul hugged me so hard it hurt.

"I tried calling your mother," Paul said, the words coming out in a rush. "She would barely talk to me, said you had a nervous breakdown. Of course, I was worried sick but she wouldn't tell me what hospital you were in. She said no visitors and to send letters to her. She'd get them to you. You got them, didn't you?"

I nodded. "I couldn't write back. I forgot a lot of things."

"But you're fine now, right? You sounded strange when you called last week and I thought, he's tired or something."

I just looked at Paul for a long time.

"Right," I said. I hadn't remembered any of this. Not the apartment, though I knew we'd shared it. Not the personal belongings, some of which I figured were mine. Not Paul. I only knew what I'd read in the letters and they told me Paul and I had loved each other. It didn't seem like much to go on.

A grand piano took up most of the living room. I wandered in to look at it while Paul made tea, lifting the cover off the keys and staring at them, black and white. I couldn't hear the chords now, but my fingers twitched. Paul came in with the tea.

"Are you going to play?" he asked. "I guess this is the longest you've ever been away from it."

"Not right now," I said. My fingers wanted to strike the keys, but in what order? "Not just yet."

That night we made love, quietly so the neighbors wouldn't overhear. I'd been anxious on the train ride, wondering if I'd know what to do and when to do it. Paul kissed me and led me into the bedroom. My body knew the rest. It felt Paul's heat, pulled us together, our mouths and tongues joining, coming apart and joining again. When he entered me, I wasn't sure I liked it and for a moment Paul seemed to thrust almost apologetically.

"Are you all right?" he kept asking. I just nodded and waited until he was finished. Then we lay very still in each other's arms.

"I want to tell you something," I said much later, "something that may sound pretty weird." Neither one of us was getting any sleep. I still clung to him, resting my head on his chest, and his arm still encircled me. "I don't remember ever seeing you before today. I know I have. I just don't remember."

Paul sat up, pulling away from me.

"What do you mean?" he said in a tone that almost annoyed me.

"Just what I said. I don't remember you or the apartment or this city. It's like I've never been here. It's funny, isn't it?" He didn't say anything, so I sat up, too, and looked at him. "You're taking this personally?" I said. I didn't know whether to slap him or laugh. "It doesn't have anything to do with you, you know. What's the matter with you?"

For a minute longer Paul didn't speak. "I don't understand what you're saying to me." He sounded a little angry.

I put my hand on Paul's leg gently, feeling something like emptiness and something like desire.

"I'm kidding," I said.

Paul remained silent, then stared down at me, his expression blank and unreadable.

"A bad joke," I said, understanding exactly where I stood, exactly how alone a person could be when he's not alone at all.

Slowly, Paul lay down next to me.

"Don't do that again," he said.

I feel a warm wind moving through my head and I open my eyes. The clock says 3:30. It's very dark but I can make out the figure of a man lying asleep at my side. Then the panic comes.

Where am I?

Who am I?

What's my goddamn name?

I remember to breath. Slowly. In and out.

Slowly . . .

Later I think: *Some day I'll be on a street corner and an old woman will grab my arm. Please help me, she will say, I don't know where I am. I'm so confused. Could you just stand by me for a while until I get my bearings? She looks so terrified, so powerless. I take her to a coffee shop and we talk. She calms down, her memories returning to her. Soon, she feels better. I walk her to a bus stop and hold her hand.*

Later I think: *Some day I'll be on a street corner and everything will connect. All my thoughts—accessible. All my memories—retrievable. Some day I'll forget everything for the last time. The panic will occur for the last time and everything will be in place. Everything will be quite clear and I won't be alone anymore.*

Later I sit at the piano. The white and the black keys stand ready, though I'm not sure in what order I'm supposed to strike them. My fingers are poised, twitching. I bring one finger down, pressing firmly. A note. I bring down another finger. Another note. The sounds slide into each other, faintly familiar, incomplete. Another finger, this time on a black key, changing the sound, brightening it. Then, as another finger twitches above another key, I hear something. In my mind, I hear the chord. I bring the finger down.

Ben's Eyes

LOUIE CREW

I loved Grandmama's. I loved the tin roof, the smell of the wood stove, the taste of the metal dipper, the tiny roof above the well, the tomatoes we picked and ate off the vine, the rope swing that hung on the tall hickory, but most of all Ben's eyes.

Long before six others and I integrated the high school in Stewartville, Georgia, or before I became the drum-major and broke the heart of the white football captain, back before I was a teenager, when we lived on an Air Force Base in Texas, I used to spend two months of every summer at Grandmama's house back in Clinton County, in South Georgia.

My older sister Hattie, 13, teased me before everyone as her "country kid-brother." She went to Georgia with me the first time, but didn't like the single room house, the bed she had to share with Grandmama, the goats in the yard, the weeding and the hoeing, collard greens every day of the week, no radio and the six mile walk, one-way, to the movies. She stood it for about three weeks and then cried until Grandmama let her return early to "Texas civilization and the twentieth century," as Hattie boasted to her girl friends at our large playground on the air base.

Ben was my older cousin, sixteen or seventeen, and he had gorgeous round, bedroom eyes, with long lashes like the kind women pay to have made up false. Ben's face was a richer black than mine, with not even a hint of tan. He had generous cheeks and a lean chin. His strong red lips could not conceal the slight smile he kept as I stared at him for minutes at a time, not just when we rested in the shade to guzzle water from the mason jar, but even while I rode with him on the rented single-seater, plowing Grandmama's field. I probably wasn't much help, but he made me feel that I was.

We watched for any rocks down the row. "Go get it, Cleveland," he would squeeze me, and I'd jump down, run ahead and put it in the big drum which we had hung on the back of the tractor for our collection. At the end of the row, we would add these to the border, built up for more than 50 years around this field. Yet and still this field continued to yield new chunks with each plowing.

"God makes them during the winter," Ben told me.

Ben had dropped out of school at 14, but anything he said convinced me, at least at the time that he said it. Most of the time he just sat silent, concentrating on the noisy tractor. Still short enough not to block his view, I braced myself on the narrow metal strip meant for his feet, and leaned against Ben's legs, just looking and looking and looking.

Ben was Grandmama's only help. Ben's mother, my aunt, and his father both had been killed in separate automobile wrecks, a week apart, when Ben was 13.

"Fancy. Mighty fancy," my mother used to tell me about them, "but a bit dangerous too."

Grandmama kept a picture of Ben's mama and daddy on the chifforobe near where she slept in the room. Ben's mama, my daddy's sister, a pleasantly fat woman with a broad, pretty face, sang the blues at backwoods clubs for black farmers all over South Georgia. His daddy, lean and less noticeable, more or less tagged along, or so I thought then from what Grandmama said whenever I asked about the picture.

Later, while at Stewartville High and no longer going to the farm for summers, I learned that Ben's daddy's accident had happened cause the Clinton County police had driven him off the road at high speed. They used the six cases of bonded whiskey in his trunk to prove that he was into "big crime."

Ben's sister and brother had already grown up and moved away when the two accidents happened. The sister worked as a hair-burner up in Macon, and the other brother worked for a packing house in Tallahassee.

Ben didn't talk about his people much, nor did he seem interested when Grandmama would answer my questions. While Grandmama and I cleaned up after supper, he usually sat over by the kerosene lamp looking at a *Jet* magazine, or studied his mustache with a pair of trimmers and a small hand mirror.

"You gonna break some gal's heart iffen you don't stop trying to be so pretty," Grandmama would tease him; "God done already give you sexy eyes. Why don't you leave well enough alone?"

Ben would laugh and continue to groom.

After we'd put away everything, sometimes we lolled around on the porch, or swang. In the top of the hickory, Ben had built a treehouse back when he had been my age, but I never got to see the inside of the treehouse. Long before I ever came to visit, Bessy Craddock, the girl who lived at the next house down the road, stepped on a weak limb, fell, and broke her arm. After than, Grandmama laid down the law: the hickory tree was only for swinging.

Sometimes I seem to convolute all evenings into one, so much did I enjoy our times in that swing, but I remember one particular evening as distinct, just for its sunset—dark reds and oranges, and then a streak of royal purple appeared just about as fast as Ben blinked his eyes. He sat on the seat and I sat in his lap, nose almost touching nose, my legs tight around his hips, his large hands clasping my ribs, my arms thrown loosely over his shoulders, as we swang higher and higher and higher. I did not grasp. I knew he held me.

Grandmama went to bed early, got up early. Sunrise. Sunset. That's what her "early" meant. "You young'ens can do as you please, but if you want to live as long as I have, you'd better be payin' attention. Leastaways, don't disturb my rest with no kerosene lamp. Those folks' pictures in *Jet* seem a bit highfallutin' anyways . . ." She would natter on until she gave us the cue: "Now I'll get into my night clothes."

Ben and I would dutifully step outside. When we came back in, we'd make our way in the dark to our own side of the room. Even without a moon, starlight sufficed. Each of us had a special chair to hang our clothes on. I slipped into some short pajamas Mama had made for me, but hot as Georgia stays at night in summer, Ben slept in his birthday suit.

Some nights, after we'd swung, Ben would not come to bed at once, but would go down the road to see Bessy and her brothers. One night a storm came up unexpectedly after he had left and I had gone to bed. It thundered and lightninged something terrible. Grandmama snored through it all, but I lay awake at least until well after midnight, listening to the rain batter our tin roof, looking at the green hands on Grandmama's wind-up alarm clock, wondering whether Ben was dry.

I awoke when I heard the tractor revving in the dark. He had stayed in the Craddock's barn until the lightning stopped, but had come back to put the tractor under the shed.

A few minutes later, the room deadly dark without even starlight, I felt cool air rush over me. He even sounded wet. I heard him sniffle as he closed the door. I heard him drip as he unlaced his shoes. I heard him peel off his socks. I heard a chair scrape the floor slightly as he tiptoed past it. I heard the zipper. I heard his buckle jiggle on the wooden floor. I heard him breathe and knew he must be arcing his t-shirt over his shoulders. It slapped the chair gently. I heard underwear ping his knees.

Then silence. An interminable silence. Even under the covers I shivered knowing he stood there wet, exposed, although I could see only his black-ness shadow the slightly lighter darkness of the room.

I feared my eyes might glow in the dark like the hands on the clock, that he might know that I stared, so I slitted them. I held my breath to hear him breathing, slowly, evenly. A board squeaked slightly. I expected our bed to tilt to his weight, but still he stood there. It seemed an eternity.

When he did get in, he moved to me at once, not after he was asleep, as he usually did. His wet chest sent goosebumps down my back. His thick thighs seemed a bit drier at my hips. He sighed pleasantly through his nose as I warmed him. "Sleep well, my little heater; sleep well," he whispered softly.

I didn't love the outhouse. That's about the only place where I ever thought of Hattie and her "Texas civilization" during the entire summer. Hattie had made it worse, by telling me even before we went to Georgia that first time together, "Snakes lay down there in the holes just waiting to bite any ass black enough and delicious enough to sit there, particularly if they decides to sit there too long. And the spiders. You just look up to the ceiling. They be waitin' for you, country bumpkin!"

Mama had told me I should try not to use nasty public restrooms except for liquids, and to plan my days so I'd be near home when I had to go. So the first time that I went to Georgia, already warned by Hattie, I fixed my mind to see the outhouse as a public restroom. When I peeked at it and saw that it was a 2-seater, that cinched it. Besides, the shack stood separate from Grandmama's house. How much more public could you get? I decided to wait all summer until I got back to Texas before I would go again, except for liquids.

By the third day, I must have looked mighty ashen. After supper Grandmama asked, "Boy, you feelin' all right?"

"Yessum," I lied.

"You don't look it. Have you vomited or something?"

"Nome."

"Ben, you be out there with him all day on the tractor. Has this child seemed sick to you?"

"The boy probably just taking time to get used to eatin real food," Ben said, lost in *Jet*.

"You regular?" Grandmama asked.

Hattie snickered. "Have you gone down with the creepy, crawly snakes every day?" she asked. She had not yet thrown her screaming fit to escape.

"Hush your mouth, girl, or I'll creepy, crawly you," Grandmama said to Hattie. Ben laughed like he was on my side. I bowed my head.

"Answer me, boy," Grandmama said gently.

She finally got out of me that I had been too scared to go. Grandmama wouldn't hear a word of it when I explained that Mama had told me never to use a public restroom.

"Ben, you go down there with him and don't either of you come back until he's done a job, you hear?! Land's sake, all this Texas civilization will be the death of him for sure."

I thought I could not do it with someone else there. At least the restroom at school had partitions for those that dared to use them. Here Ben's thigh touched mine and I nearly choked on the cigar which he lit, "to scare away everything," he said. "Take your time, Cleveland."

It began to get dark fast. We left the door open for the clean air, and looked far down the field where we'd plowed all day long.

"I didn't know that you is circumcised," Ben said.

"What?"

"I didn't know that you is circumcised," he repeated.

"What's that?"

He reached over and touched the head. "That," he said.

"What's 'circumcised'? Ain't you?"

"Nope. See."

He held his up into the twilight. "Pull back the skin like this," he said. "Your's been cut that way by the doctor soon as you born."

I looked at his, then at mine. "Is that why yours hard and mine soft?" I asked.

"Soft?" he asked. I had not noticed the hard knot mine had made.

"Why the doctors do that to me?" I asked.

"Beats me," he said. "Must have something to do with Texas civilization." I did my job easily now.

Don't be 'fraid, Cleveland. Just tell me when you want me here witchya. Besides, see this stick." He leaned and reached just outside the door for an old broom handle he kept there. "You just take this pole and beat on the side before you ever come in here. That'll scare away anything that might harm you. Don't you listen to Hattie or everwho talks that way. Nobody can't make no sissie outa man like you."

I did not fear the outhouse anymore. Yet and still I waited most times until I knew he was going so I could go at the same time.

I liked being with Ben even better outdoors on the tractor, leaning against his lap, or in the swing, or taking a break in the shade at the far end of the field, or having him snuggle up after he thought I'd gone to sleep. One night while he was still out, I took off my pajamas and hid them on the floor next to the wall under the bed, so Grandmama wouldn't see them and remember that I'd had them on.

One day right there on the tractor I took mine out and studied it. "Why the doctors do that to me?"

"They didn't hurt it none. It's as good as mine," Ben said.

I felt him grow stiff. I turned and tried to straddle him as in the swing.

"Just a minute, child, lessen we kill ourselves on this here machine." He idled it at the end of the row. Far at the other end clean white bedclothes whipped in the sun. In the shade I looked long into Ben's eyes before and after I inspected uncircumcision.

Before Daddy left the air force, we got stationed back in Georgia. When Grandmama fell sick, one of my aunts moved in to take care of her, cause Ben was away in the army. They did not have time or space for children then, and I was too busy with my paper route to laze away a summer in the country.

By the time I took home ec at Stewartville High, my sisters and brothers had gotten used to me, and were plenty proud when I brought home a national prize for one of my recipes. Besides, I led the parade and had the captain of the football team sneaking over to see me four nights a week.

After I graduated, I took up modeling in the North. I head that Ben had married, not Bessy Craddock, but a jazz singer named Eula Hines, from Macon. My Mama said Eula was as much a looker as Ben's mama had been, and that she and Ben lived just as dangerously as Ben's mama and daddy had.

So I had not seen Ben for about eighteen years when Grandmama died. I wanted to bring my lover with me, but he decided it wouldn't be right to make our lives upstage theirs, especially at a time of grief. Anyways, Mama and Daddy had already met him and liked him a lot. I can't believe he would have surprised the others. But I didn't insist, since probably he would have been bored. He didn't grow up in the South.

Neighbors and family came all over. They brought at least twenty kinds of deviled eggs, ten styles of fried chicken, and as many more of cornbread and collard greens, plus platter after platter of other good eatins. They laid it out on long picnic tables in the pecan grove between the church and the cemetery. Eula's band played gospel music all day inside, before the sermon and the burial in the late afternoon. Since the church was too small to hold all of us at once, we went to and fro, from feast to the funeral in shifts.

About one o'clock, Ben himself arrived. He had filled out lots more, but was still muscle, not fat. I recognized him first by his eyes.

"She was a good woman, Cleveland; a good woman. A real loss to the world."

All those outside came to greet him. Then Ben went in for some of the music. When he came out again, I eased to the same side of the food table so that I could strike up a conversation with at least a touch of privacy. I wanted to get off somewhere to ourselves, maybe alone in Grandmama's room, so I could tell him how much it meant to have learned about myself from someone who loved me, who was gentle, who taught me how to scare away the snakes. Before I met my lover, I discovered many people, women and men, who didn't seem to know that you can also love the person you hold through the night.

I never had heard "gay" when Ben and I were together. When I hit puberty, I needed the word to describe myself, but I never thought Ben was. I still think he is not. But I knew that he had loved me when we did those things together.

"You remember the outhouse?" I asked.

"Cleveland, you were one scared little boy, yes indeed!" he said, and moved on down the table to get some ribs.

"You remember the night you came back from Bessy Craddocks's all dripping wet?"

"No. I can't say as I do. Which time?"

"You remember the swing and the tractor?"

"What about 'em?"

"You don't remember?"

"Cleveland, you've grown up a fine young man. I always said you'd go farther than most of us. You may have begun scrawny, but like the turtle and the rabbit, you passed us all!"

"You really don't remember, do you?"

"Hey, little brother, what happened a long time ago is not important. Don't go troubling yourself." He forked a deviled egg, nibbled it, and lifted his chin to catch some yolk.

"Man, it sure is good to see you!" He said it like he meant it.

With his eyes, he indicated that perhaps we ought to mingle with the others. I could not find a way to thank him.

Dressing a Wound

DANIEL MANGIN

Hi! My name is Joseph Younes. I know I'm
not really Norma Jean Baker, but I like to think I am and sometimes I dress
up like her even though my hairy chest ruins the effect. I know my life
could have been simpler and easier than it's been, but I just did what I did at
the time and this is how I turned out. I'm not complaining (well, not too
much), but it really hurt along the way, and I think it hurt the most because
it always seemed like I was trapped in situations I just found myself in and
there was only one choice I could make (usually disastrous) and no others.

I shouldn't have turned out the way I did. My father's a doctor and my
mother went to college. My brother's a dentist. I'm the black sheep of the
family.

I guess you could say my first turn off the straight and narrow was
when I took the train into Manhattan when I was fourteen and headed
straight for a peep show in Times Square. I can't figure out how I knew to
go there for the shock of my life, but before I knew it I'd snuck in and some
old guy was putting my hand on his cock and kissing me.

I used to be pretty much of a stereotype, slightly queeny. Make that
very queeny. Nobody would have ever thought I was straight, which is why
everybody came on to me. Well, partly. I guess I was just on that wave
length, but no matter what happened, they knew I wasn't going to beat
them up or anything.

Sometimes I feel like my life has lived me instead of me living my life. It's like the story's written already, so I only get minor choices about how to play out my role, like an actor would, but I can't change the main story. Maybe that was Norma Jean's problem, too.

I have to say that even though I've managed to make the best of some bad situations, I wouldn't have minded living out someone else's story. But at least now I know that those minor choices about how you play the part you get in life can make all the difference in the world, even if some of the things about who you become really are figured out in advance. It used to be just Norma Jean on a collision course, but Norma Jean's finally grown up.

My father always said I was too romantic as a kid. He used to call me "Nancy," which my mother said wasn't going to help anything. "My name's Norma Jean Baker!" I'd scream back at him.

The first guy I fell in love with was a telephone repairman named Rick. I was sixteen. We were such opposites that we got along perfectly for a while. He was twenty-nine, six feet tall, very masculine, with broad shoulders and a muscular body. I was short, skinny and kind of hunched over like I was afraid someone was going to hit me. Rick wanted to take care of me, which was fine with me because I wasn't doing all that good of a job myself. I found myself slowly changing in his direction after a while. He knew I was hustling Times Square, but it didn't bother him and after a while I stopped doing it because I knew it would make him happy and proud of me.

What I didn't notice at first was that while I was becoming more like Rick, he was turning into a raving queen. All of a sudden he started sounding more and more like *me*. I thought there must be something really wrong with me to affect a guy like that. One night when his voice squeaked like Jayne Mansfield while he was prancing around our apartment, I realized I had to get away from him for his own good.

I started going to the live female acts in Times Square after I broke up with Rick. I couldn't figure out why I'd want to see the girls there because I sure didn't get off on it, but I guess it was because I liked the outfits they wore and it was a kind of self-projection thing about dressing up like women. I used to talk on the phone with the girls behind the plexiglass windows. I never knew what to say, so I told them I worked Times Square and how the different tricks were.

In the sex show I met a guy named Kevin who was obviously there for his first time. He was very sweet looking and figured since I looked so young it must be my first time too. I started kissing him for lack of anything better to do and I guess he was too freaked to stop me. We went into a booth and had sex while the girl watched, tapping her toes and laughing at the novelty of it all. After we were through, we paid her ten dollars for tying up her booth and went to dinner.

Kevin thought I was nuts when I told him about hustling Times Square. He was a psych major at NYU and said that even though I wasn't as sweet and innocent as he thought I was, in a way he liked me more because there was so much to psychoanalyze about me because I was so "fucked up and confused." Help like that I didn't need.

About the same time I met Kevin, I started doing this fat blind man who came to Times Square to pick up the boys. He said he used to be in the movies until his eyes went bad. He'd always offer the boys extra money because he said he knew he was worse than a regular trick. Most of the boys wouldn't do him anyway, but I'd go with him every once in a while and just charge him the regular price so he'd feel like a normal john instead of a leper. He was easy anyway because he mostly wanted me to jerk off and tell him how it felt.

After girls in phone booths and the assorted perversions of hustling, I got into leather for a change of pace. It was supposed to be a joke, but the nice thing about people is they'll take you at your own word and since I *looked* butch they figured I was. I used to have the cutest little leather cap and I always tied to my belt a half-dozen metal cock rings that reminded me of some napkin holders I'd seen at Macy's.

I went to the Anvil for a while and for once in my life even I was a little shocked—candles, fists, piss-troughs—it was all too gross for me. I met this guy there from West Germany who said he'd pay me two hundred dollars to be his master for the night. I almost burst out laughing at the thought of me ordering someone around, but I can do anything if I need to, so I started getting aggressive right off the bat and threw my ice cubes at him and told him, "My glass is empty, you scum, get me another drink."

He told me his master in West Germany was nineteen and the guy beat him and humiliated him but it was mostly a fantasy trip. In his mind he was a twelve-year-old boy named Pipi, which is German for a kid's cock. Whoever was his master was "Uncle." Since he was twelve, he was all shaved, even his pubes. He was supposed to keep his zipper down and expose himself at all times. His master gave him a two-page letter with instructions for any young masters he might pick up in the U.S. He really wanted to be treated like dirt. I threw him on the floor and started kicking him and calling him a bad boy. I made him lick my boots and spanked him and told him that if he told on "Uncle" I'd kill his pet dog and have him sent to reform school. He pleaded for mercy and asked Uncle to please be a good uncle, but I kept on slapping him like the instructions said. He started crying but I just hit him and told him to suck Uncle's dick like it was his mother's tit. When he finally came (which he wasn't supposed to, according to the instructions), I came too and told him what a beautiful boy he was for making Uncle so happy.

If I stayed the night I was supposed to make him eat his eggs with Uncle's cum in the morning, but I'd had enough of him. I thought, my god, this was harder on me than it was on him, but then that was why I was getting paid. I went into the bathroom to take a piss before I left and he followed me in and wanted to be my urinal so I said OK but twenty dollars extra and of course it had to be the longest piss of my life.

I've turned worse tricks, but the thing I hated about Pipi was having to be so mean to him. It was much easier when people were getting off being mean to me because I could get off on it a little and when they got too weird I could just tell myself it was their problem and not mine. But I had to be truly cruel to make it work for Pipi and then I actually got into my part in the whole thing and really started beating him good and I didn't like to think I could be that violent to somebody, even as a fantasy. I kicked him so much I was shaking like a leaf, but I had to hide it from him because he was supposedly loving it so much.

After I got home I just had to dress up like Marilyn to soften things up. I really thought I was going crazy because I never let tricks upset me no matter how nuts they are, but somehow this one had pulled a private part of me into the proceedings and that hadn't happened before. But when I was Marilyn, I comforted myself about all the bad feelings and the world didn't seem so cold or cruel any more. I'd tell Marilyn that even though people could be very mean, at least we had each other to count on and to dress up and play with each other like little kids having fun. I think Norma Jean was abused in a way and even though it looked like she was having a good time on the screen she was hurting inside and needed everybody to be nice to her to ease the pain. She could bring out the kindness in you, too, because she made you just want to hug her and kiss her and tell her everything's going to be all right.

As I look back on it, it's been a funny way to be nice to myself to dress up as Marilyn and be nice to her, but since she's me it all works out to the same thing because I get some comfort and don't have to feel so sad.

I think I must have been really shocked by Pipi because I started looking for "sweet" guys after him, which I hadn't done for a long time because I didn't think I deserved one and because those kind always gave me the creeps. I fell in love with the piano player at an old-timers bar on Long Island. Robert was twenty-four and so nice that I asked him to be a *little* mean to me, but he got afraid I was into S&M, so I had to drop the subject. We felt like brothers right off and the night we met I drove him home and he more to less seduced me, to a certain extent, in the back of my car. Even though he wasn't cute or anything, it was quite enjoyable because of the emotional aspect of it combined with his innocence and sincerity.

But I have to admit there was a kind of fine line between having sex with Robert and with somebody who was paying. All in all, I was more used to sex for money. Sometimes I'd be bored for a minute with Robert while we were having sex—not that he'd done anything wrong, but you can't be with it a hundred percent all the time—and I'd just space out and realize later that I'd tripped into my trick mode and started oohing and aahing without any real feeling on the subject. When you get right down to it, for me there really was something more intense about having sex with people who paid. Not a "good" intense, particularly, but there just seemed to be more at stake and that part was a rush. It's funny because I'd always say I didn't feel a thing when I got paid for sex and I didn't in the sense that the actual sex usually wasn't that good, but there were two sides of me that felt a lot whenever I was with a trick. One was shocked to death and couldn't believe he was there and the other was getting off on the dirtiness of it all because the people were usually either sleazy or at least wanted to talk sleazy.

I must have felt something one way or the other, though, because whenever I stopped tricking out for a while I'd miss the charge of it and want to get back into it again. Of course, after I'd start back again I'd remember that most of the tricks were creepy or even mean and I'd wonder why I thought I had to get back into it other than I'm always making wrong turns in my life.

By the time I was twenty, a lot of my friends were dropping like flies from drugs and general hard living and the ones that didn't were getting meaner by the minute, so I started thinking it was about time to change. I started going back to the sex arcades, though, and one night I had a dream date with a cop who earned extra money watching the arcade and keeping the sleaze out of trouble. It was the great uniform fantasy come true. We talked at the bar and he bought me some drinks. He was your classic tall, dark and handsome, thirty years old with a wife and two kids, and ever so earnest. He was so naive about gays and said he was straight as an arrow. I didn't dare try to come on to him because he was a cop, but he got very protective after a while and wouldn't let any other guys get near me, which was fine with me. He drove me home and when we got to my house he said he couldn't understand it but he felt the urge to go to bed with me. We started kissing in his car and ended up getting a motel room. He said he couldn't figure out what it was in me that brought out these urges in him, but he was so passionate it didn't matter to me as long as he wanted to be with me. He really didn't know what to do in bed, but he was really great at kissing so we made out a lot and hugged each other and finally I blew him until he freaked out and said he had to go and that he'd beat me up if I ever came near him again.

I was so frustrated by this I ran down to the Strap just to occupy my mind for a while. I met a guy there who looked like Jackie Gleason in Nazi drag. Another guy came over to us and offered us poppers as we all headed into the back room. As I stopped to take a sniff, the second guy bumped my elbow and the poppers went straight up my nose. I thought it was on fire. I bent over trying to snort out the sting but it burned on like crazy. After a few minutes it stopped and I discovered that my pocket had been picked so I went over toward Christopher Street to find a trick to get the money to go home. My friend Stephen was outside Taco Rico and asked me to show him how to turn a trick, which I didn't want to do because he was too young and his boyfriend was a vicious hairdresser who would have kicked me to death if he found out I was helping Stephen make it on the streets.

Stephen kept bugging me so I finally said OK, but he was so pathetic I had to get into the cars myself to make sure the tricks paid. I couldn't find him after his second trick so I made some old man drive me around to try and find him. At five in the morning the man said forget it so I walked the streets until a cab driver picked me up and said he'd drive me around looking for Stephen if I'd sit up front and let him play with me, which I did but we didn't find Stephen.

I forgot to mention that at this time I'd gone back to school and was studying political science. Of course I missed a few classes with the hours I kept, but I did a lot of studying, for me anyway. I think I was finally a sophomore after five semesters of college. I studied a lot about nuclear arms control, which I felt very strongly about. I wrote a paper about seventeen pages on that, twice as long as any other kid. I kept thinking I could do so much better than Carter on arms negotiations and I could be the first woman president of the United States! Back then I wasn't sure if I could be president because my mother is Israeli and my father is Lebanese, but it turned out I was American anyway because I was born here so I could have been president after all.

After school was out I started working at A&S because I was almost twenty-one and figured I'd better get a career going. I couldn't believe a department store in New York City paid only four dollars an hour to start, but I wanted to "go straight" so I went to work. The third day I went there some sleazy state senator from Albany came into my department, linens, and told me he'd take me to Puerto Rico for a week if I'd have sex with him. I couldn't believe my ears, right there in linens! It was time for a vacation after three days, so I said OK if he gave me two hundred dollars up front, which he did. I didn't have that bad a time because he went to sleep early and I got to hang out with all the hustlers in San Juan, who seemed a lot nicer than some of the ones in New York even if the living conditions were a lot worse. I fell in love with one named Carlos who still writes to me.

When I got back to New York, A&S believed my story about being sick with hemorrhoids (my department head was so sweet she even offered to let me use her padded toilet seat the next time if she wasn't using it herself) and I went back to linens vowing to be a good girl and stay on the job.

I started going to bed early and being on time for work and what have you, and that's when I started thinking about how I'd lived my life since I was fourteen. I guess seeing all the middle class ladies shopping made me think of how I was brought up and how far off course I'd gotten. I couldn't win either way because my parents weren't happy that I was at A&S when I should have been at Columbia or some such place instead, but they would have been even more unhappy if they'd known I was the *belle* of Times Square. A&S seemed like enough of a compromise to me, but since they didn't know what we were compromising about, they didn't realize how far I'd come.

Anyway, I was happy because I knew I was straightening myself out and I didn't really care about having less money because I never did much with the money I had and since I wasn't a high-priced call boy I never made all that much anyway. In the calm of A&S I wondered how I'd survived getting raped two or three times, being driven at gunpoint to Yonkers, fist-fucking a man big enough to be a whale and other such sordid adventures that aren't fit to be related here. I felt like it didn't matter ultimately because I got through it all alive, but I got scared when I went to see a psychic who used to be a nun who told me that everything we see and do stays with us and that we are the sum total of all our experiences, even the ones we've forgotten or would like to forget.

I kept thinking I was ruined because all of those tricks and humiliations and bad moves I'd made weren't just in the past, they were in the present, so I asked her what I should do about all the sights I'd seen in my life.

If there was a turning point in my life, I guess it was the day I went to the psychic, but the process of change wasn't all that quick because I was back in Times Square later that night because the hustler part of me felt like it was being destroyed. I think that night was the night I enjoyed turning tricks the most because the hustler part was trying its best to convince the rest of me that *it* was the real me. I kept thinking I was just a weak human being, but the psychic told me that I wasn't weak at all and that I should realize that my true self had always been around trying to protect me even while the hustler part was getting me into hair-raising adventures. I always assumed I was a weak person because I'm so passive—I speak passively and can never make a decision—but now I see that some people go to the loony bin when only one of the things that happened to me happens to them, so I must be strong and if I can figure out how to be strong without being coldhearted, everything will be fine.

I don't think I've ever been coldhearted to the core, but I've had to get pretty numb at times and I've spent a lot of time in a cold, dark place one way or another. People even come along and want to help you, but you figure you have to shut down the vulnerable part of yourself in order to survive, so you don't let them help you because you can't tell if they're going to be like the other ones trying to grab a piece of *you* along with your body. Instinct tells you they won't, but you can't be sure so you pull in and the energy inside you gets tighter and colder because the warmth from the outside never gets in to thaw you out and the only people you feel comfortable with are your own kind, which is miserable, haunted people.

I used to think I didn't feel anything I didn't want to feel, but what happened was that most of the time I just ignored the part of me that told me I was feeling a particular thing. When the psychic told me that all those things were still inside me, I knew just what she meant and I felt, my god, I'm just like a lump of that hard tar they use on roofs in the city and if they melt me down a lot of pain and skulls and people crying out for mercy will come rolling out for everyone to see.

One night I got the idea to sit like a yogi and let each one of the haunted people out of me, one at a time. I was amazed how I was able to remember every one of them and in chronological order almost. They were all struggling inside of me like aspects of myself and a lot of them didn't want to get out because I'd been a nice way station for them and they were afraid if they left they'd be treated badly again, but I told them each that I loved them and wished them well, but I had to get my own house in order now. I packed them all nice box lunches in my mind, gave them each a kiss goodbye and blew three short breaths and sent them on their way.

It was just a ritual, but it started me on the way to cleaning things out and opening myself up because with them gone there was more room for me to grow. It all changed slowly, though, and I always felt like I was going two steps forward and one back, but at least I wasn't losing ground ultimately. The psychic told me that I'd already changed in a spiritual sense, but I still had some old habits I hadn't broken and that all of me hadn't caught up with the changes yet.

Getting started was the worst part because all the doors to the inside were shut so tightly when I first sat down and as my sadness came out I was shocked at how ugly and violent it was from being locked up. I had a vision one day that all the hurt of me and all the people I'd come into contact with was like molten lava inside me that I was letting bubble to the surface and it was thick and hot but not yet hot enough to flow out of me so it bubbled around for a while. That scared me because I couldn't be sure the explosion was really going to happen and if it didn't I was going to be stuck with all the pain festering like an open sore for all the world to see.

I was so mad at everything at that point because all my sadness and pain was right there on the surface and the least thing would set me off because I felt so worthless and ashamed. I'd always notice that the more sadness I'd let myself feel without trying to distract it with sex or drugs or whatever—just really feel it and not fight it and almost meditate on it and then send it off on its way like the haunted people—the more free I'd feel. But I'd also always remember later on that right after those times I'd have gone on a drinking binge or something because I'd probably let out too much pain at once and needed to cut the shock some.

So it's always two steps forward and one back. You let a little out, see how it feels, rest a little and start again. I could tell you I'm living happily ever after and all that, but really I'm just started. Like I said before I sometimes wish I'd gotten someone else's story to live out. I still turn tricks—a girl's got to make a living—but not in Times Square. I've got an ad in the paper now: "Get a sensual massage from 25 yr. old boy/man. 5'5", 125 lbs., 8", cut." Sometimes they actually want the massage. I also work the hotels out of an agency but I don't like that much because I have to give them half the money.

I still dress up as Norma Jean. I have to. She watches over me and I watch over her and together we get through most of our jams. I think of her as my twin sister. She told me the other day that she's been feeling better too since we started changing things around.

Sheet Music

SAM RUDY

Harlan watched Rachel walk down the hall-
way and wondered how much longer it would be until he'd have to grease
her to get her through there and into that part of the trailer. She let very little
light get past her as she lumbered toward the bedroom, her thighs brushing
the panelled walls as she went. Brush, brush, brush. It reminded Harlan of
the sound the shredded wheat box made when he shook it every morning to
see how much was in it.

Sitting on the piano stool, he tried to recall if there had ever been one
day, one particular day recently or some time ago, when it occurred to him
that Rachel was really fat. She'd always been what her mother called
"hefty," and he remembered thinking that the night they eloped when she
loomed above him two rungs up. She moved less-than-spritely even then,
and he worried they'd be found out by her parents before Rachel made it
down the ladder. But they had managed to get away unnoticed in his '57
Chevy, and it seemed to him now that they'd been gathering weight ever
since: broken-down cars and trucks that clogged their unpaved driveway,
furniture that grew lumpy under Rachel's girth, and bills that were often
nearly impossible to pay. Excess weight, all of it, nothing that mattered to
him, really, sometimes not even the kids, it seemed. They'd grown up to be
duds, too, he thought, assuming the kind of life he had with Rachel: going
to church, sticking mostly with family, and behaving as though a drive

across the county line were the grandest adventure they knew of.

Harlan closed his eyes to block out the mental picture he had of Rachel as he knew she'd be just then, bent over the chest at the foot of their bed, one mound of fat cascading onto another. He could almost smell her sweat oozing out from between the folds of herself like icing on a layer cake as her fat fingers fumbled through the stacks of sheet music. He hoped she would find what she was looking for because he didn't want to have to go in there to help her. He hated being alone with her in the bedroom anymore. He worried that she would expect something of him, and he just couldn't do it, not anymore.

"I found it," Rachel called out. Harlan felt a wave of relief wash over him like a tonic.

"No one's asked us to sing this in so long," she said as she brushed her way back down the hallway, "it got shoved underneath a bunch of camp songs and show music. That book of Irving Berlin songs is still back there, you know."

Harlan hadn't thought about his show music in years. He'd bought an armload of it in a great excitement just before he and Rachel were to have gone on a bus trip to New York City with the Ladies Auxiliary from the Elks Club several years before. He'd longed to go to New York since he was a youngster. Their group was to have seen a Broadway show on that trip, and gone to Macy's and the United Nations and some fancy Italian restaurant and done all kinds of things. But the night before, Rachel got an attack of appendicitis and Harlan got stuck pretending to worry about her all day and half the next back home at the county hospital.

"Here," Rachel said reaching over his shoulder to place the sheet music on the piano in front of him. Her flabby arm brushed against his ear as she arranged the music, and he felt a tightening in his stomach, as though he might now become sick.

"You used to know this by heart," she said.

Indeed, when he and Rachel began performing at weddings in and around Foster's Mills some 20 years before, he had been able to breeze his way through most traditional wedding songs without once needing to refer to the music. That, however, was before brides attached new meaning to John Denver songs, or to the Carpenters; as brides' tastes changed, so did his repertoire.

Harlan leaned forward to get a closer look at the music. He squinted his eyes to bring the tiny black notes into focus. It was written in the key of F, which wasn't at all what he remembered. The chords were simple, certainly, but he looked down at his fingers to make sure they were on the right keys. He played the first chord tentatively, intending to give the first few bars a practice run. Rachel, though, charged ahead with the lyric, loud and strong.

"Oh promise me that some day you and I will take our love together to some sky . . ."

She'd been away from the song a long time, too, and was singing flat where she needed to be sharp.

"Where we can be alone, and faith renew, and find the hollows where those flowers grew . . ."

This is terrible, Harlan thought. We'll ruin the entire ceremony.

"Those first sweet violets of early spring, which come in whispers, thrill us both, and sing . . ."

But Rachel kept on warbling as though there were no tomorrow.

"Of love unspeakable that is to be; Oh, promise me! Oh, promise me!"

Harlan stopped quickly before she had a chance to attack the second verse.

"I'm not sure this is a good idea," he said turning to look up at her red, puffy face. "Maybe we should try something else."

The first time Harlan saw a car he recognized parked in the lot at the roadside rest, he decided to be more careful about when he went there, and how often. Just by going there at all he ran the risk of being spotted by someone who knew him or Rachel, or the kids. He'd gotten carried away, anyway, in the month or so before that, stopping sometimes every other day to loiter in the toilet or wait in his car for a truck to pull in. He'd done that, originally, to establish whether or not there was a pattern to when a certain young man came to the rest stop along the highway. But after two weeks of daily visits when the young man hadn't returned even once, Harlan pretty much gave up hope of ever seeing him again. He kept coming back often anyway, because he'd gotten into the habit, or the habit had gotten into him, and it was less lonely, really, sitting in his car waiting for God-knew-what than sitting at home in the living room filled with Rachel.

Not that his exchange with that young man had turned out any differently from any of the others. It was dark in the front seat of the young man's pick-up, and not a single word was said between them. The young man was passive, and he smelled like the others, with that pungent aroma that comes from the creases where a man's legs are joined. But when Harlan looked up from the young man's crotch to see if he was pleasing him, he thought he saw in the young man's eyes a look Harlan knew he'd had himself for a long, long time. A look that you could feel, really, like an ache, it was. A painful throbbing that filled his eyes and made them sting. A look that said, please, won't you help me? I hurt.

Harlan sat up quickly when he recognized that look, and buried his face in the young man's neck, as if to say, I know how you feel. I hurt, too. And when the young man came and his body went stiff for those several seconds, he turned his face into Harlan's, too, and nuzzled him back; his lips felt warm and dry, pressed against Harlan's flesh.

But it ended there, like all the others, in silence and awkwardness. The young man turned away, cleared his throat, wiped his hands, buttoned his pants. When he turned the key in the ignition, Harlan climbed out of the truck and slowly walked away, all the while hoping the young man might come after him, stop him, call out to him. But he didn't, and when Harlan stole a glance through the windshield as the truck pulled away, he saw that the look had gone from the young man's eyes as though he and Harlan had never shared a thing.

And as he watched the truck's taillights glowing like flares as they wound down the mountain road, growing smaller and smaller into dots as they went, Harlan felt the look in his own eyes burning hotter than it ever had before.

"I could just bawl when I hear that pretty song," Rachel's mother said, "and think you never had your own wedding to sing it at."

They were seated at a small table in the corner of the banquet hall where acquaintances of the bride and groom were expected to sit. Family and close friends filled up the tables around the happy couple's and popped up for pictures or nosed through the gifts.

"Eloping, what a fright," she continued. "It's a crying shame, it is."

Harlan watched his mother-in-law stab her fork into what remained of her cake and ice cream. He doubted there was enough juice left in the old biddy to produce a tear for crying. She had never been the sentimental sort and was even less so now that her husband was dead and she rambled alone around a two-story house that had seen so few happy times in 50 years.

"Oh, hush, mother, please, and finish your cake," Rachel said as she carefully scraped the melted ice cream onto the side of her spoon and licked it. "That was 25 years ago. You wouldn't talk like that if Daddy were here."

Harlan had never heard Rachel speak of her father as anything other than "Daddy," and she did so always in the manner of a little girl, turning the pitch of her voice to a whine that accented that word alone in a sentence. She sounded especially silly now, Harlan thought, as she sat spilling over the folding chair; she was all dolled up in a dress too frilly for a woman of her disposition and size.

"Your daddy, God rest his soul, should be happy he's not here, I would think," Rachel's mother said. "To see what's going on in this town. Families splitting up right and left, divorcing. People from places we never even heard of on every block now. A Jewish family living above the post office. And his own niece carrying some man's baby, and that man's married to another woman.

"It's disgusting, the things I hear," she concluded, and Harlan wondered if the way her eyes flickered in his direction meant he was somehow or other included in that remark.

He looked around the room, and from where he sat he saw a great deal of happiness and mirth, as though this were a marriage that enjoyed the blessing of everyone in the room. He would have liked 25 years ago to have had such a celebration for Rachel and himself—to have given their marriage at least that sense of tradition—but he was in a hurry then, in a big hurry, actually, to get rid of the feelings that grabbed at him so often. The feelings that lurked inside him like the boogie man who hid under his bed at night when he was young. Those "unnatural feelings" he'd read about in a pamphlet a minister once pressed into his hand at a church synod meeting. That look he felt in his eyes sometimes. He wanted to shake all that, so he quick asked Rachel to marry him, as if trying to throw himself off his own scent, like a hunter training his dog. And he made her say yes, right then and there, for fear something would happen if he waited too long.

But a lot of good it did him, he knew now, because nothing had changed except Rachel kept getting fatter, and her father never forgave him because Harlan "stole" his only daughter, and her mother never stopped bitching about anything, ever. And he still felt unnatural, like he was wicked and sick, and he grimaced at his own expression when he looked in the mirror and saw how desperate he'd become over the years. That look in his eyes stung more than ever, even when he closed them tight and tried to get it out.

"I said, did you hear about the Hoover boy?" his mother-in-law was saying in a louder voice than usual. Startled, Harlan turned to look at her and realized they were alone. Rachel had no doubt waddled off in search of more refreshments.

"Ricky Hoover's moved into his mother's old place off the mountain road," she continued. "He's dying, I hear. Got that disease men his age who don't marry are getting.

"You know what I mean," she said. "AIDS, they call it. Seems no one will go near him. He had to go all the way over to Lewistown to find a male nurse that would come in once in a while to check on him. Make sure he's still alive, I suppose.

"I can't say I blame them, his cousins and the others that are staying away. It must be a terrible burden to have in the family. He never did fit in, really. His mother put up with his queerness somehow or other, but this

AIDS business, well, I think it would have killed her if she weren't dead already."

Harlan turned to see Rachel walking back to the table. She held another plate laden with ice cream and cake, and he wondered what compelled her to such excess.

"I must ask Rachel if she'd heard anything about this," his mother-in-law said. "If she did, she didn't mention it. Or did you know?"

On his way that night to the roadside rest, Harlan stopped to look down the Hoover lane. He pulled his car off to the side of the road and sat and looked at the house through the trees. A light shone through one window downstairs, and the rest of the house was as black as the night. Harlan thought about tip-toeing up the gravel driveway to have a look in the window, but that seemed a foolish thing for a man his age to do, so he pulled back onto the highway and drove the rest of the way to the mountaintop.

Once there, he stayed in his car and just looked. He didn't get out. He watched the man in the station wagon next to him get out of his car and walk behind a thicket near the restroom. He watched another man smoking a cigarette disappear behind the same bush. He saw a third man, a young man, duck into the bathroom.

What Harlan did know about the Hoover boy, he thought, was why he didn't fit in, but he didn't know he was dying. He had thought he would call the Hoover boy had they made it to New York on that bus trip, but he supposed it wouldn't have mattered much if he did. A phone call from a man he hardly knew in his hometown 200 miles away couldn't have meant much to a young man living in New York City. Harlan imagined Ricky Hoover's life filled with friends and events that didn't come at all close to what life in Foster's Mills was like. So much excitement. So much to do. So much freedom and opportunity. So many people. Harlan imagined the Hoover boy didn't need to sit in parking lots and on cold toilet seats in search of comfort, relief from pain.

The first man who'd gone behind the bush came into the open and walked across the gravel to his car. The second man came out, too, lit another cigarette and walked in the opposite direction. The third man, the young man, came out of the bathroom and stood next to the doorway, his hands on his hips, his body cocked in a seductive way. He seemed impatient the way he looked around, as though he were expecting someone late in coming. He saw Harlan watching him and threw him a stare, a cold, hard look.

Harlan shuddered and gripped the steering wheel. He turned on the ignition and backed up the car. When he pulled onto the mountain road, he didn't even look in the mirror to see if the young man was still standing there.

The Hoover house had sat empty for over two years until the Hoover boy came home to die. And it was dust he smelled, not death, Harlan thought, when he stepped into the vestibule. He knew from having watched for several nights that week that the Hoover boy rarely left the front room in the corner of the house. Occasionally, the boy's figure broke the light as he moved through it.

And so it was that Harlan knew where to find the boy. As quickly as he'd gotten Rachel down that ladder years before, did he find himself now in the musty hallway one second and at the Hoover boy's bedside the next.

The boy was sleeping facing away from where Harlan stood. His breathing was shallow, raspy, uneven. Although he'd not seen Ricky Hoover in years, Harlan would never have guessed this to be him, even in sickness. His pajama top hung over his back as though it didn't belong there, as if it had been haphazardly tossed across the bed. His hip pushed up against the bedsheets like a tent pole, and it was hard to tell what might be a fold in the blankets and what might be his legs.

Harlan remembered Ricky being a vibrant boy as a teenager when he had come with his mother to church. She'd sung for a while in the choir when Harlan first became the accompanist, but she dropped out when her husband was shot in a hunting accident and, indeed, never returned to church after that.

The room where the Hoover boy now slept had once been a parlor or study, Harlan guessed, for it wasn't very large. The boy's bed took up half the room and around it there was clutter: an end table scattered with medicine bottles, wadded-up Kleenex everywhere, books and magazines were strewn about one corner of the bed. Harlan supposed the boy had no interest, really, in how the place looked, just in staying alive in it.

Harlan found a folding chair in one corner of the room and brought it next to the bed and sat down. He watched Ricky's chest move up and down slowly with each uncertain breath and remembered the Sunday he'd glanced up from the piano in church and saw the boy sitting in the pew a few rows back. He was staring at Harlan. It was a piercing look, actually, a look that unsettled Harlan and made him blush. In fact, he could remember it now just as well as when it happened: he had stared into the open hymnal on the piano and only looked up from it when the service was ended.

Harlan sat on that chair then, dozing on and off until morning, and it wasn't until that evening when Ricky's fever broke that the two of them exchanged words. Before then, the boy had only looked at Harlan a few times dreamily, through glazed eyes half-opened. When that happened Harlan tried to look cheerful and bright so the boy might know a friend was nigh.

"Hi," Ricky said in a voice more full of life than Harlan would have imagined. "Mr. Miller, is it? I dozed off. I'm sorry."

Harlan explained to the boy that he'd been asleep for a long time.

"I hope you don't mind. I straightened up a few things," Harlan said, indicating the room with a nervous gesture of his hand. "It gave me something to do to pass the time."

Ricky raised his head from the pillow and glanced around the room. It was tidy and spotless.

"That's nice, Mr. Miller," Ricky said smiling. "Thank you. You didn't have to. Could you help me sit up so I can get a better look at things?"

Harlan stood next to the bed and looked down at the boy. He worried that if he touched him he would collapse in his hands. There was so little to him. He looked fragile and frail. But the boy said to grab him in under the arms and pull him up until his back rested against the pillows. When he did, it was easy—there was strength left in Ricky—and Harlan was relieved that the boy seemed more comfortable after all was said and done.

"Thank you," he said. "That's great. Now maybe you could help me get washed and changed. I feel like I've been sweating in these same clothes for weeks now, you know?"

The boy's lack of pretense disarmed Harlan, though it pleased him to be approached so informally. Ricky's manner implied that they had a history together and that this was yet another part of it. As he carried a basin of warm water from the kitchen, though, Harlan was embarrassed to think of the boy naked in front of him, lying there so vulnerable and wasted. Yet as his fingers undid buttons and pulled the boy's pants to his ankles, Harlan marvelled at how smooth and lovely Ricky's skin felt, like a soft velvet cloak, or the cotton suit he saved for weddings and special occasions. The boy's breathing was steady as Harlan moved the damp cloth the length of Ricky's body, studying its contours and imagining how grand it must have been in better times. By the time he had washed every spot he could get to, Ricky had lapsed into sleep again. Not wanting to awaken him, Harlan pulled the blanket over the boy and sat on the chair again to watch and wait.

When he thought about it later, Harlan realized there was no turning back the things that happened after that. Like a piece of printed sheet music on which the notes, chords and tempos are already arranged, so it was that he fell in love with the Hoover boy that night and again each day they were together after that.

His mind was possessed of nothing else, and he lost all track of time. He only knew when the room took a chill that a day had ended, a night begun. He couldn't help wanting to be near the boy, hovering always close to the bed, feeding him or bathing him. He read to him, too, and mopped his brow when even the smallest drop of sweat came to it. He fussed with the blankets, the bedsheets, the pillow. And he especially loved to finger the boy's long blonde hair, thinking how his ears reminded Harlan of treble clefs as he pulled the boy's hair around them at night while he slept.

But the Hoover boy, though thankful and always quick to say so, remained indifferent to Harlan's touch. Harlan supposed he'd been touched by strangers so many times during his 18 months in and out of hospitals that Harlan's felt like just another pair of hands. In fact, one day when the boy was feeling the strongest he had since Harlan came to him, Ricky said, "I've been pulled at and prodded by so many nurses and doctors, I stopped feeling like a private citizen a long time ago."

So Harlan imagined his touch—though imbued with more love and adoration than he had ever felt for anyone—must have felt to the boy like so many nameless others trying to bring temporary comfort to a hopeless situation, as though applying a small bandage to a savage wound.

It was on that day when the boy seemed his most alert that Harlan first ventured outside the house. They'd talked all morning about a great many things: about how Foster's Mills had changed, of the people who still lived there, and what the boy had done with himself since he'd grown up and left home seven years before. Of his time in New York, Ricky spoke mostly of his career in the theatre and seemed to avoid talking about much of his personal life. When he did, he rarely gave names to the people he spoke of, as though Harlan knew them or as though they should be forgotten. His voice broke once as he spoke of one man, but when Harlan reached to smooth his hair and calm him, the boy turned his face away and did not speak for several minutes.

Nor did Harlan speak of Rachel and their family, for when he thought of them at all, they seemed fabled, somehow, like the characters in a morality play that had ended the day he arrived in this house.

The boy became tired from their talk eventually and said he wanted to take a nap. Braced with the feeling that the boy was getting better, Harlan decided to walk outside as soon as Ricky had gone to sleep. When he stepped onto the porch, he reeled slightly at the smell of the fresh air. He'd become so accustomed to the air that he and Ricky breathed between themselves that this seemed strange. But he filled his lungs with it and squinted his eyes in the noontime sunlight. He watched cars passing by on the mountain road at the end of the lane and felt as though that were another world, a world filled with Rachels and Rachels' mothers and brides and grooms and men in trucks at a roadside rest . . .

He turned to face the house and glanced through the window of the room on the opposite side of the house from where Ricky was. It was filled with furniture hidden by sheets and dustcovers. The boy had said that he hadn't gotten rid of anything since his mother died two years before, and Harlan now looked into what must have been the living room. Beneath assorted coverings he made out the forms of a sofa, a rocking chair, a coffee table, bookstands and lamps. In the far corner, at the opposite end of the room from where he stood outside, Harlan saw what he thought at first was some sort of packing crate. He realized as he studied its shape that it was, in fact, an upright piano beneath an old, yellowed bedsheet.

He went into the house and opened the door to the living room. As he pushed it open, he felt how still the air was inside, as though the years and dust had settled everything—the past and present—into one, quiet mood. He walked to the piano and spread his arms wide along the top of it until his fingers came to rest at the square corners of the lid. He grasped the bedsheet in each hand and gently pulled it to the floor where it lay rumpled about the piano legs. He sat on the bench and lifted the cover from the keyboard. As he always did the first time with an instrument, he brushed his fingers across the keyboard to get a sense of it, of whether or not it had been well-played or misused. The softness of the keys, their smoothness, reminded him of the boy he loved in the next room, and he knew the piano had been treated kindly through the years.

From under the lid of the piano bench he pulled out several pieces of sheet music and ambled through the first few bars of some—"After the Ball," "Send in the Clowns," "Nearer My God to Thee"—until finally he settled on "All Through the Night." He couldn't remember if he'd ever played it before, but it felt familiar, somehow, and his fingers moved across the keys with ease, as though the chords were remembered in them. He imagined the song soothing the boy the way a lullaby should—"Sleep, my child, and peace attend thee all through the night"—and when he reached the end of the page, he played it again. It seemed so right and pretty—"Soft the drowsy hours are creeping, hill and vale in slumber sleeping"—that he played it another time.

He'd lost himself in the music—"I, my loving vigil, all through the night"—when he suddenly heard Ricky coughing. He stopped playing and quickly stood up from the piano. He kicked away the sheet as it had become tangled around his ankles, and hurried out of the room and across the hall.

126

As soon as he stepped into Ricky's room, Harlan could tell the boy had run a fever, for his breathing was labored and he looked flushed. He'd thrown aside the bedcovers and with both hands was fumbling with his genitals through the opening in his pajamas.

"Here, let me help," Harlan said, assuming the boy needed to urinate.

Harlan reached for the empty plastic bottle they kept handy for that purpose, but the boy took the bottle from him and let it drop to the floor. He grasped Harlan's hand at the wrist and held it tightly. He looked up at Harlan and then looked down at his own groin. Then he looked again at Harlan and again at his penis poking through the slit in his pants.

When he looked up at Harlan a third time, Harlan blushed like he had years before in that church, yet this time he managed to look back at the boy, managed to look him square in the face, and when he did, he saw the look he'd seen in another young man's eyes, the look he'd felt in his own for so long. That look that said, please, won't you help me? I hurt.

And he took the boy's penis in his hands and let his testicles rest in his palm. He held them as though they were the most precious and delicate things on earth. And the boy responded, not as he might have to a nurse or a doctor but, Harlan imagined, the way he might to a lover. For when the boy closed his eyes, Harlan knew it wasn't in shame, but in pleasure, for his release from all pain was near. And when the boy came and his body went stiff for those several seconds, he turned to look at Harlan again and reached his arms up to pull him near.

Harlan hugged him while leaning over the bed and then lay next to him and nuzzled the boy's neck. Together they stayed that way all through the night.

D.O.M.

DONALD VINING

Otis had often vowed he would never let it come to this. Today, when his mind was clearer than it had been in some time, he remembered that distinctly. Visiting his two unmarried aunts as, one after another, they were confined to nursing homes, he swore he would never share their fate. Yet here he was.

As nursing homes went, he had to admit Sunset Gardens was superior. In its pleasant garden, where he now occupied a bench, one could in seasonable weather escape much of the unpleasantness inside. There was the odor of flowers instead of the smell of incontinence which the best efforts of the staff could never entirely remove from the lounges. In addition the more troubled and troublesome ladies seldom came out, those forever crying out demands that husbands perhaps long dead, or fathers, or children get them out of here. The men, very much in the minority, seemed mostly so docile as to fade into the wallpaper but so many of the women were querulous, shrewish, or noisily addled. There were even one or two from whose once-genteel mouths poured a stream of foul language from which, in their prime, they would almost certainly have been the first to recoil. Even if more of the women were in their right mind and nice, there would still have been too many of them. Otis had, after all, lived most of his life in an atmosphere that was just the reverse, largely male. He had socialized little with women and at work, well, in his day not too many women came into sporting goods stores.

Otis' mother had escaped the fate of her sisters, he was happy to remember. She had lived, he and her less fortunate sisters agreed, long enough but not too long. Otis had hoped to share her fate of a quick, easy, and timely death instead of her sisters' prolonged twilight. The passing of the last aunt to survive had, he'd hoped, meant that he'd seen the last of nursing homes. But here he was, indubitably a patient rather than a visitor, though he couldn't remember how he got here. He'd have to take the word of the social worker, who'd told him it was the only recourse once the hospital was ready to discharge him and his former neighbors organized to protest his return to his apartment. They felt he had endangered their lives by falling asleep while smoking just once too often. At any rate, the social worker had said, though he was taken to the hospital initially because of smoke inhalation, he had been found in very bad physical condition generally, the result of malnutrition and neglect or overdose of various medications. Clearly he wasn't, she said, able to look after himself any longer.

Otis remembered that he had once been full of stratagems to avoid this fate. When Aunt Rose first went into the home, Otis had felt smug in the knowledge that Chester was twelve years younger than he, a vigorous athletic type who swam every day of his life at the Y, and not just to have a gander at nude young men in the locker room. Who expected a car to mount the sidewalk and strike him down? Even with Chester gone, leaving Otis as alone as the unmarried aunts, he'd felt he had resources they lacked. Used to being independent, they could never be persuaded to live together and pool their strengths, nor to take a younger person into their home who might be leaned on in case of emergency. Otis, accustomed to sharing, had figured that when the time came that he felt he couldn't manage by himself, he would let Chester's room to a student, or perhaps find another gay widower who was willing to share.

It had never seemed to Otis that that time was quite at hand. He'd had lapses of memory, of course, forgotten doctors' appointments and things like that, but on the whole he'd still felt capable. He'd hired that Korean boy, whatever his name was, to do the housecleaning after a few dizzy spells when bending over to dust chair rungs. He'd been scrupulous, he thought, about not trying to get one too many wears out of his clothes before having them laundered or dry-cleaned. He had tried to curb any tendencies to collect string, paper bags, magazines or any of the things that so many old people cluttered their homes with. He'd asked his old friend Noah to let him know if he saw any signs that he was becoming a "saver" or a "dirty old man" in the literal sense. One couldn't, alas, be as beautiful as one once had been, but at least one could be clean and neat.

Noah, of course, had moved to Florida, was it three or five years ago? For a while Otis had tried to see things through Noah's eyes. He's pretend that Noah was still stopping by mornings for coffee and Danish and he'd imagined whole conversations with him. A cherished coffee mug had been thrown out, in fact, because the phantom Noah had told him he was slipping in keeping a mug with a chip out of the rim just because Chester's predecessor Jake had given it to him. Good old Noah. Dead now.

The Korean boy had been gone for a while, too, he guessed, gone to New York to work in a brother's fruit store. Was there a reason why he hadn't replaced him? He remembered thinking that if he kept the windows closed tight, not so much dirt and dust would come in and it wouldn't be so necessary to clean. Somebody, he couldn't remember who, had a theory that some of his lapses of memory were a result of lack of oxygen. They'd said they could always tell when he'd been outside and had some fresh air because his mind was so much clearer than when he'd been shut up in the apartment from which endless cigarettes had drained oxygen. It had seemed a lot of bosh at the time but Otis had to admit that now that the nurses limited his smoking to the lounges or the garden, his mind was much clearer than it had been in his last months in the apartment.

He had felt so much better lately that he'd asked the social worker if perhaps he might leave the nursing home now that he was well. She had smiled and said she feared he couldn't cope. Once he left Sunset Gardens, she'd warned, he was unlikely to be lucky a second time in finding a vacancy if things didn't work out. That would mean a far, far lower level of nursing home. God forbid, thought Otis.

The meals here weren't bad, though it infuriated some of the complaining women to have him say so. They were indignant when he cleaned his plate and spoiled the effect of their refusal to eat "such garbage." There was, however, so much out there in the world that Otis wanted that he wondered if it might be worth taking a chance on a worse nursing home just to see if he could cope.

Who here could understand him, or sympathize with some of the things he missed? His gay magazines with all those lovely nude centerfolds, for instance. Here one had to make do with the magazines brought by volunteers from the churches—old copies of *Reader's Digest* or family magazines with holes in the articles where a recipe had been cut from the other side. Articles on how to keep Communists out of Central America or how to make ten easy soufflés were not exactly jerk-off material. And God knows the visible men weren't either.

Some of the orderlies, strapping young blacks who continually mopped the halls and tried to keep the odors of age and incontinence at bay, would have made good centerfolds for certain tastes, but not his. He certainly wasn't above taking a look at the outline of their underpants when it showed through their white uniforms as they bent over, but he had never shared the interest of some of his departed friends in darker-skinned people. Though he could admire their looks, certainly, as he could admire the looks of women, horses, and children, he could never lust for them. Among the church volunteers, who came to entertain(!) them with hymns and such, an occasional buttoned-up good-looking youth would appear but they always seemed like people who still feared pimples and warts if they touched themselves "there," and likely to marry girls who shared thoughts of sex as necessary, perhaps, but not nice.

The beauty of males had always been a source of pleasure to him right up there with music and art. He was starved for it here in Sunset Gardens. On the soap operas which he had never watched till he came here but which were turned on in the lounge daily, doctors were unfailingly handsome. That wasn't the reality of the nursing home. The only staff doctor who was young was also short, fat, bald, and without any compensating charm. One hoped for visitors who might be easy on the eyes, an occasional son or grandson. But by the time their parents were in Sunset Gardens the sons were elderly themselves.

At least there was this garden and the occasional passer-by. What beauties one saw one saw only briefly, but it was better than nothing. There were, these days, construction workers passing from the building being erected in the next block and a coffee shop they favored south of Sunset Gardens. That construction project would end some day and then there would be no more of the tanned and muscled men in jeans and undershirts, in some cases so much less coarse that Otis had always imagined such men would be. There would always, he hoped, be the students, for there seemed to be a college of some sort nearby. Not that youth automatically equalled beauty. Otis had never believed that and since he'd been well enough to come out to the garden here, he had certainly learned that the student body contained at least as many uglies as beauties. On a scale of 1 to 10, many would get from Otis no more than 2 $^3/_8$. But there was that one—oh, he made up for all those that parents seemed to have put together from spare parts. It was the prospect of seeing him that kept Otis in the garden on days of good health long after he was chilled or a bit dizzy from too much sun.

That young man always seemed to have a spring in his step and his face was invariably suffused with a look that bespoke enjoyment of life. Physically he looked just a bit like Otis' favorite among the many centerfolds he had torn out to add to that collection which must have so shocked his neighbors or whoever cleaned out his apartment after he was taken to the hospital. The young man was also, Otis felt sure, gay. If anyone had asked how he knew, Otis couldn't have said, but who would be asking? To whom, in this place, could he ever say a word about such matters? He hadn't even any visitors with whom he could dish. Gay friends all seemed to be dead, housebound, or moved to warmer climates such as Otis had always felt he couldn't stand. The only people who came to see him here were the two widows with whom he had played bridge in the days when he could still remember what cards had been played. One could hardly talk about beautiful young men with women so misguided that each had nurtured hopes of making Otis their second husband. After all, one was still given to saying, on her increasingly infrequent visits, "I'd never have let a husband of mine end up here!" To escape Sunset Gardens by marrying Mrs. Katzenbach would be too extreme a measure. Otis suspected she was voraciously sexual. Well, look who's talking. If there are dirty old men, why not lusty old ladies, but not in his bed, thank you.

It didn't really matter to Otis whether or not the young student was gay. After all, he was never going to know him. He was just a vision that soothed Otis' old eyes in his quick passing. For the young man never dallied, walking along purposefully as though toward pleasure, whether he was going to or from the college with his armload of books. Otis had to undress him mentally much faster than he would have liked. It was more fun if you could stare at a man and slowly fantasize his removing one piece of clothing after another. In these circumstances, Otis had to speed things up if he wanted to get down to a vision of bobbing genitals or retreating nude buns.

There had not even been that pleasure so far today. Perhaps he had no classes, perhaps he was ill? He looked healthy, but who knew these days? It was going to spoil Otis' day if he didn't get even the quick glimpse of— what was his name now? Otis had been so happy to hear a friend call after him the other day. It had delayed him as he waited for the friend but it had also enabled Otis to put a name to him at last. And now he'd forgotten it. Well, if he didn't try too hard to think of it, it would pop into his mind in time.

Meantime, there were other passersby, though Otis took less interest in them since he'd first laid eyes on Ned. Ned—yes, that was it. He knew it would come to him when he least expected it. Ned. Ned. Ned. Ned. If he said it over and over to himself, surely he wouldn't forget it again. Such a suitable name for the young man for he looked like the hero of one of the boys' books Otis had read as a child, so many of whom where named Ned. Yes, he looked exactly as a Ned should look—scrubbed, cheerful and bright. Ned. Ned. Ned. Otis didn't intend to forget again.

132

"The name of your son?" said a voice beside Otis.

Startled, he turned to find a wizened little man he'd never seen before whose wheelchair had been rolled up close to Otis' bench.

"Son? I don't have a son," Otis said, a bit testily.

"You were saying 'Ned,' so I thought perhaps . . ."

"I was saying 'Ned?'" Otis asked. He hadn't realized he'd said anything aloud. He must watch that. Mustn't start voicing what was in his head, especially in view of the way his thoughts ran.

Suppose he suddenly said aloud, "What a gorgeous ass on that hard hat!" or "I'd love to see him when something besides his hat was hard." My God, what a commotion there'd be in the nursing home. They'd certainly heard worse from the foul-mouthed women, but he'd like to bet that those who took the profanity and scatology in stride would go into a disapproving flurry if sexual thoughts like that slipped out of Otis' mouth. Anger and bitterness the staff was used to, but frank admiration of a young man's body and looks by an old male resident might well get him forbidden to set foot in the garden. The highlight of his tedious days would be snatched away from him.

"My name's Wally," the little man in the wheelchair said, holding out a tremorous and liver-spotted hand.

"I don't give a damn what his name is," thought Otis, and hoped he hadn't said it aloud, "and I'm not going to try to remember it. I'm going to concentrate on Ted. No, not Ted. Damn, he's rattled it out of me already. It's not Ted. I know that much."

Clearly the man expected him to introduce himself, so grudgingly he grumped "Otis" but kept his eyes fixed on the sidewalk in case the youth whose name wasn't Ted but something like that came by.

"Actually, my name is Horace—Horace Walpole Austin," the little man said chattily, "Can you imagine being named Horace in this day and age? My father was an English lit professor who admired Walpole. But I skip the Horace and call myself Wally from the Walpole."

My god, Otis thought, I've always wanted more men here, but not an old chatterbox like this. If he distracts me so that I miss what's-his-name, I'll shorten his days."

"You been in Sunset Gardens long?" the man persisted. Tadpole, did he say his name was?

"I'm not sure," Otis said. "The days slip by so."

Just at that moment one of the ladies screamed and quickly vacated a chair near the flowers, in flight from a bee going about its work among the blossoms. She took refuge on a bench and Otis saw his chance to get away from this ill-timed conversation.

"Excuse me. I'm going to get that chair she just left and move it over by the fence. This bench is getting too sunny."

Moving stiffly because of his arthritis and leaning on his cane, Otis took the folding aluminum chair and set it up where, if Ned, yes, that's it, Ned, should come by, he could not fail to see him. If he thought that would discourage the newcomer, he quickly learned better. In no time the wheelchair was right beside him.

"I can't take the sun either. Had lots of skin cancers removed. I used to love the beach. Herman and I practically lived there in summer."

Otis pricked up his ears. Herman? He used to go to the beach all the time with Herman? That would bear looking into, but not right now, when Ned might be passing by. Some day he might probe to find out if he had, at last, a fellow spirit in Sunset Gardens, but this was not the time.

Oh, definitely not, because there, coming along the street with even more than his usual jauntiness was—uh—Ned. There, the name had come to him in spite of the distraction provided by Tadpole.

Otis' pulse began to quicken. Ned in any garb was beautiful to behold but, as a bonus, in today's warm and sunny weather he was wearing shorts. Not the baggy sort that the fashion world was trying to bring back, but nice short tight ones that exposed a lot of thigh. Always susceptible to nice legs, Otis could see at once that Ned's were choice.

As he came abreast of where the two old men sat, the young student turned and looked their way, which Otis had never known him to do before. On sudden impulse, Otis winked. The young man's face broke into an even broader smile than he customarily wore and, wonder of wonders, he winked back. Otis wondered if what he felt might be a heart attack.

As Ned moved briskly on toward the college, Otis heard Tadpole chuckling beside him.

"See that?" the little man asked. "He winked at me."

Otis, who had begun to feel as light as though inflated with helium, thumped to earth. He was overcome with sudden rage.

"Winked at *you?* Why would he wink at *you?*"

"Because I winked at him," the withered man said, with something like a leer.

Otis suppressed an impulse to beat Tadpole with his cane. Questions about Herman were no longer necessary, but the nerve of the old fart, daring to presume, and on top of that, daring to claim that whosis had been winking at him.

"You know something?" the unregenerate man in the wheelchair said, "I'm a student of physiognomy and body language. Just as I could tell the minute I saw you that you were another D.O.M. like me, I can tell you that boy's in love and I can also tell he's getting well laid. Never have had any trouble telling when a person's whole being is satisfied, like after first-rate sex."

"Good God," thought Otis, and was momentarily speechless.

"Not only that, but he's also gay. He's probably on his way to meet him now, judging from the spring in his step. A fellow student, perhaps, or maybe even a professor. That's why he was so kind to two old farts like us. I was always kind when I was first in love."

Tadpole's shrewd, Otis thought, but the nerve of him calling me an old fart. Then he remembered that in his mind he had used exactly the same term for the newcomer. But he was certainly presumptuous, claiming that the wink had been aimed at him. That lad had definitely not been looking in Tadpole's direction at all, but straight at Otis. Ah, well, if the illusion comforted him in these first difficult days of adjustment to the nursing home, let him go on thinking such nonsense. Otis would be kind, for he too was now very much in love, rhapsodic over the smile and return wink from What's-His-Name.

Learning Secrets

DOUGLAS FEDERHART

I knew the rumor as well as anybody, and the rumor around South Sioux City, Nebraska, was that Barry and Herb were queer. The word *gay* had not yet entered into the lexicon of the "homosexual" Midwesterner; so the terms were (in ascending order of their put-down power): *sissy, fairy, queer, faggot,* and most dreaded of all, *cocksucker.* Sissy implied a question about your masculinity, but if you devoted yourself to a regimen of trying out for all sports, and learning to smoke and drink along with the "regular" guys, redemption might just be within reach. Instinctively, I knew *I* was past *sissy;* it was just not yet a conscious admission. I hated all sports, with the exception of gymnastics. I couldn't even remember to carry my books like a guy, let alone think about smoking or drinking. Maybe I was just at *fairy,* but then, once you were beyond the first stage, what hope was there?

So, I'd heard the rumor about Barry and Herb, but should I believe it? They were older men, I'd guess mid-to-late thirties, and partners in the town's only florist shop. It was a business they were good at, and it thrived. Almost all the guys from school bought their girlfriends' corsages there, whenever some event called for flowers. And always, the rumor would start up again, flying around school on a current of whispers and snickers:

"Hey, I stopped in to order a corsage for Melanie, and boy, did those guys give me the eye! I bet they want more than my order." And somebody would usually throw in, "Yeah, and those two *live* together, too. I'm not even gonna tell you what my dad says about that."

And all over again, I'd feel panicked by that kind of talk, and at the same time caught up in an internal debate about how I could find out the truth. I tried to picture myself walking up to one of the muscle-headed jocks who fanned the flames of the rumor, and asking right out, "What's all this I hear about Barry and Herb?" Cocky, red-haired Russ Harrington was the first one I ever heard say he'd actually been to their house. And then brag about it like he should get a Boy Scout Merit Badge for living to tell. But then, Russ could get away with stuff like that, because rumor also had it that he'd gone all the way with Laurie Donaldson, so his manhood wasn't in danger. (I thought his intelligence was, though, when Laurie ended up pregnant in senior year and had to drop out.) Besides, if I slid up to Russ in the lunch line some noon and asked, "Is it true? Have you *really* been to visit Barry and Herb?" then he'd want to know what *I* wanted to know for, and there I'd be, stuck like one of our frogs in biology, because everyone knew I certainly hadn't gone all the way with Laurie Donaldson, or anyone else.

Finally, Jerry Mueller said he'd been to their house, too. Him I could approach, because even though he was sort of a jock, he was also in choir with me and sat next to me with the baritones, and talked to me. So I asked the big question.

First he gave me this funny look, and said, "Boy, you sure don't know much, do you?" That was a given, though, and when he smiled I was relieved. I could tell he liked me even if I was stupid. He went on to explain: "Some of us found out that those guys don't care if we come over and get a beer." Now, that was boring, I thought. But then Jerry added, "And, if we want it, a blow job." Jerry winked and asked, "Why, you wanna go some time?"

Suddenly it wasn't boring and I turned as red as Laurie Donaldson's fingernails. Choking, I stammered, "Uh, no—no, Jerry, I don't . . . But thanks, anyway!"

Of course I was lying. I *was* interested, and not in the beer, either. But it was too dangerous to let anybody else know that, even Jerry, in spite of the fact that I knew a thing or two that probably would have shocked even Russ Harrington. I'd learned a secret.

On Saturdays, my habit was to go overtown to the Sioux City Public Library, to get books and check out recordings of classical music. The building looked like a reformatory—ugly brown brick and blank steel-framed windows; but it did house a decent collection of recorded music. The records, kept in a large cool room down on the basement level, were my favorite browsing material. I was a rich kid there, all that great music at my fingertips, mine to take home for no more than it took to hand the librarian my card.

It's hard to pin down, but there came one Saturday when, while I was there, I needed to use the restroom. Badly. I was shy about public bathrooms and usually held it till I got back home, but this time I couldn't wait. The chili-dogs I had for lunch at the Coney Island may have been the problem, and it was one time my sensitivity wasn't going to overrule my body.

The building's architects must have been related to my parents and ashamed of bodily functions, because they had stuck the men's room way back out of the way. It was hidden in one of the stairwells, underneath the steps. Later on, I learned how in certain circles this room was notorious precisely because of its location: the creaky wooden stairs provided an early warning system, so all approaching footsteps got advance broadcast. There would come Saturdays when I'd be very grateful for that feature.

But on that particular Saturday, I prayed that the room would be deserted. Because no matter how serious my body's urges were, if anyone else were in there, I'd be unable to function. I made my way down the dim hall to the stairwell, and then down the additional three steps that led to the men's room door. Taking a deep breath, I pushed it open and went in. The single sink, the full-length urinal, the stall partitioning off the stool—and no people, thank God! From the floor and halfway up, the walls were tiled in lifeless beige ceramic. Above that, plaster, heavily stippled and painted dead-moss green. Maybe it *was* moss—down there, who could tell what might be growing? I stepped into the stall and began my business.

As my eyes adjusted to the inadequate lighting (again, more shame from the architects: "Okay, so we have to have this room, but by God, we don't want anybody seeing what you're doing!"), my nose was greeted with the dubious perfume of the deodorant cake in the urinal. I wished I would have brought one of the books in with me, but instead, I started glancing at the walls. And then I leaned closer: the partition on my right was decorated with a myriad of scribblings. At first I thought they were some sort of hieroglyphics (gosh, how long *had* this place been there?). Then, leaning closer still, and squinting, I saw not hieroglyphics at all, but a dozen or so terse messages, some printed, some in script, some short, others long—and all shockingly explicit. "Make a date. You name it, I'll do it," said one. Another said, "Come on young studs. I've got a hot 8" waiting for you." And another, practically an essay, described in detail an encounter the author had either had or wanted to have followed by a phone number.

I jerked back like someone had punched me in the face, my breathing shallow and the smell from the urinal choking me. I grabbed at the toilet paper, now in a panic to get out of there, and half the roll uncoiled onto the damp floor. Somehow I managed to pull myself together, getting my Farah slacks back in place just as I dashed out the door. I ran back through the record room, to grab my books. Back upstairs I threw them at the bewildered librarian as I rushed past her desk and out the front door. Not until I was safely on the bus and halfway across the Missouri River bridge did I feel like I could breathe again.

That night I could not get to sleep for a long time. Whenever I closed my eyes, the image of that men's room wall would flash across my inner eyelids and waver lewdly. I tried forcing myself to count sheep, only to have them turn into men—men with *body parts*—men whispering to me those horrible, obscene, *intriguing* little messages. And as much as I wanted to deny it, it was clear that my secret had slipped: *someone out there had read my mind*.

It was Barry whom I met first. When my parents and I moved from Sioux City across the state line into Nebraska, I had to give up a high school of two thousand students for one of five hundred. It meant fewer good teachers, and fewer extracurricular activities of any quality. All this so Dad could in good conscience accept the job promotion his company had offered him. It never occurred to *me* to say no. My consolation prize was that I would be allowed to try out for the first production of The Dakota County Civic Players. Their big plan was to introduce culture to South Sioux in manageable doses: start out with a one-act play and a few variety performers, and build up gradually, increasing the fare to a full-fledged Broadway musical.

That first play, the one-act, was to be *The Valiant,* something about a man in prison and a question of proper justice and a sister who wasn't his sister, or was she? Serious stuff for a first time out. The night of tryouts, Mom let me drive alone in her green Buick down to the Legion Hall. I drove with extra caution, given that I was both scared and excited about the chance to be in another play, and keyed up like that, a person could be more susceptible to an accident than usual. At my old high school, I'd been in several things but this—*this* was a *community* theater.

Even with the cautious driving, I was a half-hour early. The Legion Hall was open, but dark and empty when I walked in. Just as I was turning around, thinking maybe I'd leave and come back in twenty minutes, there was a click and suddenly the lights came on. I let out a cry and was blinded for a moment. I heard him before I saw him. "Oh, sorry—I didn't mean to startle you. I assumed I was the first one here." Then I could see him as my eyes adjusted: a neatly-groomed man of average height, handsome, a little foreign-looking, I thought, with dark hair, olive skin, and a mustache and carefully-trimmed beard. All this I took in in about three seconds, despite my surprise.

He crossed the lobby and came over to me, extending his hand. "Hi— I'm Barry Hanna." He gave my hand a gentle squeeze. "You must be here for the tryouts, too."

I'd started to sweat, and my voice felt quavery. "Yes—yes, I am. Uh, I'm Doug Hart. My family just moved overtown from Sioux City, but I decided I wanted to try out for the play anyway. I've been in some other things, but just school stuff, so this'll be my first—"

I cut myself off. The gentleman had not asked for my credentials or my life history. But when I stopped talking, one of his thick, black eyebrows rose just the slightest bit, and he said, "I get nervous at tryouts, too. Come on, let's go in by the stage until some of the others get here." As we walked into the small auditorium and crossed over towards the stage, Mr. Hanna kept talking. "Gretchen—Mrs. Youngdahl—should be here in a few minutes."

Her name rang a bell. "She's a teacher over at school, isn't she? I've seen her in the halls a couple of times, but I don't have any classes with her."

"That's the lady," Mr. Hanna answered. "She'll be directing this."

At the edge of the stage, we boosted ourselves up and sat. He proceeded to engage me in a relaxed conversation. It happened so easily, that only later did I stop to wonder at his treating me so respectfully. For that brief time, I felt like his equal, an accomplished fellow thespian and not a nervous, gangly nerd. I suspect the truth was that Barry could see through the trappings of nerdism, past my unfortunate glasses to the lanky, six-foot, blond, blue-eyed, young man beneath. No doubt I looked a lot better than I felt.

The tryouts took place and the following day Mrs. Youngdahl told me at school that I would have a part if I wanted it, that of the jailkeeper. It meant at most a half-dozen "Yessir/Nossir" lines, but nonetheless I was elated and agreed to take the part. Mr. Hanna had landed the male lead, and it meant we would work together through the two months of rehearsals. He worked hard at getting me to feel less nervous, trying to put me at ease in the very first evenings: "Doug, please call me Barry. After all, I'm going to be your prisoner, and you've got to act that role."

It was during that time I first heard him mention his friend, Herb Grey. Barry would say things like, "Herb and I cracked up at breakfast this morning over some of these lines." Or he'd say, "I feel very lucky that Herb is helping me rehearse my lines. I don't know how I'd do it otherwise." That idea pleased me, the two of them buttering their toast together, having morning coffee, and working on the lines. It filled me, even then, with a sense of longing to some day have a friend as nice as Herb.

The success of *The Valiant,* though modest, did lead to more plays, and finally, during my senior year, a musical. Barry and Herb were also involved with the musical, but an odd thing happened: whenever I saw them together, I got short of breath, my face would flush, and I'd dodge off in another direction, as if I'd just remembered some important chore. After the first few times I did this, Barry quit trying to be friendly. With a sense of sadness, I let it go like that. Besides, my days in South Sioux were numbered—one final summer there, and then I'd be bound for Lincoln, and the University, where I intended to study architecture.

Thoughts of Barry and Herb weren't easily banished, however, because something big and scary was going on in my head and heart. Full of confusion and fear, I attempted talking to Mom and Dad about it, but only once, really: it scared them more than it did me. What they wanted was for me to talk to a "professional" (meaning *psychiatrist),* and in those days that meant going first through a G.P.—in our case, Dr. Rodderman, our gruff, fat family physician. He delivered a gruff lecture about worrying too much, saying that all I needed was to go out for sports (where had I heard that before?) and spend more time thinking about girls. In the end, though, he did refer me to Dr. Bruller, his colleague and one of the town's few psychiatrists. Maybe for the first time I'd find out something concrete.

"Now, young man—Douglas, is it?—why don't you start out by telling me why you're here." I'd been expecting a round, fatherly little man with a faintly German accent, and already this skinny guy with thick glasses and eyes behind them which wouldn't quite ever land squarely on me, made me suspicious. Also, I'd assumed he'd know from Dr. Rodderman why I was there. I hesitated as I tried to frame an answer then started with the obvious. "Well, Dr. Rodderman referred me to you because—"

"Yes, yes, I know he referred you to me!" He made a motion as if to brush crumbs off his note pad. I couldn't see anything there. "No one gets *in* here without a referral. Just tell me *why* he did that, as simply as you can."

He was not going to make this easy, and for a moment I was scared. I glanced over at him again and he still would not quite look at me. I suddenly decided that the man was not much more than a nearsighted weasel so what did I really care what he thought? "I think I'm a homosexual."

In his moment of shock, he forgot himself and *did* look at me. "Oh, come now! How could anyone so young—what are you, seventeen, didn't Rodderman say?—how could you know a thing like that?"

"That's what my parents wanted to know, too."

"I should think so! Now let me say a few things about —"

"Dr. Bruller, I *am* a homosexual."

". . . what the medical profession—studies show . . ." His voice trailed off as his ears caught up with my second statement. Again, he slipped and looked at me, a twitch now affecting his left cheek. "You are? You really *are*?"

"Yes, I am. That's the part I haven't told my parents yet, but I know. I was just hoping you'd be able to tell me a little more about this. Or recommend something to read . . .?"

His eyes darted to the clock on the wall and then to the door and then ever so briefly back to me. "Uh, no—no, I can't. Tell you anything about it, I mean. Well, there are *theories,* but so little has been written. This condition is so . . . so . . . unexplored among medical professionals." He stopped and cleared his throat, pulled a handkerchief from his suit pocket and wiped his mouth. "This is so *unusual,* someone so young, I mean. This does not happen every day."

So was it my fault I was his first freak? I looked down at the rug, then back at him. "Never mind, Doctor. It's okay . . . if you don't care, I think I'll go now. My dad's coming to pick me up—I'll bet he's already down there." I got up and walked to the door.

"Uh, Douglas . . ."

I turned and looked back at him. His face was flushed.

"Well, I just want to say, good luck!"

On the elevator, I had a quick vision of the cables breaking and the car plunging downward. But the Davidson Building had only six floors—not enough, probably, to do me much damage. Outside, I glanced around but couldn't see Dad and the car anywhere. I leaned against the side of the building. Were people staring at me? Could the lady walking by tell by looking at me? What had gone wrong that I had to end up having these stupid feelings for other guys? I'd tried so hard, even having fun playing piano duets with Karen Howard, taking her to a few dances—kissing her and . . . nothing. A blank, like someone had taken an eraser to my feelings. *Damn Dr. Bruller and his stupid 'Good luck!' And damn Dr. Rodderman and the whole bunch of idiots!*

A car horn was honking, and I looked up. Dad was there, double-parked and leaning over as if staring at me would get my attention. If I moved fast, I could dash off down the alley. Or better still, run out into the traffic on Sixth Street. Dad honked again, motioning for me to get in. Cars were stuck behind him now. I pushed away from the side of the building and Dad swung open the passenger door.

"Doug. Didn't you see me? I kept honking." He put the car in gear and maneuvered into the center lane.

"Sorry, Dad. Hi." I tried not to sound depressed. Having to explain everything would make it worse.

He seemed to miss my mood. "Boy, can you imagine this traffic? Hard to believe we're getting a real rush hour in ol' Sioux City. Big time, huh?"

I made a little noise of agreement and flipped on the radio. As we headed towards South Sioux, Paul Harvey was on 'Page Two' and telling me in a confidential tone about some product that would change my whole life. I doubted it and clicked the radio off in the middle of a sentence. As we were crossing the bridge, the tires hummed on the steel grating. The brown Missouri swirled by far below us, and on the far bank, I could see a figure sitting there with a fishing rod, his small boat nearby, bumping gently against the pilings.

"How did things go, Doug?"

I started. "What, Dad?"

"I wondered, how did it go? With the doctor?" Dad kept his eyes directed straight ahead, concentrating on the sides of the bridge. He looked normal, but I could sense the tension with which he gripped the steering wheel.

"Oh, it was okay, I guess."

"What did he have to say? Did it help?"

"Nothing much. What he said was not much. We just sort of talked for a few minutes."

"Nothing much! A few minutes—what do you mean!—" I'd caught him off guard. But then just as quickly, he squelched his outburst. But not me. Suddenly, I was mad myself.

"Yes, Dad, nothing much is what he said. And you know what? I don't really want to talk about it right now!" We were in South Sioux by then, waiting to make a turn off Dakota Avenue to head over to one of the side streets. As my breathing returned to normal, all I could think of was how desperately I wanted out of this. Then it occurred to me the perfect thing to say. "Look Dad, I'm sorry. And don't worry, it was a good idea for me to see the doctor. Everything's going to be all right."

A silence settled between us, one that would continue for years, at least about this topic. I don't know what he said to Mom; I went right to my room as soon as we got in the house and disappeared again right after supper. But I picture it now, him standing there in the kitchen doorway, as if the issue were between him and Mom. And he says, "Don't worry, honey. The doctor was a good idea—everything's going to be all right."

Half the summer passed, and the hot weather parched lawns and people all over town. I kept trying to grasp the concept of being a high school graduate, but the only feeling that came with it was that somehow I had tricked them all—the teachers, the principal, the other kids. And every time I was over on Dakota Avenue, no matter what other business I had to do, the one store I really noticed and diligently avoided was the florist shop. With school done and no more need for corsages, my business there was done, too.

So it was probably late July when I called. After three or four aborted attempts, I finally let the phone ring until someone answered.

"Good evening. Avenue Florists . . ."

Shoot, I'd called them at work! What was I thinking of?

"Hello! Is someone there?" The voice sounded cranky.

I either had to say something or hang up. "Uh, is this Mr. Hanna?"

"No, it's not. Who's calling?"

"Mr. Grey?"

"Look, who *is* this anyway?" Now, *very* cranky. *God, had I ever made a mistake.*

In a voice barely audible, I said, "This is Doug . . . uh, Doug Hart."

"Doug Hart . . . oh, Doug! From the theater! What a surprise to hear from you! What on earth do you want?"

Oh, thank God he remembered me! "Is this Herb . . . uh, Mr. Grey?" It was. "I feel stupid to have called you at work, Mr. Grey. But I was wondering if . . . if I could talk to you for a while. In person, I mean. Not on the phone . . . please?"

"You sound disturbed, Doug." His voice softened. "Is something the matter?"

"I—I can't say over the phone, Mr. Grey. But I *have* to talk to you. Would that be okay?"

"Look, Doug, I can tell you're really upset, but the fact is, I'm exhausted. You only just caught me by chance because I came down to finish up some things that have to be done for tomorrow. I'm afraid all that's on my mind right now is getting home to a hot shower."

My eyes welled with tears, and in spite of my determination not to let them loose, it was my voice which betrayed me. "I understand, Mr. Grey." I felt panicky, though, like I was a drowning swimmer and a life preserver almost within reach was being withdrawn. "It's just that—just that, *I'm going crazy.*" My whisper was desperate, and I fell silent.

"Doug, are you still there?"

"Yes."

"Okay, listen. I'll be home in less than an hour. Give me that much time, and you can stop by, just for a bit." He paused, then said with a sudden wariness, "Say, this *is* Doug Hart, isn't it? Because if this is some sort of joke—"

"Yes, it's me, Mr. Grey—I mean it's really Doug!"

He sighed. "Okay, I believe you. It's just that I can't trust very many people lately. I'm sorry if I sounded mean."

I wanted to say, *Oh Mr. Grey! The last thing you could ever sound is mean!* But I just said, "It's okay. And, thanks a lot! I'll be there in an hour."

I started to hang up, but he stopped me. "Wait! Do you know where to come?"

"It's the house in back of the shop, isn't it?" I asked.

"No, not any more. We moved. Just outside of town, out past the grain elevators on Highway 20. It's the blue two-story duplex, north side of the road. Come to the door for the lower half."

"Sure. I'll be there, Mr. Grey . . . And, *thanks!*"

My hand had gotten so sweaty, the receiver almost shot out of it. *My God, I'd done it! I'd finally gotten up the courage and was really going over there!* But then I stopped to wonder, maybe I was crazier than ever? No, maybe I was scared, but definitely not crazy! Because at last I'd made contact, and maybe, after all, I wasn't such a wimp.

The forty-five minutes before I could leave seemed to last forever, but finally I came out from my bedroom. I'd have to play things just right to get out of the house without a lot of questions, but I was, after all, an actor.

I stopped at the kitchen doorway and said as calmly as possible, "Mom, I don't have much of anything else to do—I think I'll go out and ride my bike for awhile."

A moment of suspense while she tore off a piece of Saran Wrap to cover the meatloaf. But she barely glanced at me at all, just said, "Okey-doke, honey. But be sure to be back before dark. You haven't got a light on that thing, you know."

Simple as that, I was free. Except that I hadn't taken into account my growing nervousness. Once out of the house and a ways along on my bike, I was trembling so badly I could hardly steer. When I got to the edge of town and onto the highway, the sidewalk ran out, and I was forced to do battle with the gravel shoulder. Every so often, weeds got caught in my chain, threatening to throw me off balance and send me veering onto the blacktop, where the traffic sped by.

At last, just up ahead, I could see the house, and after another minute of anxious peddling, I turned onto the dirt driveway. It was not so much a driveway as a spot in the yard where the grass was worn away—evidently the tenants' only parking area. The door I needed to go to was obvious: I knew from having seen them around town that Barry and Herb drove a red Thunderbird, and there it was. I stashed my bike between the house and the car, so it would be out of sight, and stepped up onto the cement stoop. Summoning the last of my courage, I rapped as loudly as I could on the screen door. To me, it sounded like thunder. I was sure the knock could be heard all over town, and everyone would soon show up to see me, standing there, at *that* door.

The inside door opened, and though the screen blurred his outline, I realized it was Herb.

"Well, so it really was you, and you showed up. Come on in, Doug." He unlatched the screen and held it open for me. I stepped in, still trembling, but now obliged to follow through.

"Hi, Mr. Grey. Yeah, it's me alright."

He shut the inside door and seemed to lock it again. "Please, after all this intrigue, call me Herb. 'Mr. Grey' makes me sound ancient!"

"Gee, I'm sorry," I stammered. "I didn't mean that—I mean, I'm sure you're not as old as I thought—" My face lit up with embarrassment. *Damn, could I please just this once not be a dork?*

Herb laughed. "Relax, Doug. I know what you mean. Now, come all the way in and sit down." He pointed to the sofa. "Do you want something to drink?"

My thoughts fell into a jumble—this was a question—I nearly blurted out, *Yeah, how about a bottle of beer and a blow*—I slammed shut on the thought, unnerved, found myself able to say, "Umm, how 'bout some pop? Coke, if you have it."

"Is Pepsi okay? That's what I've got."

"That's fine."

He walked towards a doorway that apparently led to the kitchen. Only when he was across the room from me did I notice that all he had on was a terrycloth shower robe. *God, did I have my eyes closed when I first walked in, or what?* The room seemed suddenly hot and stuffy.

From the kitchen, I heard the clatter of the ice, the fizz of a bottle being opened, and in a few seconds Herb was back in front of me handing me a metal glass full of pop. Now that I was seated, with him standing, my eyes were at the level of his midsection; my ears started to burn as I realized I was staring at his muscular stomach and a deep-set navel. I nearly dropped the glass he was giving me, but he just smiled and nonchalantly drew his robe closed. Then, instead of joining me on the sofa, he crossed the room to a chair and sat down what seemed like a mile away. The light from a lamp on the table beside him cast a golden glow, turning his skin the same color

146

as his sandy hair. Then another surge of panic: *the lamp on! God, could it already be dark outside?* I was supposed to be home . . . but then I realized that Herb's drapes were tightly closed, in fact the whole house seemed shut up as if he were expecting a hurricane.

"So there must be something on your mind, Doug."

I jumped when he broke the silence, in the process spilling some of my drink on the sofa's arm. "Shoot! I'm sorry, Mr. Grey! I'm sure a klutz . . . sorry!"

"Doug, will you stop saying you're sorry? It's no big deal. It's landlord furniture, and frankly, it would be a favor if you set fire to it. And anyway, I'm not sorry you called. I was tired, but after my shower, I feel human again." He took a sip of his drink. "I *am* sorry, though, for giving you the third degree earlier. It's just that I've been pretty cautious lately. The reason I agreed at all for you to come over was that you were honest with me and identified yourself. Not everyone's doing that." He set his glass down on a coaster. "So. Be honest with me again, Doug. Why *did* you insist on coming over?"

There I was, face to face with it. And after all the pride I'd felt an hour or so ago over my courage, it now seemed gone. My thoughts went into another tumble, until the only thing I could think of to say was, "It's about things I've heard at school . . . about you . . . about you, and Barry . . ." I stopped.

"Oh?" Herb retrieved his glass. "Tell me what sort of things."

I cleared my throat. "Well, that you're—that you and Barry are—"

"That we're homosexuals? Is that what you're trying to say?"

I choked. "Yes! Gosh, how did you know?"

Herb chuckled. "Well, I was probably the *first* to know. Besides, it's not the first time the rumor's gotten back to me."

"It—it's not?"

"No. And anyway, what difference does it make? It's not a rumor."

If he kept this up, I was going to be doing a lot of choking. "Then you mean it's not a rumor—it's true?"

"I may not be long on logic, kid, but that's the obvious choice, isn't it?" Herb smiled at me. "It's the truth, Doug. Barry and I have been lovers for, oh, eleven years it will be."

I was stunned. I looked across at Herb, expecting to read in his face some sort of embarrassment or shame as he said those words. But there was nothing like that at all. He was as calm as ever, drinking his pop and looking right back at me. He went on with a question. "Is that what you want to talk about, Doug? About being homosexual?"

I could only look down at the floor. "Yes," I said softly. "If it's okay to discuss it."

Gently he said, "Look at me, Doug." I raised my eyes to meet his. "Listen, it *is* okay to talk about it, because I know, believe me, what it's taken for you to get here. And I want you to know that right now, right here in this house with me, you're safe. No one's going to get you, or hurt you."

Before I could stop them, tears were streaming down my face. Though I was mad at myself for losing it, at the same time, it felt good. And it felt okay for Herb to be seeing it, too. He let me cry for a while, then asked me another question.

"Has it been a long time, hiding these feelings?"

I managed to pull myself together enough to answer. "For as long as I can remember, actually. I mean, not with words to go with it. At least, not with words that weren't horrible, like the rumors at school and those stupid jocks teasing and looking at me funny. And I've been so scared, scared that if I even ever slipped and someone caught me looking at them, well . . . they'd kill me."

Herb sat quietly for a minute, then sighed. "The fear will lessen, Doug, over time. And, you'll find places that are safer to be yourself than a small-town high school. You sound really pretty sure of your feelings, after all?"

"Yeah, I guess I am. And, I've had some experiences."

"Ah, you have. I wasn't going to ask. But it's okay to talk about them, too, if you need to."

I was close to crying again, but this time in relief over having someone to whom I could finally say this stuff. "It's not exactly easy," I began. "It seems pretty crummy."

"Some of the early stuff is, Doug. We don't have a lot of choice about how we get our educations. So, what's been happening?"

I told him. The sight of him so calm, and the sense of his real understanding, encouraged me, and out came the stories of the Saturday visits to the Library. I told about the messages on the walls, and about the first man who found me there, how he seemed so old, and how when I couldn't force myself to do everything he wanted, he made me feel even more of a pervert—so dirty, so sick. And how terrified I was, yet still I found myself going back, time after time, swearing after each visit that I'd never do it again.

When I stopped and looked back over at Herb, I was astonished to see tears, this time on his face. Immediately, I felt ashamed. "Herb, what's wrong? Oh God, I shouldn't have told you all this stuff!"

But he cut in right away. "No—stop, Doug—that's not what it is." His voice tightened up. "But you don't know, do you? You don't know anything about what's happened?"

A shiver went down my spine. "No, I guess I must not . . ."

"Barry's not here, Doug, because he's in jail. He was arrested at the Library three weeks ago." Herb let out a long breath. "You didn't see the stuff about it in the papers?"

"N—no—I really don't read them." *Jez, was I ever dumb! Why hadn't I thought anything about Barry an hour ago?* I was so wrapped up in my own stuff . . . "But why'd they arrest him?" I asked, betraying my naivete.

Herb's voice was full of sarcasm. "He was picked up on what they call a *morals* charge—indecent exposure, or solicitation. I suppose that's what he's actually booked with. What they're saying is that he approached a guy in the bathroom there—the wrong guy in this case, since he turned out to be a police officer. At least, that's their version of the story. There were no witnesses."

He stopped. My urge was to rush over and somehow try to comfort him, but I couldn't move. Because several other things were happening for me at the same time: amidst the anger and sadness, a frightening possibility was occurring—*it could have been me. I could just as likely have been there, too.*

I felt like I was falling off a cliff or into some bottomless chasm with nothing there to stop me. *So this was how it would always be? Men's rooms and decoy cops and crummy sex with strangers?* Because I knew I couldn't stand that, that I couldn't survive it.

Across the room, Herb got up. "Would you like any more pop?" he asked, making an effort to recover some of his lighter tone.

"No—I've had enough," I answered. I "came to" a bit, but it seemed like I was waking from a nightmare, pieces of it still sticking to me. "Herb, what's gonna happen? To you, I mean . . . to Barry?"

"I don't know for sure, Doug." Herb tried to smile again. "But we'll pull through. Barry was advised to plead guilty, rather than fight it, so he's getting off pretty light. Ninety days. Well, plus the fine. But we're managing. I did have to move, though—assholes throwing eggs at the house, and phone calls. I changed the phone number." He came over and took my glass. "We're going to leave South Sioux, too much hassle to stay. The town's too small for us, and we've talked for a long time about moving, anyway. The only reason we stuck it out as long as we did was because of Barry's mom. She may not care now anyway."

More panic rose in me: *You can't leave, not yet! Who'll I talk to, who'll help me decide what to do?* Herb seemed to read my mind. "You won't miss us," he said. "You'll probably be going off to college, right? And you know, you might be surprised at what you'll discover there."

He took our glasses into the kitchen, then came back into the living room. It was the moment when I should go, but I just sat there, looking up at him. With the table lamp behind him, his face was in shadow and the rays of light spread out around him.

"So, do you think you should be going?" he asked gently.

"Yes," was all I could say.

"But you don't think you really want to leave just yet?"

"No," I answered.

"But you're done talking?"

This time I couldn't say even one word. I didn't need to. Herb came closer and sat down on the edge of the sofa, letting our legs touch. His hand came up slowly to my hair, which he pushed back out of my eyes. Then he touched my cheek, softly. "Go in there," he whispered, and pointed to a door which could only lead to the bedroom. "I'll be back in a minute."

On shaky legs I stood, and walked to the doorway while Herb went off through the kitchen. I heard a toilet flush, and then, for several minutes, the sound of water running in a sink.

Finally he returned, and with me still standing in a trance in the doorway, he took me in his arms. The scent of his cologne, which I hadn't noticed before, filled my nose. When I could speak, I said, "You smell wonderful. What's that you have on?"

He laughed lightly. "Well, I thought if this is going to happen, I'd better shave for you. So then I put on some aftershave—it's called 'Aphrodisia,' by Faberge."

"Afro-what?"

" -disia," he repeated. "And if you don't know what that means, well, come in here and I'll reveal its secret."

And with a graceful motion, he ushered me the rest of the way into the bedroom, and shut the door behind us.

Flying Low

TOM McKAGUE

One must, I suppose, eventually pin down one's sense of purpose. But first, one must net it. And it is as elusive as a butterfly.

What I am doing here in this charmingly decayed farmhouse, living with M., forever correcting compositions about keg parties that lead inexorably to car wrecks and instant recognition scenes, or about the river symbolism in *Huck Finn,* arguing every other day over long-distance with my daughter about money and the need to provide for the future, shaving every morning, worrying about whether my hair is growing thin, about how to pay the phone bill (which is beginning to resemble the national debt of Djibouti), taking 1/4 Valium every afternoon to take the edge off—what my flight pattern is, has been, is not entirely clear to me (nor to those, no doubt, whose orbits I tangentially touch). Perhaps I need to have an adventure. An affair. Just to reaffirm the Romantic Potential. A few candles, chablis, a clandestine smile on another's face of uncertain but suggestive significance, the hint of wonder just down the road. . . . It is after all the issue of interpretation that is most terrifying.

Last week, for example, at a party that promised to be "mixed" on the invitation (whether racially, sexually, or linguistically was never clarified), I found that everything that was said to me defied coherent response. One chubbette of a young man with a sweet face and a tie-dyed bandana around his curly-locked forehead announced that he was "baptized Angel Scarafino," and that his life "has been a living hell ever since." It occurred to me that to ask why would have been pointless, especially since his bandana was soaked with the sweat of panic. Another long blond slip of a woman with champagne bubbles in her voice giggled that "actually (she) preferred pussy to prick, but that deep-down she was tri-sexual." My imagination immediately went to work: centaurs? dogs? ripe fruit? But I could not put it together. And when the host, a tall, suave, black-suited man with a silver pompadour and only one name, Delacroix, asked me if he could "borrow M. for a teeny bit, because (he) had heard that M. had a most intriguing scar along the bottom of his foot, and that (he) was never able to resist the cool-ridged feel of foot scars," then I grasped that the evening would not yield itself to rational scrutiny.

Not that sanity is an admirable end in itself, you understand. Our Presbyterian neighbors, half an acre away through a scrubby woods, are the picture of conventional sanity. But I don't envy them their clamp on the real world. They are seventy-something, pale with hierarchical priorities, and address each other as 'Dorfy' (presumably for Dorothy) and "Evvy' (Everett? Eveline!—no, they wouldn't camp). We have a rabbit in a hutch in our intervening woods. Dorfy and Evvy coo over the rabbit each day about noon. They call it "Bam-Bam." Once, Dorfy called me up, her voice filled with a faint accusation, to tell me that "Bam-Bam doesn't have any cookies." I think she meant that I had forgotten to fill the feeder with rabbit pellets that morning. (The animal eats his own pre-digested pellets anyway, so I didn't see why it mattered much, at least for one day.) Anyway, Dorfy and Evvy, of course, don't have much to do to fill up a day, so they've taken to checking in on Bam-Bam every noon to see if he (it) is suffering from parental neglect. As fond as they are of our rabbit, I don't think they like us much. They *did* send their minister over to our house once, an imposing woman with a Bible and huge breasts (actually, her shape resembled the continent of Africa). She told us that two men living together in sin, two men drinking martinis together on the back deck regularly at 5 P.M. in good weather (Dorfy at her lace-curtained kitchen window), didn't necessarily preclude damnation. I told her that we were already members of the Church for Fallen-Away Catholics, and asked if she would like to join us in a drink.

No, one ceases to expect sanity after a while, because one comes to realize that leading a sane life requires that one have lamb chops every Thursday night, that one avoid Fettucini Alfredo, sauerkraut with pork loin, anything with garlic, anything that might cause halitosis, weight-gain, diverticulitis, a choleric disposition. My daughter strives for the unconventional. She absolutely *aspires* to it. All her Salvation Army jeans have the prerequisite rip at the base of the seat, her braless breasts droop down to her waist every time she has the monthlies. She drops courses a week before finals, schools whenever the clean whiff of closure penetrates the air, boyfriends only after they beat her up. On the other hand, she has a wholesome streak. She reads Salinger in the morning, eats regular lunches (carrot sticks, cottage cheese, mega-doses of water-soluble vitamins) and dinners (two or three kinds of lettuce, cottage cheese, Marie's creamy bleu cheese dressing, Theragram-M with Iron). She is plagued with sinus problems. It's all the dairy. I have no doubt that if her visits lasted a second more than three days I would go out to our woods and strangle Bam-Bam.

M., at least, aspires to Balance. He wears pin-striped shirts (blue, green, gray, pink) every day when he is being an Interior Architect, wearing jeans and sweatshirts around the house, Amish black hats and cowboy neckerchiefs to parties. He doesn't really understand me. He has a romantic streak, though. (We all have streaks, of many hues.) He buys candles by the dozens at flea markets, grows lemon verbena in clay pots on the kitchen window sill, even weeps occasionally when he listens to *Ariadne Auf Naxos*. And he has the most curious habit of smuggling chocolate into the house and hiding it underneath his underwear. (But why? I don't even *like* chocolate.) He reads books about Post-Modernist painting, subscribes with dedication to *Architectural Digest* and *Metropolitan Home,* feigns shock each month at the going rate for Navaho rugs (he used to own one, but sold it) and Mies van der Rohe chairs (he owns four). His revenge for never making quite enough money is to insist on living well, and just a bit beyond his (our) means. He uses a tad less Valium than I do. And nothing, absolutely nothing (Bangladesh, Lebanon, fuel increases, tax audits, Anita Bryant, Reagan, the Pope's lovable but wrong-headed paternalism toward just about everyone, hunger in America) ever enrages him. Except me. We fight a lot. But he is very good in bed.

I am in the middle of decoding a convoluted sentence about the problem of the industrial pollution of the Mississippi in Hunck Finn (actual spelling) when the phone rings. I wonder about rabbit pellets. I don't want to talk to anyone. I doubt my command of the English sentence. But I don't want to scribble another red AWK or SP. Curiosity wins out.

"Hello, this is Angel. Remember me? From the party? Delacroix gave me your number."

Long pause. I manage a "Yes?"

"Could you meet me for lunch? I think you're the kind of person I can talk to. We had such a nice conversation about the bigotry of the Moral Majority, remember? My lover's giving me hell."

Maybe it's because of your name, I think, fingering a furry verbena leaf, looking out the window for Dorfy down by the hutch. What's he after? Again, a crisis of interpretation. Then I look at the stack of papers about Hunck on the kitchen table.

I say, "Sure, why not?" without being the least bit sure.

II

I am waiting at Phoff's Garden Cafe. The prerequisite dark green walls, mahogany ceiling fans, brass rails, ficuses, staghorn ferns. I am early. I have spent much of my life being entirely too prompt. Our Mother of Perpetual Promptness. I realize that this is not virtue. Probably some kind of slick, vestigial Catholic compulsion. I order a chablis, then feel guilty. The question of whether one should drink before five on occasion is taking on political proportions in late twentieth-century culture. At least among everyone I know.

At first I don't recognize Angel without his bandana. And, I see he is far too young. But then, when one is hurdling toward forty, much of the available population is. He's more stocky than chubby, I now realize. Short, curly black hair, mustache, aquiline nose, big brown cow eyes that can never look anything but appealingly sad. I have an impulse to ask him to sit on my lap, then worry about a felony charge.

Over a salad of Romaine, jalapeno peppers, and what was purported to be Belgian endive but what looks more like chopped corn husks, Angel announces, "I'm twenty-two. You must be about thirty."

I want to kiss his baby-luscious lips, each of his untrained moo-cow eyes. Instead, I say, "About."

"Delacroix tells me that you've been involved for a long time." He says "involved" in italics, with a hint of a question mark.

"I've always been involved. It's the occupational hazard of living." I think of M., who, in the midst of scrambling eggs this morning, threw the spatula at me because I was whining about being bored with my life. Yes, that wizened, world-weary inflection is just the effect I want.

"Peter's giving me a bad time. Peter's my lover. We've lived together for two months now. I don't think it's going to last."

"Was Peter at Delacroix's party?"

"He won't go to parties. Lately, he won't even go to work, either. He sells ties at *The Silk Hat*. Occasionally."

"What *will* he do?" I ask, not certain exactly what I mean. I wipe up the crumbly bleu cheese and vinaigrette with a hunk of French bread, dimly recalling Huck and polluted Mississippis. The food is becoming more interesting than Angel.

"He likes to lick," Angel whispers.

"I beg your pardon?"

"Lick. Anything. Anyone. Ankles, hands, backs . . ."

I perk up, forgetting the salad remnants. I particularly like the hush of the ellipsis.

"Is that what attracted you to him? I mean, at first?" I ask, knowing how silly the question is. But then, this is going to be one of those luncheons. Clearly. And the salad not even dispensed with yet.

"I don't know. I mean, he's got a wicked tongue and all. But he never talks. Can you imagine living with someone who never even *talks* to you? Just hangs around and, sort of, *pants* all the time?"

I wonder why Angel doesn't see the humor in all this.

"I'm going to leave him. I'm bored. That's why I wanted to talk to you. You seemed to have such a nice . . . vocabulary."

And here I have spent much of my life admiring the laconic. Silence is a chair of great durability but one I could never quite sit comfortably in. It has become clear that this will not be a rendezvous spiced with candles and double-entendres, fingers aspiring across linened tables, breath-catching innuendoes. I will have to play Daddy to Angel's Distressed Youth.

"Angel, listen. I don't know what your obligations are to this . . . Peter (Peter the Tongue, I think, but don't say), but surely you have a right to experience as much of life as you want to. Don't box yourself into a room that is too . . . narrow for you. Where will you live? I mean, if you really decide to leave him?"

"With my mother."

I think spring is really coming. Everyone I know is thinking of revolutionizing their lives. Spring is the most tragic season, April, of course, the cruelest month. One is bombarded with new and restless sounds, snow trickling, sputtering down gutters, birds chittering in their dreams about fat surfacing earthworms, crocuses squeaking out of the cold mud. Another spring, all over again. Fasten your seat belts.

One grows weary of constant flux. Flotsam and jetsam in the huge mud soup kettle of the cosmos. I think of harbors, aware of mixing metaphors. M. is a harbor. Of sorts. A child is never a harbor. Only a storm. The grave, the final harbor. "In this little space of earth . . ." Dickinson might have said that. Maybe not. The thing is, the *Thing* is, to constantly be ready to snap to attention. To keep one's interest up. To always be on all-out alert. To accept, no, to *love,* the incoherence of it all.

Angel calls later in the afternoon. "I want you to know, you've helped me make the most important decision of my life." I seriously doubt it. Anyway, he isn't specific about which decision. I twist ice cubes into a straw basket. L. is coming for drinks.

"Hi, boys. Watcha been up to?" M. and I kiss L. on her slightly withered lips. At sixty-something, L. claims she's Mellowed Out, but she always enters rooms like whipped wind. Her hair is still entirely black, as frazzled as an unclipped poodle's. Her short stature belies her deep, raw voice, a voice cured by half a century of cigarette smoke. She wears jeans, vests, and always a shoulder-strap leather bag bursting with wads of Kleenex, scraps of paper with addresses and odd tidbits of information, a silver flask of vodka, limes (often sliced and coated with lint), odd little toys, five packs of Camels (all opened), loose photographs (mostly of herself), matches from restaurants, no cosmetics, no combs. L., like everyone else around here, is an egomaniac.

I explain to L., over vodka and sodas, about Yuppies. "It means Young Urban Professionals. It's an acronym. Preppie is out. It says it right here in *Time*." I wave the magazine at her, with the picture of Sally Ride in a sequinned evening gown on the cover. "And if you're gay and urban etc., you're a Guppie. That must make you a Luppie." We laugh. L. is a lesbian.

"Anyway," says L., wanting the stage back, "I've got to tell you guys about this little shop I came across in TriBeCa. It's *wooon*derful!" With L., the first syllable for the word "wonderful" is always about ten syllables long. "They have all these really neat things I found for my collages. Look." After much fumbling around in her grab-bag (our breath deliberately abated), she pulls out a black plastic lizard, the kind you used to find in Crackerjacks boxes. "Isn't this terrific! I love it!" she giggles. L. is inordinately fond of exclamation points, too. We love L. She keeps up one's interest. "I'm going to use it in my collage about Nixon and the Seventies."

"Albee once said that his plays were about the tarantula at the bottom of the box of Crackerjacks," I offer, pointlessly.

"Yeah?" L. asks, but it wasn't really a question. "Anyway, you guys have really got to go there, when you next get to the city. They've got early Tupperware, tombstones, fiesta pitchers, hoola hoops with rhinestones, plaster RCA dogs, all kinds of stuff. A treasure-trove of a junk shop. I spent twenty-five bucks in five minutes!"

"Is it all in your purse?" I ask. M. frowns at me. I like to tease people. M. and L. don't like to be teased. M. tells me it's a sign of repressed insecurity, low self-esteem. Sometimes. Other times he tells me it's a sign of repressed hostilities, aggressions. Everyone I know has taken at least

Intro Psych. That may or may not have been a mistake.

L.'s eyes always get glassy after her second vodka. After all, she's little, and sixty-something. Last summer I bought her a surprise birthday cake, and after two drinks, she got mad at me. Something about she didn't *want* a cake, she *told* me she didn't like cakes, and did I want to make her *fat* or something? I think she didn't want to have a birthday. But usually she's proud of her age, proud of surviving the slings and arrows. That night, M.'s mother was here. She had run away from home. Again. (Because her house was being painted, and she couldn't "stand all the goddamn mess!") She's the same age as L., but she *sits* older, if you know what I mean. Her general *interest* is dimmer. The contrast was startling. Anyway, I asked Mrs. M. if she wanted another ear of corn, and L., a bit boozy, blurted, "Aw, go ahead, why don't you just call her Ma!" After a tense second, we all laughed. Except Mrs. M.

We invite L. to stay for dinner, but she says she has to go. "I've got to get to my studio to get some work done on my Seventies box. I can't wait to show you guys my Fifties box. All black, with a ripped picture of McCarthy and his ridiculous spit-curl from an old *Life*, and, on his shoulder, a rubber worm. God, I hated the Fifties. The repression, all that crap! But I love working on my boxes. Some day they're going to put *me* in a box."

M. is snoring, fitfully. He snorts himself awake, then dozes off. I push him over on his side. The road is full of sirens tonight. M.'s foot was bothering him earlier. From when he sliced it on the broken glass. I kiss his back. In sleep, perhaps it feels like a feather. M., sleeping, reminds me of a loaf of bread rising in the oven. In the dark, in tune with the snoring, the sirens, I hear myself weeping. For M.'s foot. Angel's decision. The Tongue's silence. Dorfy and Evvy's Disneyland world view. L.'s black boxes. My chimerical sense of purpose. And I see that we are all of us here trying to pass through time with a desperate enthusiasm.

III

I can never tell a story quite right. At a party. In a room. At restaurants. I am beginning to understand why. I don't enjoy the *action* part. I am of the tribe who ask "why?" of inscrutable situations, always to the annoyance of the neighboring and much more populous tribe across the river, who want to get on with "what next?" I mean (and it is crucial that you understand this) I am not, have never been, convinced that *large* action (as opposed to, say, the trembling of a pinkie on one's shoulder, the lifting of a veil at a garden party) ever really amounts to much of anything significant. Car wrecks (unless one actually dies), weddings, the discovery of plutonium in one's breakfast cereal—all that the other tribe would call "important" action seems to me to blend right into the mud-soup river, given the long-term scheme of things. Perhaps death is one's only significant action. And the flicker-flash moment before, does one remember one's car breaking down in the Lincoln Tunnel (thus becoming the cork of New York), or one's first kiss?

My students (almost invariably from across the river) cannot cope with *The Dubliners,* Tennessee Williams (who allows nothing to happen until passion explodes, and then the play is ended), but give rave reviews to *Star Wars,* "The Lady and the Tiger," "The Most Dangerous Game." Perhaps they are right. God, if he still breathes the rarified cosmic air, has bequeathed the love of action to the Quick. And they proceed like no tomorrow, tearing grocery coupons out of newspaper inserts, sealing their driveways, leasing the local Ramada Inn for their wedding receptions. While those of us who are dying (i.e., everyone I like), spend their time wondering (whether they have quite articulated it to themselves or not) why they are not immortal. Wondering how to penetrate the gossamer shield that wraps us in time like a foetal membrane.

Hubris, of course. A Greek phenomenon. But then, so is my lust. L.'s boxes. M.'s weekend neo-Frankenthaler paintings, spread all over the floor of the garage. Aspiration = hubris. Overweening pride. Wanting to capture a fragment of perfection. Is the romantic impulse nothing more than a covert suicide wish? We all, personally, refuse the tragic denouement. And the sirens wail around us.

M. has lung cancer. I'm sure of it. Or some slick form of AIDS. A routine lung X-ray , and instant paranoia. He decided to switch companies because he, too, is falling on forty like a brick. No, a mountain top. As a matter of fact (of course none of this is fact—facts don't yield themselves to interpretation—it is all metaphor), he is a crumbling Matterhorn.

What happened was that he was told that this impossible slurb area where we live no longer needs Interior Architects, and he was demoted to "decorator" (the Northeast is dying, etc., etc.). Of course it does! It needs a fleet of bulldozers, a pipeline injection of imagination, spiked with maybe a tad of gusto (pioneer spirit? more beer)?! Anyway (L.'s word, mine, too, everybody-who-gets-easily-sidetracked-in-this-crazy-post-Viet Nam-world's word), M., being proud, a survivor, and just a wee-bit Kosher, finagled a new and even better-paying job out of Alfred. (To be honest, Alfred has been creaming his *Sergio Valente* jeans to get M. to work for him, etc., for years.)

Now, about Alfred. Where to begin? (It's so cliched!) Alfred at best has an Associate's Degree in Interior Design from some private two-year college in Manitoba (whether he actually *finished* his required "Lamps and Fabrics" course is uncertain). But his *très chic* taste, his mother's Long Island money, and his androgynous, slightly lilting attempt at a Robert Redford presence, quickly brought him local fame and success. Alfred decorates houses for blue-haired ladies who live in our most eastern, poshest suburb. Alfred says "darling" a lot to the very rich, at least those rich enough to worry about whether their loveseats should be redone in mauve tones or burgundy. (Alfred makes my claws come out, clearly.)

Well, one night, when Alfred and his lover came here for dinner (his lover is an accountant, very nice, gray streaks at thirty-one), he described over Drambuie and gooseberry cheesecake a confrontation with his mother.

She had come up to visit, and to meet Alfred's roommate. Before she arrived, Alfred and his lover had quarreled over the meringue (whether the peaks were too browned or not), the salmon mousse, the reproduction of David Hockney over the fireplace, the unused look of the second bedroom, the three bottles of Vaseline lotion in the medicine cabinet, the five alabaster statues of *David* arranged tastefully at various places around the living room—they were tense. Alfred insisted on blatancy, his lover, discretion. The dinner, predictably, was a success, and Alfred's mother was enthralled with their apartment. She raved about the black walls, the mirrored alcove, the eggshell satin bedspread in the master bedroom, the bathroom wall papered with art nouveau poster reproductions. But, after brandy, Alfred's mother made her *faux pas*.

"But boys, what do you do here, after hours?" she asked, innocently enough, one would suppose. And all the tension of the day erupted in Alfred's blurted, exasperated answer.

"I suck cock, Mother. Just like you do."

Well, needless to say, a Long Island wedding was off.

Anyway, it was clear, here at our dinner party with Alfred and his lover, that Alfred took to M. right away (I could tell by the billows of the tablecloth between them). Over salad, Alfred said to M., "If you ever want to work for me, etc., etc." (that was before he told us about his mother, etc.). And so, when M. was being demoted, along with the entire Northeast, he immediately called Alfred. A career crisis resolved in a fell swoop.

Well, not quite. A medical exam was required for Alfred's group health insurance. And this was what was found: a blot somewhere around the southwest tip of the left lung.

We await further explorations. Barium enemas. Sado-masochistic probings with rubber and plastic things. I am going crazy. Why should I

have to face mortality? Especially *his? I* am barely mortal yet! (I am beginning to understand L.'s exclamation points—does that mean I'm aging?
growing wiser? just hysterical?) My hands shake when I shave (too much
drinking?), I have a tremor in my eyelid when my daughter calls (too much
apprehension—what will she do next?), I *never* know what L. will say next
(age-differential?), I blanch when tablecloths billow (the pressure of being
a member of a minority that is frequently misunderstood and often prone to
jealous rages?), and I worry about M. (his impatience with me, his radical
career change, Alfred, his shadowed lung). And I see that, finally and for
real, I love. Because I care. And my lover is dying. So are we all.

IV

M. is not going to die. Just yet. He has, it turns out, a bizarre case of a
ripped diaphragm. The blot on the X-rays is a portion of his large intestine
which leaked through the rip to huddle against his lung. The rip will have to
be stitched up, of course, the intestine shoved down where it should be.
How did such a thing happen? Lifting large stones in our untamed yard?
Sit-ups? Shouting too enthusiastically at me? Who can say? (The doctors
can't.) One of those imperceptible but monumental things that happen to us
while we are mulling over this week's check account balance, or whether
the chicken for dinner should be stuffed with rice or chestnuts.

So now, the hospital. Waiting with L. for M. to be released from
surgery. Cream-green everywhere: walls, dressing gowns, last night's
uneaten dinners stacked on plastic trays by the elevators, L.'s face, mine
too, probably. Nurses padding in and out of rooms on erasers. L. holds my
hand as we sit in the waiting room. The young man in a maroon terrycloth
bathrobe who sits across from us, smoking, has a mere flap of skin, as white
as the underside of one's wrist, where his nose should be.

"He'll be a mighty sick boy when he returns, you know. You gotta be
strong now. But I know you." She blows her nose in a fistful of Kleenex.

"Look who's talking."

The surgeon suddenly appears, calm as a dove. "Family of M.?"

I catapult from my chair. "We're here to represent them. Is he okay?"

"He's fine, fine." I exhale; a balloon let loose. "And clean as a whistle,
too. No cancer. No complications. He'll be back on the floor in an hour."

"What can we expect in terms of recuperation?" L. asks.

"He'll be uncomfortable for about a week. We'll give him morphine
every three hours. Then he'll be fine."

Uncomfortable! I love it! They rip your back open about a yard long, pry open your rib cage, shove things around, staple you back up with a gun, and say you'll be uncomfortable! Oh, for just a tad of the objectivity of the medical profession.

L. and I go to lunch at Phoff's. We order Phoffburgers and tossed salad. The burgers arrive *tartare*.

"He could have died, you know," I announce, brandishing my salad fork.

"But he didn't." L. has a shred of lettuce on her chin. I brush it off with a finger.

"Still, he could have."

"Look. It's all one big chance anyway. A spin of a wheel. It's over, and he's fine. Don't be so damn Catholic."

"I'm not, anymore," I remind her.

"Maybe not, but you're still so morbid. Hey, this burger's raw. Waiter?"

A young man in a sort of tuxedo coat, a penguin outfit, appears at our table immediately. "Ma'am?"

"This is raw." L. slides her plate to the edge of the table. "Could you do something about it?"

"Sure thing," he smiles, taking both rather runny plates away.

"Thanks," L. says. "Hey, you're cute."

"Thanks. Anything else, Ma'am."

"Well, you could burp me, if you're of a mind," L. giggles.

M. will be home soon. Possibly by the end of the week, according to the doctors, depending on how thoroughly he can by then pee into his portable urinal. The nurses dangle catheter tubes over his bed every three hours with a you-know-what-will-happen-if-you-don't sigh. Every time I arrive, I draw the curtain, make him stand up beside his bed holding the bottle, and put my foot on the pedal beneath the sink. When M. finally coughs, or makes water, we are all smiles. In some predicaments, it takes so little to please. Still, the daisies and irises and azaleas sprouting unnaturally from every nook and cranny of the room, the balloonogram from Mrs. M. drooping over the covered radiator like a desperately tasteless morning-after corsage, (why isn't she here?), the silly cards that are entirely too cute to cheer up anyone who has gone beyond fifth grade—the facade provides little more than conversation accoutrement, something to talk about after the scars have been displayed. Thank God, M. at least does *not* joke with the nurses.

At home. My daughter calls, collect. She asks me about M. She tells me about her novel, about how the heroine will have to have an abortion.

"What are you trying to tell me?" I ask, no, shout.

"Nothing. Just about the turning point in my character's frame of reference, is all." I am, I think, relieved.

"But what about money, a job, food and stuff?" I ask, aware that I have been forever typecast as The Philistine to her peculiar version of Stephen Dedaleus. "I mean, are you okay?"

"Sure. I got a job in a pizzeria. I dust the dough, then roll it out. It's part-time, doesn't pay much, but it's fun. At least for now. Don't worry so much about me."

"I love you." What else can I say?

"Love you too. Tell M. I love him."

"Be sure to call me in a few days, so I know how you are." But cross-continental static blurs the connection. "Take care, honey," I shout, across Rocky Mountain thunder, the drone of locusts somewhere on the Great Plains, but the connection is lost. Well, at least I know she's still out there.

Alone in the deepening night, in the cavelike solitude of this old farmhouse, I make myself a martini, fiddle with the cable TV selector. Cars spinning around corners on two wheels (flick), Burt Reynolds guzzling lots of beer, his hairpiece decidedly askew (flick), Joan Collins' elegant sleaze (flick), Ingrid Bergman's victimized Perils-of-Pauline eyes (flick), the high drama of today's national weather-makers (flick), Ingrid Bergman's wizened Golda Meir (flick), the Star Spangled Banner (is it that late?). I settle for a William Inge rerun on a 24-hour movie channel, because in the fifties questions had answers, and stories, endings. L., perhaps, is wrong about the fifties, after all. Then again, L. is a far better existentialist than I am. She knows what to expect. And, more importantly, what not to.

After a second martini and a discreet 1/2 5 mg. Valium, Inge becomes less engaging. The story line, complete with all its inherent conflicts, has been clearly set up in the first five minutes; then the drama shuffles toward its inevitable bittersweet ending. My stories never have endings. This one won't. L. will never finish her boxes, but will go on to new enthusiasms (she's already hinted that she plans to blow-up reproductions of famous paintings, say *The Last Supper,* and superimpose a black-and-white photo of herself appropriately in the context, say, just behind Judas' shoulder). My daughter will continue to Do-Her-Best, and make my heart shudder. M. will come home to me quite intact, and we will continue to be happy and sad, gentle and angry, together. Angel, Alfred, others, will fade from my line of vision.

And I, poised precariously between Love and Fear, between the What-Is and the What-Might-Be, will simply have to continue to wing it.

A Rose in Murcia

RICHARD HALL

He should not have come. He knew it as soon as he boarded the rattletrap bus in Palma. The realization grew as the yellow contraption wheezed up the narrow road, over the rocks broken into pebbles by generations of Mallorcan road gangs, past the monastery where Chopin had spent that awful winter with George Sand. Why was he here, jolted, parched, the scene just ended with Alex heavy on his conscience? What did he hope to discover?

The bus heaved and groaned along the mountain road, the shifts of gear sounding like the cry of a doomed man. Every so often the hills to the left fell away and Frady glimpsed the Mediterranean, an azure blur to the horizon. Alex was probably sitting over a cup of coffee on the Borne now, his kind, seamed face under the grizzled hair showing signs of hurt and confusion. Because Frady had insisted on making this trip alone.

Well, he couldn't help it. He didn't want Alex with him. He didn't want to share this detour into the past. It belonged to him alone.

The gearshift gave another tortured cry and Frady glanced to his left. Far below, a promontory of rocks jutted into the sea. He remembered that tumble of weird shapes. They had gone fishing for bream there, he and Tom and a new British friend named Nigel. They had no proper equipment, just sticks and string and bread, and spent most of the morning staring into the water at the motionless fish, which looked delicious. Finally they had given up and scrambled across the rocks, up through the stands of olive and umbrella pine, shouting poetry, chasing sheep, stuffing huge pinecones into their knapsacks. They had reached the road, the very road he was now on, sweaty and exhilarated and hardly out of breath.

Yes, Frady thought, as the bus rounded the last curve and the little village came into view—hardly out of breath. The phrase signaled the difference between past and present as well as anything. He glanced down at his hands, noting the liver spots struggling faintly to the surface. The stains of age. He'd probably have trouble now even walking up from the beach, much less chasing sheep and shouting poetry.

The houses of brown fieldstone were coming into view now, basking like lizards in the morning sun. Above, on a rise under the Teix, the curtain of mountains that cut off the village from the rest of the island, he saw the town itself, with its little church topped with red tiles. How he had detested that church, and the priest who had looked at him and Tom as if they were carriers of heresy or corruption. When they had arrived, after a chill sea crossing, the church had been surrounded by white blossoms, the hill bright with the plumage of the flowering almond trees. He had said to Tom that they were bridal bouquets for their own wedding, but Tom hadn't been amused.

The bus creaked to a halt. Frady stood up, aware that his heart was beating rapidly. He thought again of Alex, who had been fading during the last few minutes, until he was quite dim. Well, there was no need to feel guilty. There were plenty of things Alex could do today—visit Bellver Castle, buy presents for his kids, read that history of Mallorca. But even that no longer seemed important. Now, here, in this village with its powerful freight of memory, Alex's feelings could be ignored.

As he stepped off the bus into the dusty street, everything seemed instantly familiar—the salt cod and dried beanpods in crates in front of the little grocery, the boys in short pants kicking a football, the café with its patrons in corduroy suits and berets. He might, he thought, walk in any direction and see familiar sights. Every lane, every house, would yield some richness, some association, as if the last twenty years hadn't passed, as if he were still living here with Tom.

The sound of sheep bells caught his ear. Across the street some ewes were grazing. Nearby a young shepherd rested under a tree. The Biblical scene was still enchanting. He recalled that he and Tom had stood right here, their luggage beside them, and taken in the rocky pastures, the mountains, the sheep. It seemed they had stepped into a simpler era, far from their own harsh country, where they might be truly free.

Free! The juvenile thought tolled him back to himself and he passed his hand over his forehead. He was no longer the young man who had moved here with Tom Peniman. If the nostalgia started building up again he'd have to remind himself of that. Many years had gone by—half his adult life.

Besides, he and Alex had a good present. Why should he want to wallow around in the past? "A last great autumnal passion," he had joked after they'd met at a bar in Chelsea and started spending weekends together. He'd been thinking of Zhivago and Lara—it seemed a silly but suitable image. There was only one hitch. It hadn't been a great passion, hadn't triggered the wild abandon described by Pasternak. There had been only, well, the present, which consisted of walks and meals and movies. And sex on Saturday night—nice sex, considerate sex, but not the kind that made the earth move. At first they had talked of living together but gradually, as they entered the third, fourth and fifth years of their relationship, they had dropped the idea. Nowadays they never even referred to it. It seemed to each, though they never discussed it, an invasion of privacy.

There was the path down to the house. His eye had picked it out from all the other paths leading from the town square. How well he knew that path! Several times the pebbles had slipped under him and he'd fallen on his ass. Once he'd broken a liter of *vino tinto* and some dogs had appeared to lick it up. Tom had been furious; they'd been living on a few pesetas a day.

Frady giggled slightly as he headed toward the path. How strange and distant seemed their poverty now. They'd both quit jobs to come here—Tom as a management trainee at IBM, himself as a teacher in the New York City school system. They wanted their savings—what had it been, a thousand dollars?—to last. They had chosen Mallorca, the cheapest corner of Europe. Their house in this town cost them twenty-five dollars a month.

He was on the path now, keeping an eye out for moving pebbles. His heart was still beating a crisp tattoo. The next few minutes seemed terribly important, as if he were in the theater and the curtain was about to go up.

That sound. What was it? Keeping his eye on his feet, he tried to place it. And then, as if a dam had burst, it crashed into his consciousness. *El torrente*—of course! The stream that ran through the center of the village, bringing water down from the Teix, supplying irrigation, drink for the animals, laundromat service. And there they were, the women rinsing clothes under the pink oleander. Of course, these must be the daughters of the women he and Tom had known. Still, they looked the same—the same dresses of grey worsted, long aprons, sturdy arms, reddened hands. The same harsh appraising stares, too. He wanted to speak to them, wanted to rush over and say how glad he was to be here, but he checked himself. After he waved, one of the women nodded slightly. She was the one wearing rubber gloves.

Suddenly he remembered something that had happened here under the oleander. He had brought Tom out and posed him against the stream. He'd wanted to capture the whole thing in watercolors—the crystal torrent, the wicker panniers, the bent women, Tom with his straw peasant hat, his jutting chin, his trim and sturdy 30-year-old body. He'd painted for a bit, then they'd gone back to the house for lunch. But when he returned he found his water tumbler spilled across the page and the women gone.

The injustice of that moment returned to him. The women hadn't liked being painted, hadn't liked being picturesque for tourists. Or was it something else—the idea of one man painting another? He didn't know, then or now, but it had reminded them both of the fragility of their lives, the bare tolerance which permitted them to live undisturbed. They had both been depressed after the incident, the freedom which they had come so far to find suddenly threatened. They had gotten drunk and gone to bed hanging onto each other like life preservers. Now, crossing the little bridge over the stream, he recalled how exposed and exhausted he had often felt here. They were the only male couple for miles around. Sometimes he would become unnerved by the stares of the villagers, suddenly self-conscious about his clothes, his foreignness, his shared life—and head back to the house in panic. Yearning for the sight of Tom, the privacy of their garden. In his present nostalgia he'd forgotten all the bad things—their fish tank existence, the pointing children, the whispers.

How different things were now in New York. He and Alex knew dozens of couples just like themselves. They went to movies and plays depicting relationships like theirs; they read books and attended panel discussions on how to improve their lives. The problem wasn't too much tension but not enough. Sometimes they went out looking for excitement— in a backroom bar, a park, a porno movie. With all that in his life, why should he be nostalgic about a few months in this backwater?

The next moment, it was as if the question had never occurred to him. He'd seen the stone pillar with the tile inset that marked the entrance to the house. The words on the tile, *Mon Repos,* were almost unreadable now, but it didn't matter. The sight made his head throb. He could see the gable of the house projecting over the foliage. It seemed that the play he had come to attend had finally begun.

The gate was rusty, the lock decayed, but the shrubs along the path were clipped and the patches of margaritas well-tended. The *nispero* tree and the date palm were thriving.

There it was. The sturdy two-story house of fieldstone and mortar, trimmed in blue. Built to last for several centuries of mild Mallorcan weather. They'd first glimpsed it on a gorgeous February day, standing right on this flagstone path. Each had known instantly, without speaking, that it was what they'd been looking for. After the rental agent had unlocked the front door, they'd raced through the dark rooms with their heavy Códoban furniture, sharing their excitement with their eyes only. They'd taken it on the spot, written out travelers' checks for six months' rent in advance. That very afternoon they'd moved in. "Mon Repos!" they had shouted in the echoing chambers as they ran around that first afternoon, "Mon Repos!" That night, after a meal that had been a disaster, they had made wild, joyous love in the bedroom upstairs, both uncontainable with joy, lust, faith in their destiny. Even now he felt faint stirrings at the memory of that first night.

Frady searched the facade for the bedroom window. There it was, last one on the right. And then, just as he turned around to view the garden behind him, he thought he saw a curtain twitch. Not in their bedroom but at the other end of the house.

He looked back quickly but the curtains were still. It must have been a trick of his peripheral vision. But he stood for a long moment, waiting, before he gave his attention to the garden.

This garden had been their first living room. On the blue bench right there they had had their best talks, made their happiest plans. He could almost see Tom now, his wiry body wrapped in scarves and sweaters, bent over his newly acquired guitar, trying to teach himself the chords with fingers that were chilled.

A brief jab of pain went through him. He didn't even know where Tom was now. Somewhere in the far east. They no longer wrote, no longer took each other along on their voyages—if only in imagination. The bond had been broken, the bond they had expected to last all their lives.

They had been greatly loving toward one another. Their love had burnished this house and garden, the dark rooms and ill-equipped kitchen, the *nispero* and date palm and margaritas. Everything had absorbed and reflected their affection. And the townspeople and foreign residents, for all their stares and whispers, acknowledged their doubleness. They were described, accepted, invited, as a pair. It was always "Frady and Tom" or "Tom and Frady." They seemed to share one long variable, triple-jointed name.

One night, coming home from a musical evening at the Petersons, an artistic American couple who lived on the main street, they had slipped and slithered down the pebbly path until suddenly they had heard a miraculous sound. It was a music more subtle, more romantic, than the Chopin and Schumann played earlier on the Peterson's rheumy piano. It was, in fact, a song of such crystal perfection that they had stopped and listened. And

167

then, as they stared at each other—Tom's bony face silver-plated in the moonlight—they had come to the realization at the same instant. "It's a nightingale," Tom had whispered. "Yes, yes," Frady had replied in the same breath.

Though neither had ever heard a nightingale before, the song seemed to preexist in them, an unplayed music waiting for the right moment to sound. As they stood there, not stirring, the hidden bird trembling out its tune, it seemed to Frady that he was now full of the very elixir of life. To be with Tom while a nightingale's song filled the Mallorcan night was to be fully alive. It was as if an old promise had finally been kept. When the song stopped they had picked their way across the pebbles to the stone house. They hadn't said much as they got ready for bed. And the next day they had both hummed snatches of old tunes and songs, hardly aware that they were trying to duplicate, in a foolish way, the song of the nightingale.

Frady moved to the blue bench at the back of the garden and sat down. Suddenly he realized that from the moment he and Alex had planned this trip, its sole purpose was to come here to this house, to this garden alone. It was a purpose kept hidden from Alex and, in some ways, from himself. But it had been there all along, stowed in the luggage with his underwear, in his pocket with his passport. He was coming here to find Tom, to find his joy in Tom—and it had nothing to do with the present. He shook his head slowly, appalled at the trick he had played on himself. He wanted to relive their life together, restore the old bond. It was absurd.

Their sojourn in Mallorca had been followed by several months in Paris and then home. They had arrived in New York almost broke, without job prospects, with long hair and scraggly beards. They had moved into a seedy hotel on Eighth Street. As in Mallorca and Paris, they spent long hours in cafés, cheap eateries, the barely-furnished apartments of new acquaintances. New York from this angle was not the sane, orderly place they had inhabited before going to Europe. Now it was in the grip of the flower children, the Beats, the drug explosion. They dabbled in these experiences, determined not to succumb to the forces of repression that had driven them to Spain in the first place. But it was a losing battle. The tyranny of being poor, the scruffiness of their acquaintance, the habits of discipline and order, all took their toll. The middle class reclaimed them. Within a year they were back in a small, well-organized apartment. Tom was working for a market research firm; Frady had been reinstated by the public school system. They were both clean-shaven.

But those two years on the outside had been the most exciting in Frady's life. Exciting not only because it had been his first, last and only attempt to escape the prison of his upbringing, but because during it he had discovered within himself a powerful steadfastness. He had been true—true to Tom. Through all their wanderings, all the strains of small town life and big city life, he had not once been diverted from his attachment. Although he knew Tom's faults, Frady never faltered. Tom was his and he was Tom's. Occasionally he wondered at the novelty of this—he had never been noted for his monogamy before—but there was no escape. "It must be chemical," he mused to himself sometimes. "Chemical" was the word for the mystery of his steadfastness.

It was Tom who had finally wanted out. His decision to leave had been conveyed as they both sat in the bleachers of a school playground near their home, watching some neighborhood kids play ball. "I have to get out," Tom had said in a strangled voice that Frady knew was the prelude to genuine tears. "I can't take it anymore."

He was referring to their apartment just a few blocks away, now organized the way Frady liked. But Frady knew it wasn't just the apartment Tom wanted to escape, nor even himself. It was a whole net of responsibility, obligation, that had to be cast off. Sitting in the bleachers, watching the tears begin to wet Tom's face, Frady understood that his own steadfastness was Tom's foe. While he held fast, Tom struggled to get loose. The harder he clutched, the less air reached Tom. Now their lives had come apart. There was no cure for it.

He looked up at the facade of the house, as if it might offer some solace. Why couldn't he let go of Tom? It had been a good five years and their loving friendship had continued for the next fifteen. But now it was over. He didn't even know where on the face of the planet Tom might be at this moment. *Why didn't he let go?*

This time he saw it clearly. The curtain moving, the hand withdrawing. He sat very still, his heart hammering, wondering how long he'd been observed. For a moment he felt the urge to dash out. Then he stood up and made himself wait. It wouldn't be long.

The footsteps sounded very faintly at first, then louder. The tap-tap of heels on the tile staircase. For an instant, quite irrationally, he visualized the black shoes his grandmother wore. Then the door opened.

She was much older, but her back was still straight and her eyes still bright and black.

"*Ay, señor.*" She brought her ancient hands together in a spectral clap. "Encarnación."

She stepped into the garden. Her face was lacy with wrinkles. He saw stars, flowers, snowflakes. He walked over and hugged her. She felt very frail in his arms and her skin smelled faintly of olive oil. He had the brief impression he was hugging time, or Spain, or the Old World.

"Yo le ví desde arriba!" Of course she'd seen him from upstairs. She often peered down at them as they sat in the garden, interrupting her housework, her dishwashing and bedmaking to check up on the tenants. She'd been attached to this house for fifty years. The real estate agent had told them what to pay her.

She was talking rapidly now and he barely understood. She hadn't recognized him at first. She thought he was a thief. Then she'd remembered. *El señor americano. Los dos señores americanos.*

She looked at him vaguely. She was trying to figure out which one he was. But it should have been easy. She had adored Tom. They'd hit it off instantly, communicating at some level he couldn't share, at a level where Tom's school Spanish didn't matter. Tom claimed she knew right off that he came from dirt farmers, poor Okies who'd worked a soil as exhausted as this. And she reminded him of his grandmother, a mean old biddy who sat with the hens all day and spat tobacco juice.

Now she'd placed him. He was not Tom. He was the other one. She smiled toothlessly. *"Y su amigo?"* Her voice changed from its reedy sing-song, became warmer and more alert. Frady was swept by loss as he tried to explain that Tom had moved to California and after that to the Far East. But these names had no place in Encarnación's lexicon. She blinked and repeated her question. "Ca-li-for-nia." He gave it a Spanish pronunciation. Didn't everyone know about that golden state? But Encarnación did not. He was not Tom. Tom was not here. Suddenly she lost interest. She slouched. Frady had the impression that her straight back had been only a pose, a last bit of bravery, and that underneath her bones were badly bent.

And then, as if by magic, she straightened up again. She smiled and touched his arm. He summoned up his last intuitions and made sense of her Spanish. She wanted him to come home with her. To her house across the field. She had something to show him.

She moved closer. He caught the faint smell of olive oil again. Even as he resisted the idea of accompanying her, he knew he would accept. There was no way not to go. It was all part of this day's journey.

He waited while she took a huge key from her apron pocket and locked the front door, which was a bright blue. Then they crossed the garden to the back gate, the one reserved for her use. She lived across the field now planted with artichokes—a cash crop. He followed, noting how her heels imprinted the soft soil. He had never been invited to her house before. It was one of the smaller, poorer ones in this poor village.

As he expected, the sitting room was sparsely furnished—a cabinet, a few rush chairs, a scarred table. There were some mezzotints on the wall, a Sacred Heart over the fireplace. After he sat down she went to another room and returned with a bottle of Fundador and some olivewood cups. She filled one and put it in front of him. Then she sat across from him, folded her hands and smiled. He wondered if this was what he had come for—to see her house.

After he had finished the Fundador and refused a second cup, she stood up and went to the cabinet in the corner. From it she took a large magazine, a rotogravure. It was an old issue of *Hoy*. He could see the Generalissimo on the cover, reviewing some Falangist troops. A disgusting sight. She opened the magazine to the centerfold.

She was babbling at him in Spanish that made no sense. He shook his head, trying to stop her, unsuccessfully. And then she was presenting him with . . . what? He looked up. She was beaming. He shook his head again.

"Murcia," she whispered.

He looked at the spread pages of the magazine again. Pressed flat, its leaves black, its bloom the color of dried blood, was a dead rose. *"La rosa de Murcia,"* Encarnación whispered.

His skin prickled and he felt slightly sick. It was really an ugly sight, a decayed bit of vegetation. But that wasn't it. Not at all.

He struggled with his recollections, seeking and avoiding, casting a line into the past and resisting the catch, until at last it came up.

He and Tom had been touring mainland Spain. They'd finally reached Murcia, which was Encarnación's birthplace. Tom was determined to find some souvenir to take back to her on Mallorca.

He'd spotted it while Frady was contemplating the facade of the cathedral, stirred by the sight of moonlight on old stone. He had looked around, about to repeat Goethe's phrase about baroque architecture being frozen music, but there was no Tom. He saw only two *guardias civiles,* their patent leather helmets reflecting the moonlight.

And then, unexpectedly, the *guardias* were running and shouting. Frady knew they were running after Tom.

"Frady! Over here!" He looked to his left. Tom, grinning mischievously, was behind a fence. Frady could see rows and rows of plants—small tea roses.

"Here!" Tom cupped a rosebush by its thorn-free bottom, yanked and tossed it to Frady over the fence. Then he ran off. The *guardias* chased after him.

Frady waited until they were on the other side of the plaza, then picked up the stolen rosebush. He hid it behind his back until he found some newspapers. Then he rolled it up.

By the time he got back to their hotel room he was furious. He had actually abetted Tom in the theft, helped him get a thrill from some petty and illegal escapade. The rosebush, now sitting on the dresser of the hotel room, was the evidence. The only hitch was, Franco's police weren't like the cops back home. For all he knew, they'd both get into serious trouble.

He was about to take the incriminating rosebush downstairs and dump it when the door opened. He wheeled around guiltily. It was Tom. His face was alight with glee. He was, Frady could see, vastly pleased with himself. Once the *guardias* had found out he was American they had given him a lecture about respecting the customs of the country. Then they had released him. They had actually driven him back to the hotel in one of their cars.

Frady found himself listening to all this with profound irritation. At last he said, "What the hell did you take it for?"

Tom's eyes widened. "For Encarnación! Who do you think?"

"For Encarnación!"

And then, as he watched Tom on the other bed, his face catlike with pleasure, Frady had started to laugh. At the stupidity, the childishness, the silliness of it. Of course Tom would do something like this. It was just his style—making waves, stirring things up, skirting disaster.

"If there's no trouble involved, the gift isn't worth anything. Whaddya think, I was gonna go in a souvenir shop and buy her a *bota*?"

Tom was on his feet now, inspecting the rosebush. He took it in the bathroom and dropped it into the bidet, which he filled with water. As Frady watched, it occurred to him that this little adventure was part of an old promise too—just as the nightingale had been. In his anger, his fear, his relief, he was as intensely alive as he would ever be.

Encarnación was still holding out the magazine with its hideous relic, still beaming. She didn't know anything about the theft, the *guardias,* the scene in the hotel room. For her it only mattered that the rosebush came from Murcia, her beloved Murcia. She had treasured the plant, and this, probably its last offspring, for twenty years.

And then Frady saw quite clearly that Tom had touched Encarnación's life with fire too. It had blazed up as brightly, as briefly, as his own. Tom had been an addiction for her too.

"Llévela consigo." It was Encarnación. She wanted him to take the rose. To carry it off with him. He looked up. Her hand, outstretched, was fretted with tiny lines. Her face was beatific with love. And then, taking the rose, he understood what she had in mind. She wanted him to find Tom and return the rose.

"No!" he started to shout, feeling angry and betrayed at the same time, but suddenly it wasn't necessary. The movement of his hand had decapitated the rose. Its petals, hematic brown flakes, drifted to the floor. In his hand remained a bit of dry stalk. He heard her sharp intake of breath, then he dropped the stalk. It floated to a spot among the petals.

"That's the end of the rose of Murcia," he said quite loudly in English. Then he put out his hand. She was observing him with large black eyes. He knew she had heard something in his voice, but whether it was the snapping of a chain or merely the harshness of his native tongue he did not know. At last she took his outstretched hand in both of hers. She was waiting for something more—an embrace perhaps—but he didn't make a move. It was the smell of olive oil that repelled him, but it was something else too. He turned, heading for the door. What else? As he opened the door a little breeze darted in and stirred up the brown flakes on the floor. With a good-bye nod he stepped out, closing the door behind him.

He set off toward the town plaza and the bus stop. Less than two hours had passed since he'd arrived; he might still catch the early afternoon bus back to Palma. What was it? he asked himself again, recalling a painting of the Roman soldier at Pompeii who had remained at his post even though Vesuvius had erupted and buried him in lava for twenty centuries.

It came to him as he boarded the bus and settled himself in a rear seat. She reeked of steadfastness. And then, as the bus started, it came to him that he had reached the very heart of his trouble. Faithfulness, a secular version of the love of God, had crippled him. Virtue had been transformed into vice. He had turned into that monster, the keeper of the flame. He shivered, though the bus was quite warm, and the absurd notion came to him that he would wither like the rose of Murcia unless he could forget everything that had ever happened to him in this village.

Alex was out of sorts, but Frady had expected it. He knew it from the curt greeting on his arrival in their hotel room and a reluctance to look up from the book Alex held in his hand. It was the history of Mallorca. He'd gotten as far as the Inquisition.

After a few inquiries about the presents Alex had bought for his children—gifts now piled on the dresser—Frady went into the bathroom to shower. He wondered how much to tell Alex about the day, searching for the words that would make it clear.

They went to an early dinner, at a place in the old part of town. The restaurant, under an arcade, specialized in soufflés. It was called El Siglo. Frady had often come here with Tom—it had been their special place—but that information didn't seem worth imparting tonight. Instead, he watched Alex carefully, noting his familiar habits—how he took out half-moon glasses to read the menu, how he tapped his cigarette exactly four times before putting it in his mouth, how he broke his bread neatly in half, then in quarters, before buttering it. Alex chewed very slowly; he was a deliberate eater. Once it had taken him an hour to eat an artichoke.

And then Frady saw, with devastating clarity, what the rest of his life with Alex would be like. It would consist of slow meals and quiet nights and sex once a week. There would be no fear, no anger, but a great deal of sweetness and companionship and comfort. It would be rather like life in a nursing home.

Alex hadn't spoken much through the meal. He had, of course, sensed Frady's tension, his preoccupation. In his usual mild way he was waiting. Once or twice he searched Frady's face—causing Frady a twinge of remorse. It was really up to him to explain his day. It affected them both. But he wasn't ready for that—not yet.

After dinner they walked slowly down the Borne, toward the waterfront, absorbing the soft air, the sight and sound of the other strollers, the plink of a guitar coming from a café. It was their custom to walk their dinner down. Once or twice Alex put his hand to the small of Frady's back. It was a motion that had always struck him as sweetly tender—Alex wanting to shelter him or propel him, or merely touch him. But tonight, in his unsettled state, Alex's touch struck him as the dead hand of the future. He could read the rest of his life in that slight pressure.

And then, quite unexpectedly, he knew what he had to do. It came to him in a blaze of color—the color, in fact, of one of the roses planted in the center of the promenade on which they were now strolling. He felt quite dizzy as the plan took possession of him and for a moment he thought he couldn't do it. It was too difficult, too out of character. But the next moment he knew he had no choice. If his life was going to blaze again, if it was going to be filled with the sound of nightingales, it was up to him to arrange it. There was no one else around to do the job.

Without looking left or right he stepped into the planted area and yanked up a purple rosebush by its roots. When he straightened up, he and Alex were the center of a small circle of people.

"What are you doing?" It was Alex, whispering.

Brushing at the dirt, he held out the rosebush. "It's a souvenir." Alex put his hands behind his back and stepped away. He looked mortified.

Frady started to laugh. In the next instant he was aware of a refreshing and lustful joy rising in his veins.

"Put that back," Alex hissed, coming forward. But Frady continued laughing. He knew exactly how Alex felt.

And then, as the circle of onlookers parted, a municipal officer dressed in blue stepped toward him. Frady turned, the pilfered rose held proudly, triumphantly aloft. It was not, he thought in a final moment of clarity, the rose of Murcia—that one was dissolved forever. This one was for today, and tomorrow.

A last burst of laughter escaped him. "Arrest me," he said to the guard, "I'm a thief."

The Beach

LUCAS DEDRICK

I don't know about Arlin, but what I really look forward to the most is the leaving, the slipping away in the dark, before the warm, sugary, breakfast smells invade the halls, before that first vial of painkiller is cracked open.

This time they would have said no, absolutely not, so I didn't even ask. I'm just taking Arlin to the beach for the day, and for this they'll cross me off his visitors list. It's over anyway, and what did we have but a short love affair? I can't think of more than occasional moments, usually sexual. A sort of animal warmth that's now only a memory. I suspect he won't even know I'm not there anymore. He's too far gone.

I start the car and then twist around in the seat to make sure he's okay. Arlin is groggy, near death, and he's shrunken enough to lie across the back seat without bending his knees. He's swathed, diapered, catheterized, medicated, fed. I hope that he's reasonably comfortable. I ask him, and I think he nods a little.

Beside me on the front seat is a box of Kleenex and a Coleman ice chest filled with liquids: water, broth, medicine, and juice of tomato, apple, carrot, orange.

Something I wouldn't ordinarily do is stop at all the red lights if there was no one else around, but if the police find Arlin the jig is up. He would go back to his room at the hospice, and I'd be asked to stay away, and the whole thing would seem so embarrassing. If we make it to the beach and back I may never see him again, but our journey will not have been in vain.

There's morning construction on the highway, and we're behind a Greyhound bus. I can't see around it. It seems to crawl along, forever slowing down and picking up speed. Suddenly a police car pulls out, siren screaming, it forces its way into the oncoming traffic. As it races by I thank God it has nothing to do with us.

"Arlin," I speak in a low voice, "We're off to the beach, you and I. I promised you one more time, didn't I?" His breathing is even though raspy, and he doesn't offer a signal that he hears what I've said. Ahead I study the enormous, lighted billboards which hawk a savings and loan, relief from sunburn, a purer vodka.

At a gas station a group of gypsy children—eight in all—watch me pull in. One of them, the youngest by the looks of him, comes over while I fill the tank.

"Mister," he says, "could you give us a lift to the beach?" And then five of the others have surrounded the car. None of them are wearing shoes, and their dark skin and hair look soft and dusty.

"I don't have room. There's a man asleep in the back seat."

They surround the car and press their faces against the glass.

"We could fit if he sat up," says the youngest. "We don't mind sitting on each others' laps."

"No, I'm sorry. He can't sit up. He's very ill."

One of the others nods at this. I look with the others at Arlin through the car window. It's as if I'm seeing him for the first time. His eyes and mouth are gummy, sealed tight. His body is sore-infested. His hair is thin and limp against his scalp, but his bones jut out, away from him. He's shuddering.

"I think he's cold," one of the girls says as she cranes her neck into the driver's window. Again they all press against the glass. "Yeah, he's cold," someone else confirms. But already it's roasting outside, and the morning light is still dull.

"I'll take care of him. I have to go now." I pull the door open with the young girl hanging on.

As I drive away I watch in the rear-view mirror as more dust rises above the children and settles on their soft skin. Had I been driving a van or a station wagon I wonder if I would have let the gypsies ride along. Maybe if Arlin were well, maybe if Arlin could sit up. Yes, I think I would have then.

The small of my back aches, and my shirt and shorts are soaked with sweat, but we finally make it to the beach around ten. "Arlin, can you smell the sea?"

I stab an umbrella deep into the sand and unfold a king-size blanket before I help him from the car. The ice chest is heavier than Arlin. Not far away a volleyball game is being played. I stare for a while at the men's gilded bodies; postured muscles polished by a dazzling light. Many stare back, not at me, but at the shrouded figure sleeping beside me.

"Arlin, why don't you try to wake up?" It's a gentle command, but one that seems to take. Suddenly both of Arlin's legs kick out and some sand flies. His expression darkens and he pushes his lips out until his mouth is a small black O. Under the giant umbrella I pour as much liquid into Arlin as he'll drink. He mumbles and gurgles, and though the sounds are of a baby he reminds me more of someone very old. In reality Arlin is thirty. Each time he swallows harder, and his eyes brighten and then smolder like dying planets. When he's had enough, he falls asleep more gently than he had awakened.

The late morning seems windless, but in the distance on the water the electric-yellow sail of a windsurfer is kept in motion. I strip down to my trunks and partially unravel Arlin from his robe and white sheets. My arm is across his chest, and for a while my eyes are closed until I hear someone clear their throat. An old woman squats next to Arlin with her hand on his forehead. "He's dyin'," she says. "Fever like that in a grown man is bad business. My husband's got up to a hundred and four once, made him sterile." She stands up and grinds an aluminum can into the sand with her booted foot, and then drops it into a large plastic bag already half full. Suddenly a dog barks and is upon us. He takes one of my shoes and is gone before I can rescue it.

"Whose dog is that?" and it's Arlin who asks. Somehow he's pushed himself up on his elbows. His eyes are wide, shining with a false, drugged pleasure. We both watch the dog plunge into a short wave near the shore, and then my shoe is gone.

"I thought they couldn't fit," he says, but this I don't understand.

"What, Arlin?" I ask. "You mean my shoes?"

"All those kids, I thought they couldn't fit." And suddenly I laugh because the dark, dusty gypsies have made it to the beach and have gathered around us.

"They must have gotten a ride from someone else," I say.

"What are those spots on him?" And it's the girl who swung on the car door. "What's in here?" She opens the ice chest and pulls out a plastic bottle of carrot juice.

I feel elated, not so much that they're here but to find that Arlin recognizes them. "I'm glad you made it," I say to them.

One of the small boys, streaked with the dust and sweat, lowers our umbrella, and then it's up and down and up again. "We rode in the back of a moving van, with furniture and stuff," he says. "Look!" and they open their hands for us to see. In each are the delicate, silver knobs from an antique chest of drawers.

"You have to leave us alone now, go on and play." But as they chase after the dog I notice Arlin has grown quiet again. "Arlin, I told you we'd make it to the beach again." I try to sound calm, but I'm desperate to keep the stunted conversation alive. Arlin covers his eyes with a corner of the blanket and fades away.

In the early afternoon when the sand is sizzling, and hordes of people begin to arrive, I tell Arlin it's time to leave. I wish for a rebuttal from him, a pleading to stay, to make this day at the beach last forever. But he only breathes quietly. In the heat he's as limp as a dead plant. As I lift Arlin, heads rise from the sand and turn toward us. For a brief moment the volleyball players are a group of statued gods. They watch as I carry him to the car with my shoeless foot stepping quick in the hot sand.

"Serve!" someone yells, and they're jolted back to their game, thrilled and disturbed at the same time.

During the drive back it's warmer than this morning, and the harsh, dry air burns my red face. Occasionally I reach my arm back and touch him. Arlin is alive but lifeless. He's asleep, but it's more coma-like. My wish for him now is time filled with dreams.

I stop at the same gas station from this morning and buy a pair of thin rubber thongs. A radio talks to a dozing old man behind the counter. He silently hands me my change and, with heavy-lidded eyes, stares through the screen door at nothing in particular. The place is still clouded in dust, but the gypsies are gone. I smile and imagine them back at the beach, in the sunny spray of the ocean chasing the dog with a shoe in its mouth.

At dusk at the hospice there are no police cars, there are no ambulances. No one is waving frantically outside the front gate. Everything is exactly as it was when we left. The blue light from a television seeps through the curtains of the waiting room window. Dinner was just served, and in the entryway I can smell cooked meat and medicine. In the kitchen I can hear the garbage disposal fighting with a citrus rind or some gristle, or maybe something tougher, like a bone.

"They knew it was you," says the calm night nurse as she lays down her book. Her name is Wanda. She walks ahead of us down the hall and opens the door to Arlin's room. The walls are flower-papered and before there was AIDS only nuns had ever died here.

"They're upstairs waiting. God, I think the monsignor's even up there." She pulls back the covers on the bed. "They didn't call his family, but you're in loads of trouble. You better go on up, get it over with. I'll clean him up and tuck him in."

When I kiss Arlin good-bye he stirs slightly, and sand sprinkles on the sheets like sugar.

Alida

WES MUCHMORE

I drove for miles between endless plains on the east and the foothills which modestly bordered the sudden, immense uprising of the Rocky Mountains on the west. At last the highway carried me into Alida, Colorado, the town I'd felt obliged to leave twenty years before.

The center of Alida was still two blocks long and looked about the same, except strangely renewed: the false-front wooden buildings were all painted and restored. One familiar sight after another came into view, and I felt more and more foolish and wished I'd stayed home in Denver.

Beyond the center of town I found the same straggle of dusty, unpainted houses and cluttered yards that had been there in my childhood. Fields began on both sides of the highway, and I resumed speed, heading north.

Some minutes later I passed the entrance to Larimer Mountain Park. I'd read that its roads had been improved, but I was surprised at the extent of the changes. The parking lot was no longer a patch of gravel but a huge acreage of blacktop. And the little buildings scattered among the trees had been replaced by a single large stone structure. Nobody was making big money, even decent money, off the farms and ranches in the area, I knew that. Larimer Mountain Park had to be the reason for Alida's faintly threatening vitality.

A quarter of an hour beyond the park entrance, at a break in miles of fence, I slowed and turned right, then steered carefully down a weedy, rain-ribbed gravel track. In a few minutes the farm where I was born and raised came into view. I pulled up at the gate.

All was as I remembered—house, barn, outbuildings—but far more weathered now, and the windows were boarded over. I wasn't surprised. The farm had been a marginal operation, too much of a drain on human energy. First I left, and a little later my sister Linda married and moved to California. From her I'd learned that my father had continued to work the place, with part-time help, until his health gave out. Then he went to live near her and my brother-in-law in Los Angeles. I thought it likely that nobody else had taken over the property, that it had been some local broker's hopeless case for all these years.

I headed back to town. At the outskirts I turned off the highway and circled around the John C. Fremont Consolidated High School. The homely buildings of poured concrete and the quarter-mile athletic field looked perfectly the same, as if the high Cyclone fence enclosing them could keep out the passing years.

Returning to the center of Alida, I parked, and as I got out of the car, apprehension rose inside me: what if someone recognized me? This sudden shot of fear I fought down with a barrage of facts: I'd left here at age eighteen, a thin farm boy in jeans and faded Levi jacket. Now I was almost forty, a little taller, heavier and more muscular, much better dressed, bearded and wearing glasses. And who would remember, or care?

The late summer afternoon was pleasantly warm as I strolled, tourist-like, along the uncrowded sidewalk. I turned in at Braddock's Hardware, now Braddock & Son, according to the big, new, gilt-and-black, Victorian Gothic sign over the door. Inside, all looked about the same. And surely that was Tom Braddock, once a schoolmate of mine and now looking very like his bald, handsome father, behind the counter. I wandered about the aisles, finally picked up a rectangle of thumbtacks, and took it to the scarred wooden counter. As Tom rang up the sale, I looked directly at him. He gave no sign of recognition or even curiosity.

Checking out every passerby as I went, I crossed the street and headed toward the drug store. Several people looked familiar, but I couldn't bring up a name to go with the face. Nobody looked at me twice. It was obvious that the presence of a stranger in Alida had long since stopped being a novelty. I was just another tourist looking at the old buildings. Still, safe as I now felt, my journey to the Rexall was more of a forced march than a nostalgic stroll.

There the bench was, still by the door, and a timetable was taped in the window. Yes, the drugstore continued to serve as Alida's bus depot. Duty done, I turned away and walked back to the car.

Now the late afternoon had taken on a well-remembered bluish cast, caused by the mountain peaks cutting off direct sunlight long before sunset. In this strange but familiar light I drove to the motel just north of town, where I'd made a reservation.

As I showered in the standard plastic stall, I wondered if this visit, which until recently I thought I'd never make, could possibly turn out to be anything but a useless, painful waste of time. But after six months of severe insomnia, anything that might help had to be tried. Even a return to Alida.

For some time now, after a long day's work in downtown Denver and a quiet, pleasant evening with my lover, Judd, I would go to bed and slowly be overcome not by drowsiness but by anger. At first, Judd took this personally, but I made it clear that my rages had nothing to do with him, which forced me to try and figure out just what they did have to do with. Their source seemed to be in obsessive thoughts of the past, old memories that insisted on circulating through my mind no matter how much useless pain and hate they fired up in me.

I tried everything I could, but the rages persisted, and a good night's sleep was beginning to be a fond memory.

As best I could, I picked through the facts of my situation and came up with this picture: back when all the ugliness happened, anger was a luxury I couldn't afford, for one thing, and crowded out by pain, for another. Then, as a young man, alone, naive, and poor in a strange city, I completely preoccupied myself with putting together a new life. The following many years of getting an education and then working hard served to suppress thoughts of the past, the world I had run from, my father. Recently, though, with the latest promotion, my job became more fancy gesturing than real labor. Suddenly and for the first time, my life was easy, and I guess all the held-in anger had the opportunity to come forth at last.

It helped that I was able to talk it all out with Judd. His main worry was that I had begun drinking too much at night and using too many sleeping pills. He gently suggested that a dab of psychotherapy might be a good idea "to kill all those dragons." I agreed, reluctantly, and that's when the notion struck me: I would go back to Alida, face the scene of my unrelenting memories, and then I would . . . what? I wasn't sure. But an overnight pilgrimage, invasion, exorcism, whatever it might prove to be, would cost a lot less than a shrink in both money and time. And I could preserve my sense of personal, hard-won independence. Which had a lot of importance to me.

Now, though, as I stood drying myself, the idea again seemed foolish, an evasion. So far, the visit had merely brought up familiar bad memories mixed with a lot of harmless nostalgia. Alida, Colorado existed, safe, on one side of plate glass and I on the other.

I lay on the bed for a long while, trying to nap. As the room turned dark, I gave up, dressed, and decided that this visit would *not* be a mere evasion, even if it turned out to be a mistake. I looked through the thin local telephone directory. The guy who had caused me all the trouble still lived in Alida, or very near, out on the hill road. I thought of calling him up, saying something like, "It's John Swanson, the guy whose life you wrecked twenty years ago," then cursing him out until he hung up. Or, I might go out to his place and beat him up in his front yard. And get myself arrested? Obviously stupid ideas, childish stuff, no help at all. And how silly it had been for me to look for him this afternoon as I strolled around Alida.

It seemed clear to me that the best thing was to have some dinner and drive back to Denver. At the motel office I asked the elderly manager for a good place to eat.

"You want the Steakery at Larimer Lanes," he said.

"Okay. And where's the action?" I knew that in a small town like this there's usually only one place to go on Saturday night.

"Try the bar at the Larimer Lanes."

Curious, I said, "A friend suggested I try the Pioneer Hotel."

"Not for years, now, and it's closed for restoration."

"Everything's at the Larimer Lanes?" I asked.

"Pretty much. Otherwise you've got a coupla joints in town for ranch hands and a three-two bar that gets the kids. Kinda rough places, though, and not many women. Can't miss the Lanes, right at the south end of town."

I remembered passing the cinderblock building, new and enormous, way out of scale with the rest of Alida. Now, at night and all lit up, it looked studiedly cheery. I parked my car in a lot full of RVs, pickups, and El Caminos.

The Steakery was imitation walnut paneling, fake French provincial furnishings, and wagon wheel chandeliers. From somewhere not far off came, faintly, the roar of bowling. The young woman who showed me to a table also served as my waitress.

"Not very crowded for Saturday night, is it?" I asked.

"Well, we're between times, after Labor Day and too early for the skiing crowd to be coming through."

After dinner I went through an arch into the round-up Lounge, a large, crowded space of slow curves, indirect lighting, and padded fake leather. Three men were making drinks behind the long, fully occupied bar, and two conventionally underdressed cocktail waitresses moved among the tables and booths.

I moved slowly, casually around the room. It was full of young couples, groups of older married folks, a lot of single men, and a fair number of unattached females. The motel guy was right: this *was* the place to be in Alida on Saturday night. And if the man I wanted to find was anywhere but home, he'd most likely be here. Denver could wait a little longer. I checked out every male face I could see as I sauntered about the room, surveying the crowd with what I thought must be a detective's discreet thoroughness. Automatically, out of habit, I also looked for gay people. I found none, not even one or two suspicious types. Well, this was an uptight town. Who knew that better than I?

Near the piano bar I came to a halt, and one of the waitresses took my order. All around me, people in their thirties were drinking and listening to the songs and trying to look worldly. The singer-pianist, thin and deftly handsome, had the surgery-inspired look of being twenty-eight and forty-five at the same time. Our eyes met for a moment and I knew I wasn't alone.

After a while I began to think that my nemesis must be elsewhere, maybe sprawled on the couch at home, watching television. I finished my drink, took a last look around the bar, and went down a long hall to the bowling alley. The man I wanted to find had been an athlete, after all.

Many of the bowlers were about my age, but nobody had the right face. I returned to the Round-up Room and came to rest on a stool at one end of the bar, where it curved into a rough-textured wall of sparkling beige plaster. About half the room was visible, as well as the main entrance, the passageway to the restrooms and bowling alley, and most of the other drinkers seated at the bar. Though I examined every face I could see, when I ordered another drink I knew it would be my last. Whatever I sought in Alida, I also wanted to get out of here, desired to get back to my good life in Denver.

The bartender came toward me with my change, and ten thousand alarm bells went off in my head. Yes, I was sure, that was Bill Eckers, the man I was looking for. Beneath my fast-building excitement I felt a mocking little poke of irony: I'd been so busy searching the place for Eckers that he'd served me a drink without my seeing who he was.

I sipped at my vodka and tonic and watched Bill as he worked. His looks, once sharp-cut and giving him a wicked air, were still fairly good, though his face had filled out and made his eyes look squinty. The curly, brown-blond head of hair had become a fuzzy clamp around a gleaming, freckled skull. The compact muscles of his high school quarterback body had given way to beefiness, especially around his shoulders and chest. His red vest, white shirt, and black slacks served to emphasize his well-developed pot belly.

I'm not overweight. I've worked out regularly for years, and by genetic good luck I still have most of my hair. So I thought I could just sit there and gloat away my rage while I nursed a drink or two.

But the ugly memories slammed into my mind and took over and, just as at bedtime, they would not stop. They focused insanely on that sad summer after graduation from high school, when it had become clear that I could not go to college as planned. Despite my part-time jobs and my father's budgeting, there was no chance I could attend the University of Colorado for at least another year, maybe longer if my father's health didn't improve.

Deep inside me I had a secret reason for regret: here in Alida it was extremely difficult for me to have a sex life. Surely it would be easier in Boulder.

I managed to have my first experience by age sixteen. On a Saturday night I'd loitered about after the movie until a truck driver helped me overcome my nervous indecision. As he directed, I drove us in my father's pickup out to the dark entrance of Larimer Park. The few small structures, half-hidden among the trees, were connected by narrow paths. The trucker led me along one of the trails well into the forest.

Afterwards, as I drove him back into town, the man explained how the park entry area was a place to meet guys, late at night, long after the rangers had gone.

My guilt was slight and didn't last long. Sex was never discussed at home, so I had little information and no rigid ideas about it. The drift of certain jokes I heard at school made it clear that most people disapproved of sex between men. But for me, the act validated itself: anything that felt so good and so right had to be okay. Even if it had to be kept a dark secret. After all, I didn't want to be called a queer, and everyone I encountered at the park tried to be as anonymous as possible, which was fairly easy in the heavily shadowed night under the trees.

Only Mr. Braddock, owner of the hardware store and with a son in my grade in school, was at all open with me. We found each other at the park often, sometimes arranging to meet there, but we rarely did much talking.

The park, after a while, impressed me as better than nothing, but I lived for the day I got to Boulder and the university. Then, surely, there would be more than just hurried, anonymous sex. I'd find like minds, companionship, love.

One Saturday night, late in that summer, I walked quietly along the Nature Path in Larimer Park, acutely alert for scratchy little signal noises. Just ahead in the darkness I sensed movement. A few more steps and I saw, for a brief moment, the bare grey mound of a shoulder clad in a light-toned jacket.

"Get 'im!"

I turned and ran, charging straight into a fist. Assuming I was surrounded, I swung and kicked in every direction as sudden blasts of pain shot out of the dark. I could not tell if three men or a dozen were beating me up.

With a bloom of bright red color everything stopped.

When I woke up, dew-damp and shivering, I found Mr. Braddock's face just above mine. He asked if I wanted to go to the hospital, by which he meant the little clinic in the county seat, two towns down the highway.

Taking even a slightly deep breath gave me a lot of pain, and I ached everywhere. But I was able to get to my feet, which was a great relief. "No, thank you," I said. The clinic was out of the question, of course. Nobody could know about this. I *had* to be all right.

Mr. Braddock walked me to my father's pickup. He asked again if I was okay, and I said yes. He helped me up into the cab and disappeared into the darkness. Before I started up I felt my face. It was fattened out on one side, tender under the eyes and around my nose. Both lips were split, but my teeth all seemed to be firm in their places.

On the drive home a voice came back and back, pitched at a jeering yell. It was the unmistakable bray of Bill Eckers: "Get 'im! Get 'im! Get 'im!"

I began to feel sick as I drove, and as I got near the farmhouse my sense of balance began to come and go. I became so dizzy that it was all I could do to get out of the pickup and open the heavy, wide, metal gate. As I turned back toward the Ford, I seemed to suddenly begin floating, as if weightless. From some great distance I heard a sob.

My father, as I learned later, found me a little before dawn and drove me to the clinic in Wells.

"Just a fight with somebody," I mumbled. My father and the deputy sheriff finally stopped asking questions when I held to that story.

Three days later my father drove me back to the farmhouse in dead silence. He wasn't a talkative man, but I felt he was grimmer than usual and suspected he was irked by the avoidable expense of my stay at the clinic.

Once inside the house he began shouting, and that's when I realized that while I had been lying in bed two bits of gossip met and fused in Alida: Bill Eckers, it was said, was boasting that he and some friends had punched out a queer at Larimer Park. They couldn't tell who it was in the darkness, but he had come on to them, so they beat him up. And John Swanson, that nice, quiet young man, was in the clinic down in Wells, severely injured from some kind of fight.

My father had little difficulty getting the truth out of me. When I look back, the most surprising thing in the whole hideous scene is that in some way I expected my father to understand. My virginity lay several years in the past, yes, but my innocence was still almost complete. That afternoon my father came as close to insanity as I've ever seen anyone come. I escaped a beating only because I was recovering from one.

Finally my father couldn't shout any more, could only glare and cough and stride around the room. In a sudden motion he headed for the front door and said I was no longer his son.

I stood there. I heard the pickup motor turn over, and I was sure he was going to go somewhere and get drunk, which he did only rarely. The last time had been after my mother's funeral, two years before.

During all the uproar, my sister Linda had stood in the kitchen doorway, terrified for me. Now she helped me upstairs to my room. I went straight to the closet and jerked a suitcase out of it. "Shouldn't you wait until you're better?" she asked.

"Nope. He doesn't want me here, and I want out."

Linda helped me pack. "I'm leaving too," she said. "The first decent man who asks me, I'm saying yes, even if it's some dumb cowboy. Daddy has been just awful since Mother died."

She drove me in our sickly, old Chevy to the drugstore that was Alida's bus station. When we had made the turn from the track onto the highway, Linda asked me if I wanted to get the bus in another town. I did, but I said no. I wasn't about to sneak around in front of her.

Still, my bravery was not perfect: I told Linda she didn't have to wait with me for the bus. I didn't want her to be present if somebody on the street yelled something at me. She took the hint, pressed some bills into my shirt pocket, and drove away.

I set my suitcase on the empty bench and stood there, ribs aching, bandage over my nose, feeling murderously defiant and at the same time desperately self-conscious.

As the bus carried me out of town I saw Mr. Braddock, standing as usual in the doorway of his hardware store. I waved to him. He started, recognizing me, then waved back.

Now, again in Alida, I found that Eckers' voice still sounded the same, grainy edge and all and, in his movements behind the bar, I could see occasional reminders of the lithe assurance of his high school days.

I had another drink. So did Bill Eckers, slipping a shot of bourbon into a cup of coffee.

Isn't it enough, I asked myself, to see Eckers like this, humbled by life, just another guy?

No, it wasn't enough. This was the man who was robbing me of my sleep, who had driven me from this town, and who, worst of all, somehow, caused me to end up so hungry once in Denver that I'd eaten rolls taken from the garbage can of a restaurant.

I decided to provoke a fight. The odds had changed over the years, I was sure; this time it would be one-to-one, in addition. Even if I lost, which was doubtful, giving out a few good chops would surely go far to help me reclaim my peace of mind.

A few drinkers remained along the bar counter, but the other bartenders had left. Over at the piano the entertainer sang a slightly risqué Cole Porter number, ending his last set.

Bill Eckers spiked another cup of coffee, openly this time, drank it all in one gulp, and came my way, polishing the bar top with a rag. "So, what's happening?" he asked, smiling pleasantly. "Salesman?"

"On vacation. Going back to Denver."

"Denver. Like that town a lot. Hardly ever get down there anymore, though. Nothing like a family to slow a guy down."

"Yeah," I said, "keeps you busy." Married. Of course. Who did he marry?

"Damn right, 'specially with three kids. This is my second job. Big crowd Fridays and Saturdays, Sunday afternoons." Eckers finished cleaning the counter and came to rest, leaning against the back bar in a set-for-action stance I remembered from high school. "Work in a body shop during the week. Like bartending better, great way to meet people. What's your line?"

"Real estate," I lied.

We talked a little more, the usual nothings, and Eckers moved off, went to wash cocktail glasses and mix final drink orders for the one remaining cocktail waitress.

My anger, under compression, powered a pure, cold premeditation. Words strung themselves together in my mind, making phrases that would surprise him at first, then bring him out to the parking lot with me.

Eckers came back my way. He was still smiling. "Last call."

Interrupted just as I'd opened my mouth, I nodded for another drink. It might come in handy. If he chose to ignore my words, I could douse him with the vodka-tonic.

He set the cocktail in front of me and pushed back my money. "This one's on the house."

I inclined my head in thanks, unwilling to speak them. And I didn't want to see any more of that big, dumb smile of his.

"Say, what's the hot spots now in Denver?" Eckers asked.

"Oh, no place in particular."

"Used to get down there a lot. Really liked goin' to the Rigoletto and Don's Ship Ahoy."

I had been to the Rigoletto exactly once; it was a gay bar in the seedier part of downtown. And Don's Ship Ahoy, a beer joint nearby, was supposed to have been a hustler hangout. It had been urban renewed out of existence four or five years before.

Bill Eckers?

His smile, his conversation, his pose against the back bar, the free drink . . .

He was looking me straight in the eye as he talked, and now his smile was a whole lot warmer than a professional grin. "Ever heard of those places?" he asked from just across the counter, breath heavy with bourbon.

Unable to quite believe what I was hearing, suddenly wary, I asked Bill a question in return: "No bars like that around here?"

"Nah, not till you get to Boulder, and that's mostly college kids."

"Oh . . . Well, what does a guy do for fun on a hot night?"

"Here? Nothin'. Used to be some action up at the park entrance, but that was years ago, before they changed it all around, put in the new building and all those lights."

"I see." Yes, I saw, and I was planning fast. "I'm not really sleepy," I said, "but I guess it's closing time, so I better head back to the motel. . . ." I finished off the drink and got to my feet.

"You, uh, gonna be up a while?" Eckers asked.

"Yeah."

"Well, hey, if you could stand some company . . ."

You fool, I thought. I looked him up and down. "Sure. That'd be real nice."

Eckers leaned over the bar counter toward me. "Listen, I can't get out of here for twenty minutes or so after closing, but I'll show up soon as I can and bring a bottle. Which motel?"

I told him, including the room number, and as I drove through town I worked out a vengeance that would be simple, satisfying, and not likely to cause me any legal problems.

In a short time I had my car parked right outside the door. I put a plastic bucket of ice in the bathroom sink. In the medicine cabinet was a glass of water in which two crushed sleeping tablets were dissolving. My inside coat pocket held the pad of thumbtacks and a sheet of motel stationery, its letterhead neatly removed. On the piece of paper I had printed, in the biggest, darkest letters my pen would make, the word QUEER.

Calmly I waited for Bill Eckers to arrive.

Around a quarter to three there was a soft knock on the door. I let Bill inside. He had changed clothes. Now he wore a pair of designer jeans, a fringed leather jacket, and a loud cowboy shirt. Exactly the wrong clothes for a man with a pot belly and a full behind.

"Name's Bill," he said in a half-whisper and handed me a bottle of expensive bourbon.

"Jack," I lied. "Have a seat."

He lowered himself onto the double bed, and I took the whiskey into the bathroom. I made my drink with mostly water and his with mostly bourbon, plus the liquefied sleeping pills.

When I came out I found Eckers sitting in the same place on the bed, but now he was naked. The whip-smooth, tight-muscled body I remembered so clearly existed now only in my mind. Eckers was fattier and beefier than I'd suspected.

"Not rushin' things," he said. "I always like to talk when I can, with a guy, an' I noticed in the bar, you really listen. I figure it's not often I get to relax like this, in good company."

Sitting around undressed as daring, exotic? I smiled agreeably and handed Eckers his drink. I sat down on the bed, not too close to him.

He took a big swallow and said, "Yer lucky, livin' in Denver and all. Jeez, up here all I worry about is bein' seen."

"Yeah, I guess in a small town like this, if anybody found out —"

"Whee-*yuu*! Truth is, I shoulda joined the Navy and seen the world like I planned. But I stuck around after high school, thinkin' I could get into pro ball. See, I was quarterback the year Fremont won the finals. But I was too light for the pros. Bad knee, too. Then I went and married this chick. Helluva looker, head cheerleader, great little dancer."

Head cheerleader? Donna Smith. With the pick of so many girls he married *her*? When will the pills work?

"She said I knocked her up. Had my doubts, but all that fuss made me out such a stud, so I married Donna and didn't join the Navy."

Donna Smith, the girl that almost every boy in the senior class had had.

"Well, 's not so bad, just the oldest kid keeps getting into the damndest kinds of trouble. The other two raise a little hell now and then, but that oldest one keeps needing lawyers."

I love it, I thought, lousy of me but I love it all.

"Well, hey, here I am spoutin' off. What you get for bein' so easy to talk to. Whyncha take off yer duds too? I feel kinda naked all alone like this, heh heh . . ."

His words slid all over the place, his eyelids were heavy; he'd be out very soon, I was sure. Setting my hardly tasted drink aside, I stood up and undressed.

When I was done Eckers said, "Hey, real nice. You mus' work out . . . jus' what I like." He lifted himself to his feet and came toward me with quite a gleam in his half-closed eyes. "'S funny," he mumbled as he put his hands on my upper arms. "So simple what I want, you know? But ya jus' go through hell to get it in this town. . . ."

Eckers slobbered his mouth along my chest and abdomen as he lowered himself. He thumped to his knees. His shiny head banged against my thighs as he flopped to the rug.

All that remained now was to drive Eckers into downtown Alida, dump him naked on the bus stop bench, thumbtack the QUEER sign above him, and return to Denver. I regretted that I could not be present to see the effect this tableau would make on the townsfolk in the morning. But one can't have everything, and if I got my ability to sleep back, that would be plenty.

I dressed, set the room door slightly ajar, then nudged Bill Eckers with my toe. He made no movement or sound. His mouth hung gaping, still.

He proved too heavy for me to carry in my arms, so I gripped him under his shoulders in a firm bear hug and raised the body to nearly its full height. Hugging his spine to my chest, I started to move backwards toward the door. Half way across the room I stopped, shocked at the half-lit reflection in the large rectangle of dresser mirror. I saw a fat, ugly, limp body under my head. This illusion, so startling, was too imperfect to last longer than an instant. Still, it had its effect: I lugged the dead weight back to the bed, let it fall from my aching arms, and folded the comforter over it.

I drove away from Alida seeing clearly how easily I might have been kept there, held by the farm and my father's poor health, no college, and inevitably I'd have gotten married. Would I have tried to play it straight? Probably, for a while, then back to furtive scenes. And probably the bottle as relief from the strain and loneliness.

The terms of my salvation had been harsh, true, but happy is what I felt as I drove through the darkness towards Denver. In a few hours I could slip into bed and curl around Judd's warm body. Sleep would come, I was sure, easily enough.

A Somewhat Imperfect Landing

FELICE PICANO

I'd lived nearly a quarter of a century and to my continuing astonishment, I'd found the truth to be more a hindrance in my life than it was either useful or profitable. Like Cervantes' hero I'd come to battle with reality several times already and like the noble La Manchan I'd already been trounced quite thoroughly. Because of the truth, I'd lost Ricky Hersch in the seventh grade and Djanko Travernicke just a few months after my twenty-second birthday. Because of the truth, I'd ended one potential career as a fiction writer a decade ago, before it could even be thought of as an apprenticeship and another potential career, as a film writer, only a few months past. I'd seen it coming this time around, of course, but I'd been in no way able to help myself. Reality intruded, made itself all too clear that it was something quite different than illusion. I'd jumped for the bait and bam!

This being so, when I left Europe, part of my plan was a quite conscious decision to jettison the truth wherever it seemed problematic, to let reality fall by the wayside whenever it appeared to clash with what I perceived as my best interests.

I'd already made this decision by the time I'd boarded the jet that took me back to New York City. If the passenger next to me in coach happened to ask my name, I'd tell him or her I was Herbert Stoller from Rego Park Queens, a certified public accountant for a large insurance company, traveling on business. Or Alan Stern, from Mamaroneck, a Peace Corps volunteer, on the last leg of a journey home from Sri Lanka, or . . . anyone! As it turned out no one did ask. And a good thing. Because if I was planning to return to the States free of the hindrances of reality I couldn't have chosen better circumstances than Fate selected for me.

Without knowing it, I was returning to an America about to burst into a decade of Learyesque hallucination. Without knowing that I would become part of this counter culture, I was already within it. You see, I boarded that plane stoned on hashish, continued for much of the six-hour-long flight to become even more stoned, and arrived at the newly renamed Kennedy Airport so thoroughly smashed I might have been landing at a Moonbase a hundred years in the future. Naturally, this was unintentional. It was also a most appropriate omen: I had left the States with a taste for grass and an occasional drink. Aside from one bizarre and to this day inexplicable incident—in which I drank absinthe at a party in Copenhagen, passed out and awakened twenty-seven hours later in the backseat of a Volkswagen driven by strangers on the outskirts of Rotterdam—my stay throughout Europe had been relatively drugless.

This is how I happened to fly back ripped to the tits.

I like to fly in airplanes. By 1967 I'd only been in a few compared to now, but enough to know that I very much liked to fly in airplanes. So I was in my digs south of Sloan Square, all dressed and packed and ready hours early to fly back to New York. Eager too. I was shaking the dust of Europe off my heels, a dust which had managed to accumulate with a singular oppressiveness in my last months of living through an impermissibly dreary London autumn and a despicable winter. They've cleaned up the pollution since then, but in those days when I was feeling a bit bored on a December evening, I used to go through the center of local squares picking up and helping home and sometimes taking to hospitals the barely breathing bodies of elderly pensioners who'd thought to find a short cut home and instead found their lungs stopped by the concentration of yellow-black fog and putrid air. I generally rewarded myself for these good deeds at a local Wimpy's with gluey kidney pie and a tankard of warm beer the tint of slightly hepatitic urine.

Picture me then about to make my great escape: I'm barbered, shaved, dressed in a pale blue button-down Oxford, a school tie left behind by someone I'd slept with, charcoal flannel trousers, Scottish walking buffs, pewter Harris tweed jacket—all recently purchased on Regent or Bond streets: the very portrait of a Rhodes Scholar, you'd say. I was that clean cut.

Then I remembered the hashish.

The loveliest green-brown Turkish hashish you've ever seen, it was the consistency of hand-made chocolate which has been kept in the refrigerator and taken out ten minutes ago. Using a razor blade you could carve it into strips which bent almost double but didn't break, thin as a perfect Carpaccio. The hashish was still wrapped in the baroquely embossed and highly decorative gold and pink foil I'd bought it in for several hundred dollars a few weeks before. Hell! It was even stamped through the foil with a Turkish Government tax mark. It was an inch thick and about the size of the palm of my hand. Yet my luggage was already belted up and sitting in the downstairs hallway under the ever scrupulous eye of my ginger-haired Dundee-bred landlady when I remembered the hash and took it out of the ginger jar where'd I'd been hiding it.

Smuggling drugs was hardly on my mind, though it would be a bit difficult to explain that to the authorities. "Gee, Constable, I was going to keep it and smoke it a little bit at a time for the next ten months." But that was *exactly* what I'd been planning to do when I bought it.

More to the point, how I'd gotten the hashish had given it such a personal stamp, I knew I simply *had* to be able to keep it. I could see myself comfily ensconced in my apartment in Manhattan with friends inhaling it on either side of me, as I began to narrate the adventure.

I'd been in Istanbul, staying at the Hilton during my last jaunt out of England. I can't remember what possessed me to go there, except that I'd never been and someone I'd met in a King's Road pub had told me he could get me tickets on the Orient Express for a quarter of the usual cost. The train's last stop was the Turkish city.

Five minutes after I'd arrived in Istanbul I wanted to leave. If the antiquity of London, Paris and Rome had begun to get on my nerves, Istanbul expressed the worst aspects of all three of them rolled into one. It was old, it was noisy, it was crowded, it was filthy, it smelled as though its two million inhabitants had forgotten to put out the garbage. The walls of even the most modern shops and hotels were already crumbling in the miasma of taxi fumes, horse dung and toxic mists off the Sea of Marmora. The place was undeniably picturesque—but I'd had my fill of picturesque. I avoided the Hagia Sophia, narrowly averted being dragged to Suleiman's Castle with its seven towers and to the Mosque of Mohammed II. I fought my way out of the streets that led to the Bucolean Palace where Theodora once held court, or to the Hippodrome and or to John Crystothomos' tomb and I almost paid money to avoid the Topkapi Museum. My one stroll through the huge *souk* in the center of the city—it had once been Constantine's forum—on the afternoon I detrained was enough to last a lifetime. I determined to spend the next two days, until my train left again, in my hotel which, being American, was clean, had a good bar and television, and where I might be bored by meals but not anticipate food poisoning. I envisioned a perfect, sterile ennui. I took showers repeatedly, ordered hamburgers and french fries and root beers. I was awful. I was in heaven.

This might have lasted if it weren't for lust.

Going up to my room from the lobby where I'd just purchased weeks old *Time* and *Look* magazines which I was dying to peruse, I was suddenly struck by the pale green eyes and superb physique of the young elevator operator. I stared, he stared back. I stared harder, he said hello in broken English. I said I think your eyes are lovely, he said would I like to see more of him. I said yes, all of him. His name was 'Thrakis, short for a much longer name I never quite caught, and he was Frankish, i.e., mostly of European lineage, and he lived with a huge family across the smaller bridge in Pera. He agreed to meet me when he got off a few hours later, and he didn't name a fee, but he did insist we meet on the roof, which had a pool and cabana closed to the public after twilight.

We did meet up there, and with the mist swirling above most of the baleful city, we smoked some delightful hashish he'd thoughtfully provided and made love for an hour upon a dampish chaise lounge in a humid cabana.

Almost to make conversation afterward, I told 'Thrakis how much I'd liked the hash and asked how I could get more. He told me a friend of a friend of his would sell me some. A half pound of the stuff for only two hundred dollars. American dollars. He gave me the address and suggested I go the following night as the friend of a friend was a construction worker and wouldn't be home until after dinner time—i.e., about 10 P.M. Although neither his family nor the friend of a friend had a telephone, 'Thrakis promised he'd get word to the man that I was coming. I was to ask for 'Ulema.

The next night I had dinner and caught a cab in the hotel's *porte cochere*. The minute I told the driver where I wanted to go, he stopped the car (causing a back-up and blowing horns) and said he wouldn't take me there.

"Why not?"

"It's a danger place. Very danger. I wouldn't send my mother with a pistol to that place."

That made so little sense I insisted: "I'm visiting a friend."

"What kind of friend do you have?" he asked.

"A construction worker!"

"A murderer!" he insisted. "I won't drive to that place."

I left the cab and returned to my room. There I sat and thought. 'Thrakis was a sweet boy and it was possible the friend of a friend was not a murderer. Drug deals however were notoriously perilous and I might easily be killed and thrown into the Hellespont. I had to plan this a bit better.

The silverware from my meal tray was still outside the door where I'd left it. I picked up the steak knife, cleaned it off, and tested its edge. It would do. I changed from my preppy clothing into an outfit I thought might be both less conspicuous and a bit more menacing: motorcyclist's leather jacket and square-toed boots (for a good kick to the nuts), worn denims and a torn shirt. I messed up my hair and beard. I slipped the knife into my pocket where it bulged, then slid it into my left boot, where it fit perfectly, and where if I were sitting down I'd be able to grab it instantly to defend myself.

Garbed for the back alleys of Istanbul, I walked away from the hotel until I'd arrived near the *souk*. There I found a particularly battered old Vauxhall taxi with four different colored fenders and a one-eyed driver. I addressed him in French which he didn't know, then in Italian, which he did (Venetian merchants all but owned the city for centuries, even after the Ottomans had made it the capital of their Empire). I told him where I was going and told him I wanted him to drive and wait for me—he'd be well paid. If he left me while I was out of the cab, I'd go out of my way to find him the next day. I showed him the haft of the knife in my boot. I spoke fast and hard and he thought I was a criminal. He drove me to within a hundred feet of where I wanted to be. The instant I got out of the taxi he pulled out and began to read a comic book.

It had been raining in Istanbul but once across the Golden Horn, the rain plunged in sheets. Galata's main roads were reduced to a series of puddles and Tophane, the northern dockside area we'd finally stopped in, was even worse: the wind howled across the Bosphorus and fog from Scutari whirled off the water. For about a minute I asked myself what the hell I was doing. Then I found the house I was looking for, entered a deep foyer in the windowless facade and knocked on the wooden door.

Instantly a very stooped old woman with Ghirlandiao eyes opened up, arranging her kerchief to hide the rest of her face from the stranger.

"Ulema!" I said.

She nodded and let me in, looking around outside before shutting the door, and guided me through a short corridor past a room where people seemed to be silently sitting amidst a haze of cigarette smoke, up a short stairway, around a bend and into another room with its door ajar. She gestured me to enter.

An elderly man with a scar that cut one nostril in half and crossed his cheek all the way to the ear was the only occupant. He sat on one side of the built-in-bench. When he looked up, I wondered could this be Ulema?

The woman said something in Turkish. The man grunted. I noticed that he didn't look at me again. She gestured at me again, which I interpreted to mean that I should take a seat and wait. I did so, as far away from Scarface as I could in the small undecorated room, and she disappeared.

By the clock it was only about five minutes, but it seemed an hour before anything happened. The old man was cutting his fingernails with an astonishing Swiss Army knife which seemed to bristle with contraptions for a dozen unknown purposes. In general he ignored me, but once he said "Ulema?" And I replied in Italian. "I'm a friend of 'Thrakis." He grunted and mumbled something then went back to hacking at his fingernails.

There was no doubt in my mind that this old brigand was psyching me out and sizing me up, "softening" me up until Ulema arrived, at which point they'd show me hashish, ask to see my money, and kill me. Even so, I avoided any outward nervousness. I stared at a point straight ahead to distract the penultimate moments of my suddenly too-short life by following the intricate traceries of a wooden screen. I also tried to keep the old man within my peripheral vision.

Finally he said something, or rather grunted out an entire sentence, not one word of which I understood. I asked him to repeat himself, and this time he asked in very poor Italian if I was *fratel 'd'amo'*, i.e., "love-brother" of 'Thrakis. I didn't know what to answer. Then I decided I was doomed no matter what I said and might as well admit it. *"Certo!"* I answered.

"Bell'figl'" he said, meaning that 'Thrakis was a handsome lad.

Once again I answered, *"Certo!"*

Then he said something to the effect that Ulema wouldn't be coming.

Oh, oh! I thought. Here it comes!

He asked to see my money.

Anxiously, I pulled out a wad of twenties and laid all ten out for him on the space of bench between us.

He looked at them without moving.

My left hand went to the lip of my boot, found the haft of my knife, and gripped it. I'd never done anything even vaguely homicidal, didn't know if I could, even to defend my life. And even if I should, I didn't know my way out of the house, was certain to have to pass the roomful of men who would doubtless stop me by any means, chase me outside to where the deceitful taxi driver had long taken off, and I would stumble through a neighborhood I didn't know and pound on the doors of people who wouldn't answer as I was attacked again and again, like Caesar in the Senate ante-room, clawing at the stone walls as I slipped bloody into the mud and piss and dung!

Suddenly I saw a foil packet next to the money, as if by magic. The hashish.

Take it, or touch it, he grunted.

Without for a second letting go of the knife, I picked up the foil packet and set it down closer to myself. I peeled off one section, saw the brown-green brick, picked at a corner of it with my thumb and index fingernails and tasted it. Sweet. Musky. Strong.

The money was gone from the bench.

I took another tiny piece off another side of the hashish, ate it, then pocketed the foil packet in my right boot.

The old man was back with his Swiss Army knife, carving his finger-nails.

I thought if I move slowly and can get out of the house . . .

"*Ciao!*" I said, got up and walked out, expecting to be attacked any second. I cautiously moved past any doorway, open or closed, until I'd gotten to what I remembered was the front door. Still no one. In fact, the room where the dozen smoking men had been was now empty. Were they waiting for me outside?

I opened the door and let myself out. It was still raining so hard I thought they might be hiding anywhere in the alley to jump me and I wouldn't see them until it was too late. But the parti-colored Vauxhall was still waiting. I braced myself to walk slowly, like Gary Cooper in *High Noon*. I promised myself that I wouldn't go down begging and squirming. I took one step and heard a voice behind me. I spun around, dropped to my knee and reached for the knife in my boot.

It was the old woman. She held out something wrapped in cloth. Offering it to me with one hand while the other held the scarf closed over her face.

When I didn't move, she used her veil hand to subtly lift the cloth off the package. I don't know what horror I expected to see. What I saw was pastry.

I stood up and she pushed it into my hand and ran inside.

Abashed, I walked to the cab, no longer paying attention to a dozen possible lurking assassins. I came up behind where the cabbie was still reading the comic book. When I tried the back door it was locked. I rapped on his window and through the rain-soaked glass could see him hurriedly button his flies beneath the protection of the comic and reach around to lift the lock on the back door. I got in and told him to drive back to the hotel.

Once we were in a place in Galata I recognized and I'd somewhat calmed down, I looked at the pastry and offered him some of the nut-filled baklava. He ate it using the same hand he steered with and took his fares with and masturbated with behind a comic book. Later on, I also ate the baklava. It was scrumptious.

So you see, I couldn't just *leave* the hashish, or throw it away. But what could I possibly do? I knew U.S. Customs searched like crazy, even more so than British Customs, and that they liked nothing better than to find young people—even clean cut ones—"carrying" and give them stiff prison sentences. Within Europe it was bad enough. I'd heard tales of students caught with a stick of grass who were moldering away for decades to come in jails from Madrid to Athens. I'd brought the hash to England through the Dover port wrapped in a particularly pungent group of dirty socks—the approved Provo method of carrying—but my bags were packed now, and anyway I didn't have any dirty socks.

I was so jangled by this sudden new problem that I immediately knocked a piece off the slab of hashish and placed it upon the glowing ember of my cigarette—a "quick pick me up" I'd seen frequently practiced in the darker corners of a gay disco in Amsterdam called the D.O.K. It wasn't enough to calm me down. I knocked off and smoked another chunkette and another and another. I felt somewhat better!

My taxi arrived too quickly. The landlady of my lodgings was rapping on my door. I called back that I was coming. I hastily rewrapped the hash, shoved it into an empty box of Dunhills, added a few cigarettes and slipped the box into the inner breast pocket of my Harris Tweed jacket. Then I ran down to the cab taking me to Victoria Station.

Once there, the bus to take me to Heathrow Airport was just pulling out and I had to run to catch it. The bus connected almost instantly to my flight—a rather crowded flight, even though it was at night, probably because it was cheaper. Passengers were already being called into the plane by seat numbers in groups of tens and wouldn't you know my seat was called the instant I arrived in the lobby. I hurriedly checked my bags, held onto only a largish bar of Cadbury's chocolate and a small India-paper edition of *Bleak House* which I'd planned to begin on the plane—then quietly but totally panicked. Sure, I wouldn't have to worry about the hashish next to my heart until I landed, but suddenly the Atlantic was too tiny an ocean to cross, six hours, but a brief, Beckettian moment. I was in serious Dutch: I was boarding the plane.

I have to admit I managed to forget about the hash at isolated moments during the first few hours of the flight, although it ran a constant countertheme throughout the meal, through my attempts at reading Dickens, through my wanderings around the plane. Once the meal had been cleared away and the lights put out, however, I found I wasn't at all tired. No, I was lost in thought—how could I not be? The hashish glowed in my breast pocket like a flaming ingot. I had to do *something*.

I decided to leave it under the seat when I disembarked. The hell with it! So I wouldn't have hashish—my all time favorite high—once I landed.

So I would have lost two hundred dollars. So what? At least I'd be out of jail.

Then I thought about what awaited me in Manhattan.

Not much. I did have an apartment. A small studio in the West Village that I'd been panicked into renting when I'd left for Europe a year and a half before, my East Tenth Street apartment having been burgled so regularly by junkies that I'd been able to move West in someone's car, having little clothing or furniture or anything unstolen really to transport but books and records. I'd grown up in big houses, had enjoyed the three sunny rooms of East Tenth Street with its sagging parquet floors and chipped French doors between the living room and bedroom. In Rome I'd lived in a huge suite at the Hassler, in Paris in a duplex I was "watching" for some Americans; even in Chelsea my lodgings had been large and bright—with central heating yet! This hole in the wall on Jane Street with a kitchenette and two windows was going to be a coop. While I'd been away, I'd sublet it to newlywed friends who'd written me that it was almost impossibly close, even as a honeymoon nest. I would need some serious "inner space" to make up for the lack of external area. What better way than a smoke and a Supremes record?

Another problem was that I had no job awaiting me and didn't even know what kind of job I wanted. I knew one thing: I had no interest in ever being a social worker again. It might take weeks, even months to find work that brought in money. No job—and limited resources. Just a few weeks before, I'd gone on a shopping spree to replace my clothing stolen from Tenth Street. I could ill afford to throw away several hundred dollars worth of anything.

A third problem I didn't even want to think about was that I was socially adrift. In the two years or so after college graduation before I'd gone to Europe, I'd still been surrounded by friends from college who'd also lived on the Lower East Side, and later by friends I'd made at work. Now my college chums were all gone—off to Grad School. I'd been accepted at Columbia for English Literature and at the Iowa Writing Program. But I would have gone on a diet of ground glass and cyanide before returning to school. Nor did I want, really, to see the people I'd left at the East End Welfare Center. I'd gone to Europe to change my life and I had changed my life. I was starting fresh—once again—whatever that might entail.

By this time in the transatlantic flight, the mild high I'd gotten in my Chelsea digs was long gone. Three hours had passed, I'd snacked and eaten a full BOAC dinner. I decided on another tack. I wouldn't throw away all of the hashish. I'd smoke as much of it as I could in the airplane john, keeping the ventilator on high and flushing the toilet often to get rid of the smoke.

Mad you say? Quite mad. But I was desperate. I waited until all the other passengers around me seemed to be asleep, until even the stewards were settled in their seats with magazines and soft drinks, then I pounced. Selecting the john furthest from my seat, I shut myself in and began to smoke a cigarette and to pick off chunks of hash. I kept the ventilator going and kept on flushing the toilet. Anyone listening outside would conclude that I'd contracted serious dysentery—and hopefully stay away.

It worked! At least the john never got that smoky.

I don't recall exactly at what moment I realized that I'd been sitting on a closed toilet seat in a jet filled with sleeping people thirty thousand feet above the Atlantic Ocean fervently smoking hash for twenty minutes, but I did—quite suddenly—and I managed to reach the following conclusions:

1) I was making very little progress on the sizable chunk of hashish. In fact, I'd barely picked one edge to a quite lovely ruffle. In fact it seemed more than likely that I would have to sit here smoking and flushing for the next week before I came close to finishing it off.

2) I was already so bombed that if I continued smoking the hash another minute, never mind 'til we landed, they'd have to carry me off the plane.

3) I'd never noticed before what odd wallpaper was inside BOAC jet johns. And:

4) I no longer cared what happened to the hash or to me.

I returned to my seat and promptly fell into a series of De Quincyean hallucinations which ended in my falling asleep.

"Sir! Sir!" I could barely get my eyes open. "Sir, we've landed. You'll have to wake up, sir!"

The stewardess moved down the aisle and I struggled to look around. Most of the passengers from my section of the plane were gone. I was alone, amidst magazines scattered on seats and chatting airline staff. Hurrying, I grabbed my carry-on bag, stuffed my Dickens into it, struggled to get on my jacket and disembarked into a cool and starlit April night. As I half stumbled across the tarmac into the International Arrivals Building I realized that I was still stoned: I felt as though I was moving in slow-motion, gravity rising to defy me with every step.

After wandering around a bit, as if in a dream, I located the right luggage carousel and there was my bag, virtually alone. Someone from the airline urged me to join the rest of the passengers in the customs shed. The minute I got into the big room new confusion faced me. There were four lines of people at long tables with two customs inspectors per table. The lines were alphabetically divided by last names and I found O-T with only a few people ahead of me. I lifted my bag onto the table as I'd seen others do and the first Customs' man gestured to me with his fingers several times until I realized he meant for me to open it.

He and his partner were middle-aged fellows in very official looking uniforms. One wore what I guessed to be a perpetual professional visage of bored, cynical indifference. The other inspector had sharper and more peppery features. He even looked like a ferret and seemed to enjoy harassing people. At that moment he was hassling a well-dressed woman about her clothing, asking where she had bought various items and how much she was going to declare in customs duty.

"Surely you don't think I travel without undergarments," she sniffed at him. "I'll certainly not declare those."

"Look lady, did you buy them in England or not? Anything you bought there has to be tallied into the accounting. Liquor, perfume, jewelry, clothing!" he spat out as he rummaged through another one of her many open suitcases in front of him.

Oh my God! I thought. Virtually everything I had in my suitcase was bought in London: shirts, ties, slacks, socks—even my underwear! I was going to have to pay duty on all of it!

"Well, if you can't find your receipts you'll have to step aside and look for them," he was saying to her.

"Why can't I just tell you how much they cost?"

"All right!" he pulled a heavy calculator out from under the table, and she began to roll off prices, as he continually interrupted and questioned her.

This was awful. I'd paid cash for my clothing and I hadn't kept a single receipt. How much was this going to cost me?

"You must be completely out of your mind!" the woman shouted.

"Look, lady, either we do it my way or . . ."

"I'll report you to your superior. Who do you think you are? The Russian Police? I'll have my attorney . . ."

I looked at my open suitcase and began to calculate what my clothing had cost me. Despite being in London a longish time I'd never quite gotten the exchange rate straight in my head. I had managed to figure out British prices among themselves, which was how I knew something was expensive or cheap. But in dollars? Was it two dollars to one Pound Sterling? Or . . .

"Look lady, there are other people here. You're going to have to wait until I'm done with them."

"What do you mean I have to wait? I want this straightened out now! Now!"

He moved away from her and her half dozen open suitcases, and he and his partner began rummaging through the open bags of the next person, an elderly woman, asking mechanically, "Any liquor, perfume, jewelry or clothing to declare?"

I was next! Let's see. The Harris Tweed was the most expensive item. Then the shoes. That equalled . . .

"I did get this lovely little handkerchief set for my granddaughter," the elderly woman simpered. "A real bargain. It only cost One and four."

"Next!" they said, and they were suddenly at my suitcase.

"Any liquor, perfume, jewelry or clothing to declare," Mr. Ferret demanded, all the while rummaging through my bag with two ungloved hands.

I stood there unable to say anything.

"Looks clean, Gord," the other said and moved down to a couple who'd just arrived late behind me.

"Wait a minute!" Mr. Ferret had grabbed something at the bottom of my suitcase beneath my socks and underwear. "What's this?"

What had he found? I looked and saw two small flexible pebble-covered and bound Collins' Classics.

"Books!" I said, I thought self-evidently.

"Yes!" he replied, his face becoming more vulpine every second. "But what kind of books?"

I was so startled by his attitude, that I replied, "Just books!"

"Let's see," he said, and began thumbing through *Framley Parsonage*, looking for I couldn't think what. "Books written by trollops . . ." he muttered.

"That's Trollope! Anthony Trollope. A famous British novelist," I defended.

"Funny name for a writer," he insinuated and dropped the book on top of my shirts, and began looking through the second volume, saying in a confidential voice to me, "Don't think we don't get a lot of people coming through here and claiming they're students and then bringing in all sorts of smut." He dropped *Daniel Deronda* onto my shirts and picked up the third volume. "And here!" he exulted, "is a perfect example of what I'm talking about."

He held the volume so I couldn't see what it was. I'd bought the four of them months ago as they were inexpensive and would look good in my otherwise paperback and college text library. *Bleak House, Daniel Deronda, Framley Parsonage* and . . . for the life of me I couldn't remember what the fourth title might be.

"You see," he intimated, "They bind them as though they were real books and put them in with real books. But they can't fool me. I know better. Have to. That's my job." He was leafing through the book. "Pictures too!" he all but glowed with satisfaction for an instant, then darkened and thumbed on, evidently looking for other pictures.

"What book is that?" I asked, totally befuddled.

"A bad one! I can tell."

"I didn't bring in any bad ones," I declared. "What's its title?"

He wasn't liking the pictures he'd found and now had turned to reading the text a sentence or two at a time every few pages. I was now both confused and humiliated by the many people looking on at our little scene. I was also beginning to get angry. He wasn't liking what he was reading, either, and moved from page to page, searching for who knew what.

"What are you doing?" I demanded.

"Looking!" he said, and mumbled, "Got to be here somewhere!"

"What are you looking for?"

Without stopping his search, he said, "The scenes! The scenes! The whips, the torture scenes . . . you know!"

"Whips," I fairly shouted, "torture?" causing even more people to look at us. "Give me that," I grabbed the book out of his hands. "It can't be anything I brought . . ."

I turned to the title page. Jane Austen. *Persuasion.*

"This is Jane Austen, for Chrissakes! What does Jane Austen have to do with whips and chains? Thirteen-year-old girls read this book in school. I know you people aren't educated. But to so openly show your ignorance and to do it in so embarrassing a manner to a perfectly innocent person like myself is completely unforgivable!" I was now shouting at the top of my voice. "Jane Austen! You dolt! You ignoramus! You blithering idiot!"

He shut my suitcase and threw it onto the floor and moved on to the next person.

"Did you hear that?" I shouted to the assembled passengers. "He thought Jane Austen wrote about torture and bondage. That's the quality of the employees here! That's who you're paying with your hard-earned taxes!"

Two large Customs police emerged from out of nowhere and immediately surrounded me. They said they would escort me out of the room. As I was still waving the book around, one of them took my arm, another my other elbow, they even picked up my suitcase and carry-on bag for me.

"Wait a minute!" I shouted.

Half a minute later, I found myself out of the terminal and being shoved into a taxi. They slammed the car door on me, shook their heads and, having narrowly averted a revolution, returned indoors.

I sat back in the taxi, gave my address and lit a cigarette. I fumed more than my Salem until we arrived at the Midtown Tunnel.

That's when it struck me what had just happened back there. He'd been looking for smut and he'd found a book titled *Persuasion*. No wonder! *Persuasion!* No wonder! I began to laugh and as I did, the incident got funnier and funnier and funnier. When the cab reached Jane Street my ribs hurt from laughing so much. The cabbie must have been sure I was completely certifiable. He was politeness itself, even carried my luggage to the front door.

That evening I was telling the story to my friend Barbara on the telephone when she suddenly asked: "What happened to the hashish?"

I stopped. During all the farandole at the Customs Shed I'd never once—not for an instant—thought about the hashish. I'd completely forgotten it.

I grabbed my Harris Tweed jacket which I'd thrown over a chair as I'd come in, and there it was inside the spare pack of cigarettes in my breast pocket where I'd put it.

"I'm holding it in my hot little hand," I reported.

"How much do you have?"

"All of it, less what I smoked on the plane."

"Welcome back to the States, doll. I'm really certain you're going to enjoy your stay."

Baseball in July

PATRICK HOCTEL

I've always hated baseball, I still do. In April when the sports writers start with their "Rites of Spring" and then later "Boys of Summer" malarkey, I get this queasy lump in my gut remembering the days when I was what you'd call a "conditional player." "Okay, we'll take Paul, but *only* if we bat first" or "We'll take Paul *only* if Mark doesn't pitch."

That's why I was surprised when my father leaned over from his lawn chair and with a hand on the back of my head said, "Get on up there with Jason and toss him a few. You always had a good arm." Jason was my eight-year-old nephew, one of the thousands, perhaps millions, of pre-adolescent Jasons in the country. His best friend at school was named Jason as was the boy next door he sometimes played with.

"I hate baseball," I said. "You know that."

"Funny," Dad said, "I thought you liked it. But Larry was the sports one."

Last Christmas, my father gave my mother round-trip tickets to Montreal because, as he put it, "That's the one place your mother's always wanted to go." The truth is that she's been saying for thirty years that she wants, just once, to see Hawaii. But, as Mother told me confidentially over the phone, "I can't hurt his feelings. He spent a fortune." So they went to Montreal in January where Mother came down with pneumonia. "A slight case," she'd written.

"Come on, Paul," Jason begged. "Pim's no good."

Pim blushed. He's Danish with a Dutch name. True blonds get so red in the face.

"*Uncle* Paul," my father corrected.

"Give him a break," I groaned. "He's met me twice."

"Come on, *Uncle* Paul," Jason said, more insistent. "Please."

"I throw like a girl," I said. "Pim's better." I heard my father sigh. Jason was stunned by this admission: an adult male publicly stating that he did something like a girl.

He took a couple steps toward me and shaded his eyes in my direction. "Really," he said.

"He's just lazy," my father said, covering for me. And then bending down to ear level, he whispered, "You never used to throw like a girl." Like it was something I must've learned last year.

"I never threw at all," I whispered back.

Pim, eager to please everyone, the whole town of Beaumont, Texas, where my brother lives if necessary, promised to do better.

My father fidgeted in his seat, and after a pause, said loud enough for just me to hear, "I like Pim."

But he liked anyone who was consistently pleasant—or tried to be. "So do I," I said.

"He's a real 'pitcher inner' type," my father said. A quiet followed that made me brave the July sun and study my father's face. It was his neck that got me. Stringy and red.

"His collars just hang on him," I could hear my mother saying over the phone, "ever since he dropped that weight over the kidney thing. Old chicken neck." I'd laughed because of how she states things, but it didn't seem funny now. It gave him a frailty that was more scary then endearing.

The "women," as we say in New Orleans where I grew up, the women being my mother, my sister-in-law, and my Aunt Tee-Tee, were in the house smocking the baby's christening gown; it being understood that the humidity was too much for them. *Only* an eight-year-old could enjoy himself in this weather, I reasoned. The air-conditioning unit humming on the side of the house filled me with envy. I was not a bad smocker myself.

"There's one thing I don't get," my father said, drawing me back from my bad humor. "Two men sleeping together."

Maybe it was the humidity or maybe it was having to watch baseball, but I wasn't feeling kind. "I always got it," I told him. "Even before I did it. Before I knew the words." Watching Pim, pale skin reddening in the sun, the flex of his shoulder as he let go of the ball, I didn't believe my father. Such a thing was simple, universal. "It's not difficult," I said, "if you use your imagination."

"Sex can't be that important," Dad continued, sounding sure of himself. "You're both men—and it's not like you're kids."

Picturing Pim and me as two ever-so-slightly aging bachelors living together for convenience' sake made him happy. "It is," I said.

My father sighed—one of his prolonged, sad ones—and began filling his pipe from his ever-present tobacco pouch. "You did have a good arm, though," he said. "Even if you don't remember."

Aunt Tee-Tee, as Larry and I had been taught to call her ever since we were babies, was really Theresa, my mother's best friend and former next-door neighbor of 20 years. I had always feared her, not because she was mean, but because she had the knack of blurting the most embarrassing thing possible.

At 12, when I'd taken up basketball in an effort to fit in, she'd come over one afternoon to have coffee with my mother. Right in the middle of a game, she'd walked up to me, grabbed my arm affectionately, and exclaimed, "You're just too pretty to be a boy!" And I was, high-point man or not.

I'd managed to avoid her so far. I gave Pim a push to the right—away from the den and Aunt Tee-Tee—and down the hall to our room as we came in the front door. But Dad called behind us, "Come in and say hello to Theresa. She's come all the way from Houston."

Pim flopped across the lower bunk. At first, I'd thought it was Larry's idea of a joke—to put Pim and me in a room with bunk beds—but Sharon had explained that they were fixing it up for when Jason got a little older.

"Your father's a good man," Pim said. "You're his favorite, I think. He teases you but not your brother."

That's because my father considers Larry an adult, I thought, someone like himself. "He likes you, too," I said. "They all do. Even Mom." Actually, Mom was being polite. That was her way of dealing with a person she didn't know or wasn't positive she wanted to know. Pim was trying very hard. As I watched him settle on the bunk, I was angry that she should have to pretend to like him at all.

But Mom didn't like much of anything any more. Maybe her grandchildren. Two years before when I'd come out to her and my father in their room on the 18th floor of San Francisco's Holiday Inn on Van Ness, something had stopped for us. Now we were like two people with partial amnesia. We knew we knew each other, but we weren't clear on our past connection. And we'd been the closest in the family.

My father had knocked out his pipe and then nodded several times in the direction of the ashtray. "You've been a fine son," he'd said. "It doesn't make any difference to me." Mother had looked very tired and said only, "Yes."

And then later when Pim had come into the picture, Dad, after lots of questions over long distance, indicated that in his estimation I'd made a good catch. I felt like the prodigal daughter redeemed. Mother had waited until we were through and there was a break before asking, "How's your job?" and then "Is the Honda running okay?"

I stayed until Pim was asleep and then snuck back down the hall to the kitchen, which was separated from the den by shutters running along a counter. I was a kid again, eavesdropping on the adults' conversation. Dad was telling Aunt Tee-Tee about my painting—bragging on me. It was fun to hear him go on like that, even if what he was saying wasn't entirely accurate.

"Just had a month-long exhibit in a big gallery," Dad said. "Never could use a drill, but sure is hell with a brush."

I didn't catch Tee-Tee's response. A surge of something—guilt—overtook me. The big gallery had been a well-known cafe which featured a local artist's work every month. My father had gotten the idea that I was an important artist on the West Coast, and since he was far enough away in New Orleans, I'd never tried to break him of this impression.

I did sell my paintings, though—but by the barrelful to a company in New York that used them for the covers of their romance novels. My own work had taken such a back seat that it was practically non-existent.

Instead, my studio was filled with portraits of young women, seductive yet innocent, in various states of distress and undress, men on horseback, capes flying, riding towards them, a castle or manor in the backgrounds, as their ample bosoms, prominent in the lower right-hand corners, heaved with fear or anticipation or both. Dad wouldn't want to know, I'd decided.

Sharon burst through the door with a tray of dirty coffee cups and caught me with my ear pressed to the shutters. Fortunately, she'd upset the creamer and wasn't paying me any attention. "Tee-Tee is too much," she said, depositing the cups on the counter. "She knows more about me than I do. Marie just lies there and stares at her. She's never seen anything like it. It's decaf the next go-around."

No sooner had Sharon gotten her last word out than Aunt Tee-Tee stuck her head in to find where she'd gone. "Paul!" she said. "Hiding from me! Give your old Aunt Tee-Tee a kiss if she's not too ugly."

I gave her a kiss because she wasn't ugly and she was actually a nice woman, a bit garrulous is all. But somehow I was still scared of her, tiny and round as she was.

"You and Larry both over 30," she said. "I can't believe it. Of course, men look different nowadays. Don't they, Sharon?"

Sharon was making for the den, but Tee-Tee was seeing she stayed put.

"Take better care of themselves. Used to be only women had to worry about what they looked like. Course, I was a mess. Not like your mother. Always turned out like a lady. And that house was a showplace."

"Mom was very neat," I said.

Aunt Tee-Tee reached up and grabbed a handful of my hair and shook it. "Look at those curls," she said, not letting go. "Wasted on a man."

I heard Sharon laugh behind me. I smiled, I think, at Aunt Tee-Tee. It was probably more like half a smile, half a sneer. She let go, but she hadn't lost her technique. No matter how old, a minute or so with Aunt Tee-Tee and I felt like I was wearing a yellow taffeta ball gown with matching pumps instead of my jeans and T-shirt. She had that way with people.

At 30, I'd gotten a bad case of baby fever, and it had lasted a whole year now. With that fever had come a bemused sense of betrayal. I'd been exhausting my disposable income sending baby gift after baby gift to various straight friends who'd claimed *they'd* never have children. Gay friends were having babies through artificial insemination or other means and talking constantly of parent networks and alliances between gay and lesbian households. Occasionally, my one-on-one relationship with Pim seemed distinctly passé.

Sitting there in my brother's den with the pink, gurgling Marie on my lap wasn't helping to reassure my biological clock. I was happy Pim was sleeping. He thought I got a bit silly when a baby was in the room. I wasn't gaga or anything, but I had to admit to a few kidnapping fantasies, Marie living with Pim and me, a dream nursery with a life-size giraffe and billowy curtains.

"He's a looker," Aunt Tee-Tee said, interrupting my baby reverie. "Not American."

Mother shifted her weight on the sofa beside me. "Danish," I said.

"I never heard him talk," she said, "so I didn't know where he was from. Of course, there aren't many men named 'Pim' in the state of Texas."

Aunt Tee-Tee had been watching us from behind the living room drapes. "His family came over when he was seven," I said. "He talks just like us. But no drawl."

"Where do you know him from?" she asked.

She meant how. How did I know that man down the hall? The blond in

211

the bed. I glanced at my mother trying to seem so absorbed in her grand-daughter. Maybe this one time doesn't count, I told myself. I'll probably never see Aunt Tee-Tee again and now mother is giving me a look like she's calling in her markers for the past 30 years. I was glad Pim was out of earshot, oblivious to all goings-on.

I heard Harvey Milk saying, "Come out, come out, come out!" But the picture in my head was of a scene 25 years before: I am sitting on the edge of a pool and an instructor is cajoling me to swim across its width. But I won't be moved. Not by sweetness—"You're such a good swimmer"—or threats—"You'll be the only one not to and you don't want that."

I was afraid of the deep water, having almost drowned the year before. First, I was scared, then mad at being singled out in the instructor's singsong voice. I didn't say anything. I didn't even look at the woman, but I knocked her hand off when she tried to grab my shoulder and pull me into the water. This was met with a chorus of disapproving clucks from the mothers on the other side of the pool, all gathered to see their children perform. I was the finale, but I wouldn't budge. My brother came over and squatted beside me. He whispered that Mom had said to do it. I caught her dark green lenses in their silver frames fastened on me. She wasn't smiling, only waiting. Neither one of us moved.

"We own a house together," I said. Mother looked pained.

"It's a *great* house," Larry said, coming to my rescue before Tee-Tee could jump in. "Overlooks downtown, and from the other side you get a view of the Bay Bridge. Pre-earthquake, 1885. Hardwood floors, fireplace in the main bedroom, and one in the living room. All the amenities."

Aunt Tee-Tee was momentarily overwhelmed, and before she could collect herself after Larry's onslaught, Marie cut her off. "She's wet or worse," Mother said.

"Fillin' her drawers," Tee-Tee said. "How I remember that!"

"I'll take her," I said. Marie was proving to be more valuable than I'd thought, although I hoped she was only wet. Mom got up with me, both of us seizing the excuse to absent ourselves.

"Don't help him, Janet," Tee-Tee said, her voice tracking us down the hall to Marie's room. "He'd better start learnin' to do that himself."

"I *know* how to change a diaper," I said, more to myself than to Mom or Marie. "I worked in a daycare center for a year and a half."

"Theresa means well," Mother said. "And she doesn't know about your string of odd jobs."

Mom was moving in on Marie's bassinet, handling the whole proce-dure herself. The only sounds in the room were the baby kicking and my mother's breathing, heavy from bending over the child. I didn't feel like getting into my work record, why it was how it was, so I let it go. Instead, I made Marie's mobile jump up and down for her, butterflies scattering to the left and right.

"I don't know why you had to say that to her, anyway," Mom said. She dropped the filthy diaper into a hamper. "There are other things you could've said."

"There's a limit," I said.

"You could've said you're friends or you're co-workers. I don't see why it's necessary for Theresa to know that you live in the same house."

"Right," I said. "A co-worker is going to travel with me from California to Texas for my niece's christening. That makes sense." Mother was giving Marie's bottom lots of powder; clouds of talcum were settling over the baby. "You're going to choke her," I said.

"Your Aunt Tee-Tee means well," Mother repeated. "But she talks too much. I don't know what she'll say or to whom. She comes out with anything that strikes her."

"So what," I said. This was old ground for my mother and me. "Tee-Tee lives in Houston. You don't know anyone in Houston."

Mom scooped Marie off the bassinet. "I'm 65," she said. "I don't need any more upsets. People used to care what other people said of them," Mother added. "About their reputations."

I wanted to shout, but I knew that would bring Tee-Tee on the run. "It's your reputation," I said. "That's what this is."

Mother patted Marie's back, trying to raise a burp. In the fading afternoon light as she lay Marie in the crib, I was startled to see her hair, though jet black on top, was now a dreary shade of white at the roots. "I don't gray pretty," she'd once said.

"You don't understand," Mom said, straightening up. "People can be nasty. You haven't learned that. Maybe your ways are fine for California, but here they'll smile and nod their heads—and then do something awful. I don't want you hurt."

Mother bent down to fuss over Marie and turned her back on me in such a way as to indicate that our talk had ended. I didn't mind, though. I wasn't thinking about our talk. I was thinking about how close we'd been when there was that lie of omission between us and now how she was once again the woman in the silver-frame glasses on the other side of the pool, waiting for me to swim across.

Pim was still asleep, his face to the wall. But even from where I was sitting on the edge of the bunk, I could see that his nose was turning an imposing red. Outside, Mom was waving Aunt Tee-Tee off. Tee-Tee was having difficulty negotiating her Cadillac down the gravel driveway in reverse and had come close to maiming several small trees Larry and Sharon had planted along there. Mom looked rosy in the glow from the sun's last light—younger. When she went to go back into the house, our eyes met, my face at sill level. She hesitated, then waved to me as well.

Pim stirred and sat up beside me, rubbing his forehead on my back, something he liked to do when waking up. "Is it morning?" he asked. "You're cold."

"Not quite," I said. "We're having dinner in half an hour."

He took a minute to absorb this. "Then I want a look at the appetizer," he said, sliding his hands up the front of my T-shirt.

We found we couldn't kiss. Each time our faces brushed, he'd wince and pull away. "Do I look bad?" he asked as if he already knew the answer.

"Like a Maine lobster," I said, "but very cute."

He made several baby noises I pretended not to hear. "Cuter than Marie?"

He was slightly jealous of the baby. Though he liked her, he didn't share my fascination. "Much cuter," I said. Pim reached for the buttons of my 501s, and I glanced around to check the door. "It doesn't lock," I said. His hand had reached the third button.

Pim let button three alone. "I'm afraid to go out there," he said. "And you keep looking over your shoulder." He stood but didn't take a step, his knee right on a level with my nose.

When he walked into a room, my whole family would look up, even Jason, as if on cue, and smile. Except the smiles were the sort you might give someone who stumbled out of an alley on a darkened street late at night and asked you directions to the nearest bar.

"I don't know what to do," Pim said. "When I catch myself in a mirror, I'm Mr. Sardonicus. Your family and their smiling. Even Marie."

"She's a baby," I said. "That's her job. Smiling is a part of politeness—hospitality." Pim groaned but didn't fight me when I grabbed his shirttail and dragged him down beside me. "You all recall," I said, affecting my best Southern twang, "that I told you about hospitality. It's how we make strangers, even blond, Yankee-lookin' strangers, feel welcome down here."

I pushed my weight onto him and forced him down on the bunk. I began to kiss him, lick him, all over—his hands, his shoulders—anywhere he hadn't burned. A knock on the door froze us. "Dinner in 20," Larry said. We listened to him walk off.

"I should get dressed," Pim said, trying to rise.

I put my elbow in his chest, just enough to keep him in place. "You haven't tasted true Southern hospitality," I said, "till you've had mint juleps on my veranda."

"Mint juleps are too sweet," he said.

"Not the way I make them." I undid the other buttons myself, and Pim and I made love in a new way, face to face, with our eyes open on the other.

The Presbyterian church where the christening was held was a copy of the one Larry and I had grown up in. Everything about it was brown: the pews, the carpet, the pulpit, the choir loft—the same monochromatic dullness throughout. The reverend in his dark purple robe was the only spot of color and that a pretty dour one.

As I held Marie in my arms in front of the baptismal font, I realized that the last time I had been in a church was when Larry and Sharon had gotten married. Here I was promising, in front of the congregation along with Sharon's sister, to see that this baby "would be raised in the ways of the Lord."

My favorite Durrell quote jumped before my eyes, as if it were plastered across the reverend's chin: "For those of us who stand upon the margins of the world, as yet unsolicited by any god, the only truth is that work itself is love." My gallery of Harlequin heroines presented themselves like a bad joke, and I remembered that in my mother's armoire in New Orleans was a pin with seven bars hanging from it. Each bar represented a year of perfect Sunday school attendance.

I gazed down at Marie, who seemed right on the verge of something. She had that omniscient look that comes from knowing what's going to happen next. When I went to raise her so the reverend could sprinkle the water on her forehead, I couldn't find her in the enormous gown my mother and Sharon had made, and she started to slide out of my arms.

"Where is she?" I said to Sharon's sister. "Where's her arm?" Sharon's sister, a nurse, grabbed Marie by the back of the dress and pulled. Fortunately, she came up with the dress and not out of it, never losing that look on her face.

After the ceremony we gathered in front of the church for pictures. Larry had hired a photographer. Devoted father that he was, he left no event in his children's lives undocumented. Reverend Gardner was explaining to me how I'd understand babies when I had one of my own, and I was thinking heterosexuals are so proprietary, reverend or not. But I kept my grin, imagining what Reverend Gardner would think of the turkey-baster method of conception. Besides, as Pim pointed out, my family smiled a lot.

To my right, Larry was trying to organize everyone into a group picture. It was like my brother to do the photographer's work for him. I saw him motion to Pim, and then my brother made me smile even wider when

215

he said, "Come on and get in here. Next to Mom and Dad." And then my mother turned to Pim. I was the only one besides him who heard her because I could see her lips move—as if she were telegraphing the words to me. "This is a family portrait," she said.

I felt my face burn. It was like someone had dipped it in kerosene, then switched on a low flame at my throat. Reverend Gardner was going on, but regarding me uneasily. From down on my left, Jason popped up with, "Mom said you weren't ever going to get married."

"Some men have husbands," I said, then Reverend Gardner said something about the weather, a glorious day. Larry called us over for the portrait, but I watched Pim walking out to the parking lot, hands in pockets, red face fixed on the white, chalky shells crunching under the dress shoes he'd bought for this trip. Jason was already on the church steps, and Larry was still motioning me over. Sharon pulled his arm down, and the photographer took the shot.

I started walking towards my mother, locking eyes all the way. Larry raised a hand. I'm not sure for what. Restraint. Supplication. Don't spoil the day. After all those years, Mother was getting what she wanted. I was crossing the pool, but I was going to make sure she'd wish I'd stayed on my side.

Mother couldn't really see me in the noonday glare, although her eyes remained focused in my direction. She knew I was coming. "I know what you're up to," I said when I'd gotten right next to her. "That was a rotten stinking thing to do." Aunt Tee-Tee had backed off a few steps. We were all alone.

"These are family pictures," Mother repeated, looking around her as if we weren't having this conversation at all, just surveying the scene, "for your aunts and uncles and your grandmother."

Despite her calm, measured voice, she was flustered. Her glasses had slipped down the bridge of her nose and were crooked on her face. "Don't ever do that again," I said.

Her mouth narrowed into a crease. She was ugly for a moment. "You, your father, and Larry," she said, "trying to throw dirt over it. But what do I tell your grandmother—'He's the man who owns a house with Paul?' Oh, I know what *you're* up to," she said, "but it's not that easy."

I wanted to take a hold of my mother and shake her. The way she did when I was little and refused to understand what she was saying. "Grandma doesn't know who I am all the time," I said. "Tell her he's an usher."

"I shouldn't have to make explanations," Mother said. "'Be accepting'—that's what I keep hearing. Like I should be a zombie and plaster a smile on my face."

Fiery splotches had appeared on her neck and were working their way up behind her left earlobe. Hives. I could make out the bumps under the make-up on her right cheek. That's where they always started. "You're making your mother nervous," Dad used to say. In spite of myself, I felt sorry for her.

"Pim and I are different," I said. "I can be nasty. I can be polite. He can't do those things. So he walked off."

Mother was teetering slightly, and I was feeling a bit lightheaded myself. The humidity, I thought, and almost laughed—the foolproof excuse. "That's it," I said. "That's all."

We were silent. The others seized this opportunity to break us up. Marie, fast asleep, her christening gown brushing my knees, was thrust into my arms, one of the few things sure to make me feel better. Everyone was so hushed that I wondered if Mother and I had been hysterical at some point, going at it like two fishwives.

Aunt Tee-Tee took my arm, and we headed for her Cadillac where Pim was leaning against the trunk, still studying the shells he was pulverizing with his heel. My father had my mother by one arm, and Larry was on the other. Sharon, her sister, and Jason brought up the rear.

Whatever had exploded in our midst, we were physically unscathed if somewhat shaken. Reverend Gardner had disappeared back into the church, the double doors firmly shut. Pim glanced up when we were about ten yards away—his face lowered in a hangdog expression, color approaching vermilion, hair as blinding as the baby's white dress in the overhead sun. Chalk from the shells he'd been grinding covered his black shoes. One melancholy "goo-goo" escaped him, followed by the lamest of smiles.

"He *is* a looker," Aunt Tee-Tee said.

In the night, I didn't hear Marie crying, but Pim's getting up shook the bunk bed frame and awakened me. "I'll go," I said.

"Stay put," he said. "I had a hard enough time getting you up there."

I'd spent the christening party outside with Jason, away from the adults, relearning how to throw a baseball—at least to an eight-year-old's satisfaction. Each time my arm got tired, I'd send Jason in for another glass of champagne punch, which I was downing in the 90-plus Beaumont heat.

"I don't feel that great," I said, but Pim was already beyond my moan. I could see his pale back disappearing into Marie's room and the light going on beneath her door. I couldn't make out a thing but the sound of his words soothing her. The door opened again, and from my vantage point in the top bunk, my mother's bright, almost iridescent, pink housecoat flashed at me for a second.

217

I imagined that one of them would beat a hasty retreat to a neutral corner, but they were in there for a while. I could hear their voices, my mother's and my lover's, very even in the dark. Occasionally Marie would cut in with a cry or exclamation of some sort, but they were halfhearted at best, as Mother and Pim were doing their utmost to lull her to sleep.

I was dozing when Pim woke me up again. He was singing. A broken version of "The Impossible Dream" wafted up to me. Except for a few words, Pim only knew the chorus, but there was a kind of glee in the way he was singing it.

"What happened in there?" I said, knowing already that he was going to prolong this.

"'To fight the unbeatable foe,'" Pim sang a la Tony Bennett or Jack Jones, with exaggerated feeling. "'This is my quest, to follow that star, no matter how hopeless, no matter how far. . .'" His voice trailed off as he began to mix up the rest.

"What did Mom say?"

"She said—she didn't know—I could change—a diaper."

Pim inserted long pauses between phrases, pretending to be drifting off, a few snores for my benefit. He was full of himself, enjoying making me dig.

"Neither did I," I said. "What else?"

"I thought you knew everything about me," he said. "I do have five younger brothers and sisters."

He was going to make me work for it. He'd spill it eventually, though. He couldn't resist when he was so pleased with himself. It was a contest to see who could hold out the longest. "More?"

"Nothing," Pim said.

I rolled over and let out a great yawn, the yawn of someone on the verge of deep slumber. "Swell," I said.

It came in a rush. "She said that I'd be a good father. And that she was happy for me. But I think she meant you." This was what he'd been saving: Mother's concession, his victory.

"Okay?" Pim said and kicked the bottom of my bunk three or four times.

Unfortunately, I was curled on my side, and the kicks, mixed with the afternoon's sun and champagne, caused a delayed reaction minutes later. "I don't feel so good," I said, but Pim was again beyond my voice, managing to elude me a second time. I lay there in the upper bunk, alternately holding and massaging my stomach, convincing myself that the nausea was getting better, as Pim's snores and the now-subsiding rumbles from below tricked me into sleep.

Morning came and went without my being aware of it. The first hint I had that it was a new day was the slamming of a car door. I peeked out the curtains, and there were Larry and Pim carrying my parents' bags down the driveway, while Jason ran around opening the trunk and the doors to the back seat.

I figured they were simply loading up, something they usually did a few hours before they left anywhere, just to make sure they had everything they'd come with. I lay back down for what I hoped would be another good half hour, but a knock, which became a rap, made me sit up, muttering to whomever was on the other side of the door.

Dad poked his head in, looking first at Pim's bed, even though he knew he was outside. Maybe he hoped to discover something there, a clue. "We're pulling out, son," he said.

Dad always likened traveling to a cattle drive. "I thought you were leaving late," I said. My brain was the consistency of a bowl of oatmeal that had been left outside for three days. "At least have breakfast."

"It's one o'clock," he said. He stepped gingerly into the room like a cat does into new territory. My parents had never come in before, only knocked. Being with Pim had finally given me the privacy I'd never had living with them.

"You're not what I'd called an early riser," Dad said.

I watched his eyes settle here, then there. He's trying to puzzle it out, I thought. Perhaps it's a scent or the way the bedclothes are arranged.

"Aren't you going to say goodbye to your mother?"

This was my least favorite parental ploy—asking for the other when it was something they wanted. "I'll say goodbye to you, too," I said, "if that's okay."

"Joker," my father said. "But your mother's not so young anymore. And I'm older than her." He said this last bit as if it were of no great mind. "This could be the last family get-together."

I sincerely wanted to lie back down. The oatmeal in my head was bubbling violently now. "You've said that before."

"It's true," he said.

"Is he sick?" I heard my mother whisper in the hall.

"I don't feel wonderful," I said, loud enough for her to hear.

Mother's face appeared in the doorway where Dad's had been, although lured there for different reasons. For her, it was a combination of motherly concern and fascination with illness of any sort, even a lowly hangover.

Dad was peering out the window. "They're loading that birdhouse in the back seat," he said, "and they haven't even got a towel down." He left us to go supervise.

"It's late," Mother said, coming completely into the room. "Jason will enjoy this in a couple years, won't he?"

"I guess." It could've been the hangover, but I didn't want to spend these last moments on small talk, a string of banalities designed so we could hear ourselves speak more than anything else. "Pim told me the nice things you said last night."

"It was *very* nice of him to check on Marie," she said. The tone of her words served as an all-clear that everything was back to normal as far as she was concerned. The church scene yesterday had not taken place, and it was now forgotten, if never entirely forgiven.

My brain had gone from days-old oatmeal to molten ore, and someone was stuffing cotton up my nose. I was not in the mood for discretion.

"That time in the Holiday Inn," I said. "I wish you would've told me how you felt."

"I was trying to be supportive," Mother said, so fast I realized that the response had been rehearsed.

She couldn't see me from her vantage point; I was a kind of disembodied voice, floating down to her. But I could see her as she examined the wallpaper: Early-American—eagles alternating with the spirit of '76.

"This is nice for a boy," Mother ventured, getting us back onto safe ground. She traced the paper with her index finger, outlining an eagle's head. I lost sight of her as she bent down to inspect the carpet.

"It was a blow," she blurted, as I was propping myself up on one elbow. "We'd come there for a vacation. I didn't know what I felt. I wanted to go back in the bathroom and finish my hair. Get away from you and your father and his damn pipe."

When she stood up, her face had that pained expression it'd had when I'd told Aunt Tee-Tee about owning a house with Pim. Something unexpected had broken through the surface to disturb her. Her small mouth, the one she'd passed on to me but not Larry, had resumed its semi-pursed shape—not tight, just shut, and I knew that was all I'd get from her.

Mother came over to the bed and reached up and patted my hand. "Don't get up," she said. "You look terrible."

I considered that I must be looking bad, but then I remembered that she couldn't see me. It was too late to ask her about this as she was on her way down the hall—and calling out to anyone at this moment was beyond me.

But when I saw them from behind the curtain getting into the car, I got up in a rush and jumped down to the floor, my stomach and head outraged. I passed the open door of the room where Sharon and Marie were napping. Jason was in the backyard on his bike.

From the front doorway, I spied my father struggling to get behind the steering wheel. His knees were bad that day, and he had to brace himself against the frame and then lower himself in. And his damn neck. So scrawny. He *is* almost 70, I thought. And you're a terrible child. You won't get out of bed to tell your parents goodbye.

Mother spotted me on the steps. "Don't come out like that," she said.

I was in my underwear. Even now she was worried that a neighbor might see me in my jockeys. Larry and I laughed at the same moment, bound in a conspiracy of children against parents.

"I won't," I said and retreated behind the screen door.

Mom blew me a kiss, and Pim helped her in. It wasn't easy. She was heavy, and her body didn't turn like it used to. There was a moment when they were directly facing each other. Pim raised his eyebrows at my mother and sort of grinned by pressing his lips tightly together and then drawing them out. She gave him a quick one on the cheek and then disappeared, seeming to vanish into the upholstery.

With the sun shining on the windshield, I couldn't actually see my parents, although I could make out their hands moving, so I waved back. Pim went to the other side of the car and shook my father's hand. My father leaned out and said something to him I couldn't catch.

They started down the curving driveway, in reverse, swerving to avoid the small trees planted there like an obstacle course. I kept up the waving, imagining they were, too—even though they couldn't see me through the screen and I couldn't see them through the windshield.

"You're wearing your underwear," Jason said. He'd appeared by my side and was waving madly at his grandparents who'd managed to reach the street without harming themselves or the flora.

"It's hot," I said. Larry and Pim were huddled on the lawn, examining some brown patches.

"Let's play," Jason said. "Dad got me a new glove, you know."

From inside the house, I heard the baby's first stirrings and the unmistakable intake of air that would turn into a cry a second later. "All right," I said. "I feel about good enough for that."

Contributors' Notes

GREG BAYSANS co-founded *The James White Review* in 1983 and serves as editor, designer and production manager. He is a native of North Dakota and has resided in Minneapolis since 1980. His poetry has appeared in *The Evergreen Chronicles* and *Northwest Literary Quarterly*. His criticism has appeared in the *Minneapolis Star Tribune* and the *St. Paul Pioneer Press*. He is also the creator of crossword puzzles for *Outweek* magazine.

WALTER RICO BURRELL was a radio and television host interviewer in the Los Angeles area and a movie publicist. He was a journalist on Black involvement in the entertainment industry and contributed to *Ebony, Jet, Soul, Black Stars, Black Enterprise, New York Times, Rolling Stone*. Burrell died of AIDS in September, 1990.

LOUIS CREW was born in 1936 in Anniston, Alabama. He has authored over 760 published essays, poems, and stories. He is a professor at Rutgers, the State University of New Jersey, and is married to Ernest Clay.

LUCAS DEDRICK was born and raised in Wichita, Kansas. He studied English and Creative Writing at Wichita State University. In 1983 he left the midwest and moved to Washington D.C. where he worked as a Program Specialist for the Literature Program of the National Endowment for the Arts. He currently lives in San Francisco with his partner of six years, Michael Cuesta, and is working on an anthology of short stories.

DOUGLAS FEDERHART is a native of Iowa now living in Minneapolis. He was formerly a managing editor of the *Evergreen Chronicles*, a journal of gay and lesbian writing. He is currently involved with the Radical Faeries.

DAVID B. FEINBERG'S first novel, *Eighty-sixed*, was published in 1989. His fiction has also appeared in *Mandate* and *Torso*. A graduate of the Massachusetts Institute of Technology and New York University, he lives in New York City. *Spontaneous Combustion* will be published by Viking Penguin in the fall of 1991.

RICHARD HALL is the author of a novel, *The Butterscotch Prince,* a volume of plays, *Three Plays for a Gay Theater,* and two collections of stories, *Coupling* and *Letter from a Great-Uncle*. His latest book, *Family Fictions*, will be published by Viking Penguin in 1991.

PATRICK HOCTEL lives and works in San Francisco. He is the assistant editor at the *Bay Area Reporter*. His short stories have appeared in *Mirage, Men on Men 1*, and *Christopher Street*. He has written film reviews, interviews and arts features for the *Sentinel, SF Weekly,* and the *Bay AreaReporter*.

ISAAC JACKSON'S writing has appeared in numerous gay and lesbian political and literary publications. His poems have been anthologized in the volumes *Not Love Alone: A Modern Gay Anthology* and *Tongues Untied: Five Black Gay Poets*. He is working on a new collection of poems. His first children's book, *Somebody's New Pajamas*, will be published by Dial Books next year. He is pursuing a doctorate at the Massachusetts Institute of Technology's Media Lab and lives in Cambridge, MA.

DANIEL MANGIN'S short fiction has appeared in the *San Francisco Sentinel*. He is currently the Arts Editor of the *Bay Area Reporter* and teaches a course in lesbian and gay film at City College of San Francisco.

PETER MCGEHEE lives in Toronto. His latest book is a novel, *Boys Like Us* (St. Martin's Press and Harper Collins). He is also the author of two collections of stories, *Beyond Happiness* and *The I.Q. Zoo*, and two musical revues, *The Quinland Sisters* and *The Fabulous Sirs*.

TOM MCKAGUE is an Associate Professor of English at Onondaga Community College of Syracuse, NY, where he teaches composition, literature, and creative writing. He has published short fiction and poetry in a variety of journals, including *Art Times, On the Edge, Bitterroot, Third Eye, Embers, Poet's Pride, Blueline, The Blue Unicorn, Lake Effect, Esprit, Wordsmith*, and others.

WES MUCHMORE is the co-author of *Coming Out Right,* a revised version of which was published in September, 1990, and of *Coming Along Fine*. He also has had a number of short stories published and currently is working on a book of short stories and a play. He lives in San Francisco.

FELICE PICANO is the author of seven novels including *The Lure* and *Late in the Season,* a collection of short stories, *Slashed to Ribbons in Defense of Love,* a book of poetry, *The Deformity Lover,* two volumes of memoirs — *Ambidextrous* and *Men Who Loved Me,* and two plays produced Off-Broadway. He was an Ernest Hemingway award finalist in 1975, and won a PEN Syndicated Fiction award in 1986. In 1981 he edited *A True Likeness: Lesbian and Gay Writing Today,* the first anthology of its kind. He founded the SeaHorse Press in 1977, publishing many noted gay novelists, dramatists and poets and has been co-publisher and editor in chief of The Gay Presses of New York since 1981.

SAM RUDY earns his living as a theatrical publicist in New York. His list of clients includes scores of Broadway and Off-Broadway productions including *La Cage Aux Folles*, *Other People's Money*, *Vampire Lesbians of Sodom* and *The Lady In Question*. Raised on a dairy farm in Pennsylvania, he is a graduate of Penn State University.

DAVID STEINBERG grew up in Niantic, Connecticut; graduated from University of Hartford, 1976. He completed his M.A. in Creative Writing at San Francisco State University. He lives in San Francisco.

LEONARD TIRADO is forty-three, South Bronx-born and Brooklyn-bred. He is a counseling psychologist working currently in the field of substance abuse in Albany, New York. He divides his time between practicing Buddhist meditation, ACT-UP, writing and studying the connections between religion, psychology, race, culture and sexual politics.

JAMES TUSHINSKI grew up in Lombard, Illinois, and now lives in San Francisco. He has been a bartender, factory worker, computer programmer, file clerk, editor and teacher, but prefers writing fiction. His short stories, articles and reviews have appeared in *PRISM International*, the *Bay Area Reporter*, the *San Francisco Sentinel*, *Au Courant* and *darknerve*. He is working on a novel, *The Boy Who Changed Places with His Shadow*.

DONALD VINING, a Pennsylvanian by birth, New Yorker by choice since 1942, studied playwriting at the Yale Drama School and had a dozen one-act plays published. He is the author of the four-volume *A Gay Diary* (covering 1933-1975) and of a book of essays on gay life and relationships (his lasted 43 years) entitled *How Can You Come Out If You've Never Been In?* A contributor of fiction and non-fiction to major gay periodicals, he also does a monthly column on diaries for the straight publication *Diarist's Journal* and is assembling these for a projected book on diary-keeping.

JAMES L. WHITE was born in 1936 in Indianapolis. He wrote four books of poetry, *Divorce Proceedings*, *A Crow's Story of Deer*, *The Del Rio Hotel* and *The Salt Ecstasies* (Greywolf Press, 1982). After a career as a classical ballet dancer, White took two degrees in English literature and went to New Mexico and Arizona to live with and teach Navaho people. He edited two books of contemporary Native American poetry for Dacotah Territory. He last resided in Minneapolis where he died of heart disease in 1981.

PHILIP WILLKIE co-founded *The James White Review* in 1983 and serves as publisher. He has studied writing with Natalie Goldberg in Minnesota and with others at Naropa Institute in Colorado. A native of Indiana, he now, with his lover, Brent Derowitsch, divides his time between St. Paul and a cabin in northwestern Wisconsin.